Clinical Social
Worker Misconduct

D0874744

Nelson-Hall Series in Social Work

Consulting Editor: Charles Zastrow
University of Wisconsin-Whitewater

Clinical Social Worker Misconduct

Law, Ethics, and Interpersonal Dynamics

Ronald K. Bullis, Ph.D., M.Div., J.D.

Nelson-Hall Publishers/Chicago

Project Editor: Rachel Schick
Typesetter: Alexander Graphics, Inc.
Printer: Capital City Press
Cover Painting: *Darklight* by Suzanne Hanson

Library of Congress Cataloging-in-Publication Data

Bullis, Ronald K.
    Clinical social worker misconduct : law, ethics & interpersonal
dynamics / Ronald K. Bullis.
        p.   cm.
    Includes bibliographical references.
    ISBN 0-8304-1327-8
    1. Social service and sex.   2. Socal workers—Sexual behavior.
3. Social workers—Malpractice.   4. Social workers—Professional
ethics.   I. Title.
HV41.B85   1995   94-43290
174'.9362--dc20   CIP

Manufactured in the United States of America

10   9   8   7   6   5   4   3   2   1

The paper used in this book meets the
minimum requirements of American
National Standard for Information
Sciences—Permanence of Paper for
Printed Library Materials, ANSI
Z39.48-1984.

To Amy, for her kind words and compassionate ear

Contents

Introduction

Usually, the introduction is designed to entice the reader to buy (and read) the book. This introduction takes a different approach. It lists some reasons why readers may want to avoid this book. First, social worker sexual relations with clients is an unpleasant topic. No one wants to think about the vulnerable being exploited, especially sexually exploited. Second, professional misconduct is professionally embarrassing. No social worker wants to think about other social workers exploiting clients. The exploitative acts of one social worker demean the work and status of all social workers. In short, it is personally and professionally embarrassing. Third, as this book discusses, such actions place social workers and other professionals at legal risk. No one wants to think about being sued or placed under arrest.

The fourth reason differs from the previous three. This is the suspicion that law and legal actions are not the proper province of social work education or practice; the assumption is that a great deal of effort should not be expended on a few rotten apples and that, in any event, such matters are best left to other disciplines.

Ironically, these four tensions are the very reasons this book should be read by social workers and others in the helping professions. While no one wants to think about social workers sexually exploiting clients, it is increasingly hard to deny these incidents. For some time now, courts of law have addressed this issue; increasingly, the courts of mass media and public opinion are openly discussing it. Chapter 1 and later chapters recite these findings. While social workers may think that revelations of sexual misconduct among colleagues are embarrassing, to avoid these issues is professionally detrimental. Individual social workers, social work educators, social work supervisors and administrators, and social work professional organizations must address these issues to maintain professional competence and public confidence.

While no one wants to think about being sued or placed under arrest, this book offers preventive means to avoid legal vulnerability. A systematic approach to understanding ethical mandates is also presented. Without knowing the language or the standards by which clinical social workers will be judged, without knowing the rules by which the rules will be applied—in other words, without knowing the lay of the legal landscape—clinical social workers are ethically and legally vulnerable. They are at the mercy of unseen, unknown, and often unmerciful obligations and consequences. Clinical social workers, taking a proactive stance in their professional lives, will use this book as a primer in their practices; they will become familiar with sexual misconduct and other ethical problems. In the world of law and ethics, what you do not know *can* hurt you.

Social workers have no choice but to begin to conceive of their profession as interdisciplinary. Social work is increasingly influenced by state and federal law as well as professional ethics. This book's first three chapters discuss both the criminal and civil liability to professionals, particularly to social workers, arising from client sexual exploitation. The book then discusses the varieties of harm to clients and the varieties of harm to the profession arising from client sexual exploitation as well as a whole range of dual relations. "Dual relations" refers to conflicted loyalties caused by conflicting roles between social worker and client. This book ultimately attempts to prevent future client abuse by taking a long, unblinking look at the legal and ethical issues arising from professional misconduct.

One popular way of teaching both law and ethics is the "case study" approach. This book employs that method by discussing a number of different law cases applicable to social workers. The book also examines ethical cases from other professions. Sometimes these facts are explicit and painful to read. However, the recitation of these facts is necessary to understand the rulings in cases and to facilitate a psychodynamic understanding of social worker misconduct. I have tried to preserve the litigants' dignity as well as to remain faithful to the facts.

It is only prudent to end this introduction with a set of disclaimers—to protect both the author and the audience. First, this book is not intended to provide legal advice on civil or criminal matters of sexual misconduct or other ethical misconduct. No book can specify the legal liabilities or suggest legal options for any particular set of facts in any particular jurisdiction. To do so would misrepresent the capabilities of this book and jeopardize the defendant's case.

Second, this book is not intended to replace competent legal counsel. They alone have the capacity and authority to assess probable liability and to suggest legal courses of action. Part of this book's purpose is to help clinical social workers understand legal standards for their behavior and how laws (both statutes and judicial decisions) establish both the standard of lawful behavior and the standards by which unlawful behavior is sanctioned. The law profoundly influences clinical social work practice. Clinical social workers need to know the legal issues inherent in dual relations, the legal processes used to adjudicate such issues, and the legal language used to state the rulings. Without knowledge of the legal issues, processes, and language, clinical social workers place themselves in an extremely alienated and vulnerable position.

Chapter 1

▶ ·························· ◀

Defining Sexual Misconduct and Its Cross-Professional Context

▶ ·························· ◀

This chapter establishes the legal and ethical context of sexual misconduct. While "sexual misconduct" is strictly defined in the next chapters by statute and by case law, a brief note about defining this term is important here. Neither the *Social Work Dictionary* (Barker 1991) nor the *Social Work Encyclopedia* (NASW 1987 and 1990 Supplements) specifically defines sexual misconduct. However, the *Encyclopedia* contains references to sexual misconduct in three of its entries. "Legal Issues and Legal Services" notes that sexual intercourse with a client is usually considered grounds for a malpractice suit. The entry under "Professional Liability and Malpractice" notes, "Sexual contact or the innocent extension of the professional relationship into private domains is inappropriate. Sexual restraint is widely accepted as an ethical principle among professions." The entry adds that professionals should avoid even the appearance of impropriety. Finally, the entry "Profession of Social Work: Contemporary Characteristics" notes the definition of "misconduct or malpractice" from *Black's Law Dictionary* (Black 1979) as "unreasonable lack of skill."

Applying definitions from a law dictionary to social work has two results. First, it provides a legal definition. *Black's Law Dictionary* defines misconduct as "a transgression of some established and definite rule," and also as "carelessness or negligence of such degree or recurrence as to manifest wrongful intent or evil design." This

1

definition is specific enough to require an *intent* to engage in the wrongful conduct and general enough to include related offenses such as sexual harassment. (Sexual harassment is addressed in chapter 3.)

The legal definition of sexual misconduct, applied to professional groups, can also be defined by statute. For example, the state of New Hampshire prohibits sexual misconduct by psychologists (§§ 330-A:10—14, 1988). Sexual misconduct is defined as "sexual relations with a client or a former client." Sexual relations is defined as the "intentional touching of any part of the client's body or any verbal or non-verbal communication for the purpose of sexual arousal or gratification." Again, the sexual misconduct must be intentional but can include a broad variety of acts.

The second result of applying a definition formulated outside the profession of social work is to incorporate interdisciplinary knowledge and insights into social work professional conduct. Social workers now are obliged to know the legal context of their professional conduct. This obligation has come about by force of legal constraint, if not by choice. As the next two chapters demonstrate, the law did not require social work's permission when asked to litigate alleged sexual misconduct of social workers. The law applied its principles to social work conduct whether or not the social work profession was aware of legal principles.

The professional problems inherent in sexual misconduct must be addressed from an interdisciplinary perspective. While this book considers clinical social worker misconduct, especially sexual misconduct, it is important to address such misconduct in light of the law and the humanities. The next section considers some elements of sexual misconduct through the cinema.

SCENARIOS FROM THE CINEMA

Films have a long history of depicting professional sexual misconduct (Ansen and Springen 1992). Sometimes the media seem to both anticipate and mold attitudes on social topics. Important questions might be asked about each of the following scenarios. These questions include what kind of obligations are owed to whom and precisely what those obligations are.

Presumed Innocent stars Harrison Ford as deputy district attorney Rusty Sabich, a man who has had an affair with a female colleague— another assistant district attorney. The plot thickens when Sabich's boss orders him to become the chief investigator in the murder of the assistant district attorney with whom Sabich had the affair. Sabich does not initially tell his boss that he has had an affair with her. Indeed, the district attorney has had an affair with her as well.

Presumed Innocent is a film that explicitly and seriously addresses the issue of sexual misconduct. The film makes it clear that Sabich must lie and compromise his professional duties to keep his misconduct a secret. He destroys pertinent evidence of his involvement with the assistant D.A. and asks a detective-friend of his to overlook obvious leads to maintain the charade. The film makes clear at both the beginning and the surprising ending that Sabich's relationship with his wife suffers because of the deceit.

It is also clear that Sabich's professional reputation is seriously damaged. He is eventually charged with the murder of his former lover. The movie protrays Sabich's agony over his betrayal of his wife and his professional disgrace.

Another movie that depicts sexual misconduct is *The Prince of Tides*, which stars Barbra Streisand as Susan Lowenstein, a psychiatrist, and Nick Nolte as Tom Wingo, an out-of-work coach from South Carolina. Wingo's sister, a poet who has moved to New York City, has once again attempted to commit suicide. Wingo travels to New York to offer his insights to Lowenstein so that she can better treat his sister. At first, Wingo and Lowenstein seem to studiously dislike each other.

As one might expect, the distance does not last. Wingo begins to teach Lowenstein's son how to play football, has dinner with her, has dinner with Lowenstein's philandering husband, and has an affair with her—ultimately revealing his tragic and brutal family secret.

These two movies place important issues before the public and the professions. First is the temptation of professionals to engage in sexual misconduct. Sabich, the otherwise solid citizen, is willing to risk his professional prestige, his family, and his finances for the affections of his attractive colleague. If Sabich is willing to take such risks, are other professionals also at risk? If Sabich will risk his professional persona for his sexual self, are other professionals equally sexually accessible?

The second issue is the harm caused by professional sexual misconduct. In *Presumed Innocent* two negative consequences occur. First, Sabich is used by his female colleague to gain access to information and cases otherwise unavailable to her. Second, she is murdered by Sabich's wife.

In *The Prince of Tides* there are no negative consequences. Noting that Wingo is not strictly Lowenstein's client, the perception that a sexual contact with those in the helping professions is somehow therapeutic is a dangerous misperception. The *Dutton* case in chapter 2 is an example of a professional using such a subterfuge. While these movies may be dismissed as Hollywood versions of life, sometimes life really does imitate art. The following sections are brief, real-life studies in misconduct.

MEDICAL PRACTITIONERS

Physicians obviously have an intimate relationship with their clients, and the medical profession has an early prohibition against violating that intimate relationship. This prohibition is codified in the Hippocratic Creed (ca. 460–377 B.C.E.), which states:

> . . . in whatever house I enter, and will go into them for the benefit of the sick; and will abstain from every voluntary act of mischief and corruption; and further, from the seduction of females and males, of freemen and slaves. (Adams n.d.)

Obviously, if there were no sexual misconduct problems in fourth century Greece, there would be no need for such an oath. While the antiquity of sexual misconduct is no excuse for its persistence, such antiquity is evidence of its prevalence and pervasiveness.

Another type of alleged misconduct among physicians has recently come to national attention. A potential conflict of interest occurs when physicians refer their patients to laboratories, diagnostic imaging centers, and physical therapy centers in which the physicians have a financial interest. In a recent study, the Florida Health Care Cost Containment Board found that doctors' ownership of such facilities tends to increase both the use and the cost of services, with no improvement of services to the poor or to rural residents (Pear 1991). Critics of such investments by physicians specifically raise the issue of a conflict between the real needs of patients for such treatments and the financial interests of the physicians.

As a partial remedy, the federal Department of Health and Human Services has issued guidelines for physicians on how to comply with 1972 anti-kickback law. The new regulations do not prohibit physicians from referring Medicaid or Medicare patients to their own clinics, but mandate that the referrals be based solely upon medical grounds, limit the percentage of physicians who may invest in such facilities, and limit the percentage of revenues received from the facility by those who invest in it (Rich 1991).

COLLEGE PROFESSORS

Against a backdrop of allegations that scientists and other researchers forge or misrepresent research data and overbill the federal government for research costs, a professor at the University of Tennessee is under investigation by the university and the National Aeronautics and Space Administration for a scheme to exchange his approval of students' degrees for lucrative government contracts (Putka 1991). The professor, who served as advisor for about sixty-five master's and doctoral students and had his own consulting firm, is accused of allowing students to copy his own work. In exchange, some of his students awarded his private firm consulting contracts. Faculty committees have recommended that some degrees be rescinded and that the professor be dismissed. The professor has since retired.

These allegations offer possible conflicts of interest in four areas. First, the professor owed a duty to the university to verify the originality of students' work. Even with his own permission to use his work, there may be an independent duty to require that students provide original research for their degrees. This independent duty would at least guard against collusion of student and professor of the type alleged above. Indeed, it is the *university* that grants the degree, not the *professor*.

Second, the professor had an obligation to the contractor to win a contract based fully on his firm's merits, not on a private relationship between the consultant and the person awarding the contract. This duty protects the integrity of the process by which governments award contracts and protects the public against unwise government spending.

Third, the professor had an obligation to the students to provide them with an untainted degree. This obligation is extremely important because the major professor is in a controlling position relative to the students' degrees. The person who controls the degree-granting process bears the most responsibility for ethical behavior.

Fourth, the professor had an obligation to his profession. Such an obligation may lie with the professor's contract with the university or with professional organizations. In any event, this case provides a scenario where the potential for personal gain places the professor in a clear conflict of interest, or dual relations.

CLERGY AND RELIGIOUS PROFESSIONALS

The reader does not need to look far to find examples of sexual misconduct among religious figures. Recently, there has been a proliferation of indictments and convictions against the clergy. However, the Bible itself furnishes a prime example of a high religious figure who used his authority and power for his own gain and to the detriment of others to whom he was responsible. In the Book of Second Samuel (RSV), there is a story about David's love affair and subsequent marriage to Bathsheba. David, King of Israel, was married to Michal, and Bathsheba was married to Uriah the Hittite. David saw Bathsheba bathing alone late one afternoon. He sent for her, "and she came to him and he lay with her."

The story does not relate whether David's wife became a problem in his scheme; however, David was threatened by Uriah. David ordered Uriah's military commander to send Uriah into the deadliest part of the battle—and Uriah was killed. David then married Bathsheba—"but the thing that David had done displeased the Lord."

The prophet Nathan was sent to facilitate David's repentance. Nathan recounted a parable that marked David as a murderer and adulterer. The parable allegorically demonstrated the nature of David's conflicted interests in Bathsheba and Uriah. David repented; yet, the child born later to Bathsheba and David died.

Another source of sanctions imposed for such alleged improprieties were uncovered recently by a historian examining previously overlooked records in the Library of Congress. The story was published by *The Washington Post* (Ringle 1990) under the title "The Scandal that Rocked Old Virginny." The records documented the only full-fledged church trial in colonial Virginia, which resulted from allegations that a cleric, Reverend Charles Green, attempted to debauch George Washington's sister-in-law, Ann Fairfax Washington.

Ann's husband accused the Reverend Green, a long-time friend of the Washington family and a physician, of frequent attempts to debauch Ann in the years previous to her marriage, and asked the bishop to remove him from the parish. Interestingly, Ann's husband did not press to defrock Green, but only to send him to another parish—a practice not unknown to this day.

Green denied the charge and countersued Ann's husband for slander. The trial testimony, given at the Chapel of the College of William and Mary, was conflicting. Damaging testimony was offered against Green by Ann's stepmother, who stated that Green admitted to an indiscretion, but that no harm was done to Ann because she remained *virga intacta* prior to her marriage. On the other hand, defense witnesses, anxious to discredit Ann, brought in testimony that Ann "kissed and patted" Green on at least one occasion.

Apparently, the trial was as sensational to eighteenth century Virginia as many trials are today. The trial ended in a plea bargain, when the Virginia governor and head of the Anglican church forged a compromise. All charges against Green were dropped, but Green agreed to drop the slander charge and pay all court costs—a penalty usually reserved for losers in a modern civil court fight. Ironically, Green lived to see his reputation restored; George Washington himself befriended the cleric and employed him as a physician.

This case reveals a tangle of duties owed by Green to a number of persons in his parish. He owed a professional duty to Ann and her family as members of his parish; he was bound to maintain the precepts of his Anglican ordination; and he had a legal duty of care toward a young woman.

In the appendices of this text, examples of religious denominational policy statements are included. These statements illustrate how religious organizations address the problem of sexual misconduct by clergy and other church officials.

SOCIAL WORKERS

While this book addresses with depth and breadth the legal and ethical nature of social worker sexual misconduct, a brief section is included here to give some background. First, it is difficult to establish national statistics for the frequency of social worker sexual exploitation. According to Elizabeth DuMez, adjudication associate at the National Association of Social Workers, that organization will begin compiling statistics by type of infraction beginning in 1992 (personal communication 1992). Research from a variety of sources will describe the nature and frequency of sexual misconduct in a variety of profession groups—including social workers.

DuMez outlined the range of sanctions imposed by the NASW. From most severe to least severe, they include: outright expulsion, suspension with prescribed remediation (close supervision, counseling, practice limitation, and supervision), notification of state licensing boards, public notification of sanction in the *NASW News,* and employer notification of the sanctions imposed upon their employee. Public notification of sanctions in the *NASW News* includes the sanctions imposed and a very brief description of the infraction. These sanctions are not mutually exclusive.

In one of the few, if not the only empirical description of ethical complaints of social workers on the national level, Berliner (1989) studied the 292 available ethics cases filed in NASW state chapters

Table 1.1
Ethical Complaints Against Social Workers on the National Level, 1979–1985

Category	Number	Percent
Conduct as a social worker	24	25%
Ethical responsibility to clients		
Sexual misconduct	8	8
Breach of confidentiality	6	6
Fee splitting	3	3
Soliciting another's clients	2	3
Ethical responsibilities to colleagues	26	27
Ethical responsibilities to organizations, the social work profession, or society	27	28

between 1979 and 1985. Most of these complaints never reached the adjudication arm of the NASW chapter for a variety of reasons. Ten percent of complainants did not pursue their allegations. Another 10 percent of the claims were rejected by state chapters. Forty-one percent of the remaining complaints were sustained by the NASW chapters. These complaints were broken down by type, as shown in table 1.1.

This study revealed that one in twelve complaints dealt with sexual misconduct. It is worthwhile to consider the time gap from the incident of misconduct to the client's awareness of the harm done. A more thorough discussion of the dynamics of sexual misconduct is represented in chapter 4. Other ethical issues (fee splitting, etc.) are also categorized in table 1.1. Confidentiality, fee splitting, and other ethical issues are discussed in chapter 6.

The above examples of misconduct from various professions have brought to light the contexts in which conflicts of interest or conflicts in loyalties are created. The next section of this chapter surveys the literature on the extent of divided loyalties and conflicts of interest—particularly sexual misconduct—among professionals.

DEFINING MISCONDUCT AND RELATED TERMS AND CONCEPTS

Misconduct and sexual misconduct are components of other ethical and legal terms and concepts and may be prohibited under different terminologies. It is important to understand terms and concepts related to sexual misconduct because they form the ethical nomenclature with which professionals define the parameters of acceptable behavior.

Part of the problem with using only terms such as "misconduct" is that the definitions are either nonexistent, very narrow, or very broad. Without a clear definition of related terms and concepts such as fiduciary, conflict of interest, integrity, and loyalty, clinical social workers are placed in the untenable position of complying with terms they do not really understand. In the United States, definitions for legal and ethical conduct must be both public and consistent.

Neither the 1987 version of *The Social Work Dictionary* nor the 1987 version of the *Encyclopedia of Social Work* have entries for "fiduciary duty," "loyalty," or "conflicts of interest." However, several provisions of the NASW Code (1990) address such terms, including the main section of "Integrity" (I, D), which states: "social workers should act in accordance with the highest standards of professional integrity and impartiality."

1. The social worker should be alert to and resist the influences and pressures that interfere with the exercise of professional discretion and impartial judgment required for the performance of professional functions.
2. The social worker should not exploit professional relationships for personal gain.

These provisions do not provide consistent definitions and conceptions; therefore, social workers must adopt and adapt definitions from other disciplines. It is logical to begin with definitions from the legal field. Conflict of interest, for public officials, is defined by *Black's Law Dictionary* (1979) as a "clash between public interest and private, pecuniary interest." In terms of the private relationships between clinical social workers and clients, the concept might be thought of as the clash between the interests of the client and some competing, contradictory interest.

Related to conflict of interest is the concept of loyalty. *Black's Law Dictionary* defines loyalty as "faithfulness." A faithful social worker cannot hold contradictory loyalties with respect to a client, or properly act as lover and as objective counselor or helper at the same time. One cannot be loyal and have conflicted interests at the same time.

The nature of a conflict of interest can be illustrated by an important survey of 1,021 psychologists, psychiatrists, and social workers (Borys and Pope 1989). The study found no significant differences among the professions in reporting sexual, social, or financial relations with clients. The two behaviors engaged in by most of the respondents with at least one client were (1) accepting a gift with a value of less than ten dollars, and (2) providing counseling simultaneously to a client and a client's significant other. These conflicts of interest illustrate the nature of divided loyalties.

Another important term, which case law will illustrate later, is "fiduciary," defined by *Black's Law Dictionary* as "A person having [a] duty, created by his undertaking, to act *primarily* [author's emphasis] for another's benefit in matters connected with such undertaking." "Duty" here can be defined as a legal obligation; in the case of an ethical duty it means an ethical obligation. Thus, a clinical social worker is in a fiduciary relationship with clients. This means that, absent other legal obligations, the social worker has a legal duty to act primarily in the client's best interest. Defined positively, there are no divided loyalty problems when a clinical social worker has no interests other than to serve the client. Defined negatively, there *can* be a misconduct problem where a clinical social worker has other interests than those of the client.

The term "fiduciary" has its roots in Roman law, in which a person serves as a "trustee"—often of someone else's money. The trustee is paid to hold someone's money, and has a corresponding legal duty to safeguard that money, maintain confidences in connection with that duty, and candidly offer such advice as is warranted with that duty. In the same way, a clinical social worker has a set of rights and obligations arising from the client-clinician relationship. The clinician has the right to be paid for services rendered. Under a fiduciary duty, the client has the right to adequate preparation for termination and adequate referral, as well as the right to demand that the clinician keep confidences and tell the client the truth (Kutchins 1991).

The term "primarily," as italicized above, is a word that recognizes other legitimate interests than the client's. Usually these other interests are well defined in law. For example, a now common limitation to the putative direct interests of the client is the legal duty for the clinician to protect third parties from the dangerous acts of clients. This now-famous duty was first enunciated by the Supreme Court of California in the case of *Tarasoff v. Regents, University of California* (1976). In that case a counselee at the University of California at Berkeley killed his girlfriend after informing the counseling staff of his intent to do so. *Tarasoff* held that counselors can be sued if they do not take necessary precautions to protect third parties threatened by counselees under their care.

The duty to protect third parties may directly conflict with the interests of the client, but it is subordinate to a larger interest, public health and safety. While public health and safety is a conflicting interest, the "duty to protect" is now fairly well established in statutory if not in case law.

BRIEF EXAMPLES OF LAW AND SEXUAL MISCONDUCT

Case law from two professions, the clergy and the law, illustrate how the law can address sexual misconduct among non-social worker professional groups. These illustrations are an attempt to examine cases dealing with professional sexual misconduct from an interdisciplinary perspective.

Clergy

In *DeStefano v. Grabrian* (1988) a priest and his archdiocese were sued by a couple who had sought and received marriage counseling. The allegations included the fact that Father Grabrian represented himself as a professional who could help solve the DeStefanos' marital problems, that Grabrian had an intimate relationship with Edna DeStefano, and that Grabrian knew or should have known that such behavior was likely to result in the dissolution of the marriage.

The court affirmed that Grabrian's fiduciary duty extended to both the husband and the wife. The Supreme Court of Colorado defined fiduciary as having the duties of loyalty, exercising reasonable care and skill, and acting in an impartial manner with beneficiaries. The court further found that Grabrian, as a counselor had a duty to engage in no conduct likely to harm the DeStefanos' relationship, and concluded that if the allegations were true, the priest breached his duty when he had sexual relations with Edna.

This case illustrates several important points. The first is that this is a civil case, not a criminal case. Civil cases adjudicate private wrongs between parties and the penalties consist of money damages. Conversely, criminal cases try public crimes through a governmental body such as a district attorney, police, sheriff, or other government-sponsored law-enforcement body. The plaintiff (the one who initiates a trial or legal proceeding) in a criminal proceeding is the government. Thus, the city, county, state, or federal government brings the alleged perpetrator up on charges in a criminal proceeding. In a civil case, private individuals may initiate the proceedings. The sentences for violations of the criminal law include jail or prison as well as fines. In the *DeStefano* case, the plaintiffs (the husband and wife) used the civil law to press their grievances. The civil law is often used to impose liability upon clinicians for sexual (and other) misconduct. There are at least three reasons for pursuing sexual misconduct allegations against clinicians through the civil courts rather than the criminal courts.

First, many states have no criminal statutes that prohibit sexual conduct between clinician and client. Where no criminal statutes exist that prohibit such activities, no criminal charges may be placed against the alleged perpetrator. Although most states and national organizations that license clinical social workers may impose sanctions upon clinicians who violate their codes of ethics, the sanctions placed address only the perpetrators' licensure, and are not criminal charges against them.

Second, civil liability often requires a lower standard of proof than criminal liability. A criminal defendant must be proven guilty "beyond a reasonable doubt." This is a relatively high standard for the government prosecutors to meet. However, in most civil trials, the standard of proof may be the less burdensome "preponderance of the evidence" standard. This means that generally it is easier to prove a civil case than a criminal case. The reasoning for this disparity in the standards of proof is that more is at stake in a criminal than a civil trial—loss of liberty rather than loss of money.

Third, plaintiffs in a civil trial generally have a better chance of collecting money than those in a criminal trial. While governments increasingly provide for some monetary compensation for the victims of crimes, and sometimes judges require those convicted to pay their victims restitution, basically criminal trials provide little beyond satisfaction (if that) to crime victims. It is left to the civil courts to provide victims with money damages as compensation for wrongful acts done to them. Indeed, it is not uncommon for an aggrieved party to civilly sue defendants after the defendants are convicted in a criminal trial.

The fourth reason is the expedient doctrine of "deep pockets." The deep pockets doctrine means that plaintiffs want to sue someone who has the ability to pay damages. Successfully suing someone who has no money, or not enough money to satisfy the judgment against them, is a hollow victory. Thus, plaintiffs search the list of possible defendants to include those who have deep pockets. While this doctrine may sound rather cynical or mercenary, it bears repeating that even deep-pockets defendants must be proven liable before a judgment can be awarded against them. The point is that the deep-pockets defendant may not be the only party at fault.

For example, when a clinical social worker works for a private or public agency and is accused of sexual misconduct, it is likely that the clinician's employing agency will be named as a defendant as well. Even if the agency did nothing directly to aid or abet the alleged misconduct, the plaintiff's attorney will likely try to allege agency responsibility through the legal doctrines of *respondeat superior* or "vicarious liability," on the premise that an agency may have more money than the individual clinical social worker. A fuller discussion of *respondeat superior*, vicarious liability, and related aspects of civil litigation are included in chapter 3.

Another important element illustrated by the *DeStefano* case is how the court viewed the beneficiaries (the couple) of the fiduciary (the priest). There was no discussion of payment on the part of the clients to the priest. In fact, the counseling might have been free. Nor was there any discussion of the incidentals of how they became clients. The court identified the couple as the priest's clients when the judge accepted the fact that the priest *represented* that he was both willing and able to provide counseling services to a couple, who accepted such services. This seemingly nonchalant exchange introduced to the court was neither simple nor nonchalant. By such an exchange, a clinician-client relationship was initially formed— without such a relationship the priest would have no duties whatsoever to people who are legal strangers to him. Legal strangers refers to relationships without corresponding legal obligations.

Clinical social workers need to know that they create clinician-client relationships, whether they know it or not, by responding in the affirmative when asked for help. These relationships are formed regardless of an exchange of money, regardless of the setting for counseling, and regardless of the clinician's expectations. It is the *client's* notion of whether or not the clinician has agreed to a professional relationship that courts are likely to consider dispositive. In other words, if the client thinks the clinician has agreed to help him or her, then courts are likely to find that a professional relationship has been formed.

Lawyers

A telling example of attorneys accused of sexual misconduct involves a recent Illinois case. In the second recorded case alleging malpractice for sexual misconduct against an attorney (*Suppressed v. Suppressed* 1990), a client accused her divorce lawyer of taking sexual advantage of her. The client-plaintiff alleged that after she retained a lawyer to litigate her divorce on behalf of herself and her children, her lawyer induced her to have sexual intercourse. The plaintiff says she agreed to intercourse because she was afraid that the lawyer would not advocate fully for her or her children during the divorce proceedings if she refused.

The court based its decision on one main issue: whether or not the client-plaintiff set forth facts that state a proper cause of action for breach of a lawyer's fiduciary duty toward his or her client. A legal "cause of action" refers to the facts that give a right to judicial relief (Black 1979). The appeals court refused to allow a cause of action for legal malpractice based upon sex with a client for three reasons. First, while the court agreed that a fiduciary duty means that the lawyer has to deal fairly and in good faith with his or her client, the court's definition of the nature of the fiduciary did not address sexual intercourse with clients. The court ruled that a lawyer's fiduciary duty means a duty to provide competent legal services. Therefore, the duty does not necessarily include refraining from sexual contact with clients.

Second, the court rules that the plaintiff did not claim damages that are measurable. Even in cases where courts allow emotional damages to be compensated, courts require alleged damages to be verifiable in order to avoid the possibility of fraud.

Third, and perhaps most interesting, is that the court does "not disagree with the plaintiff's suggestion that there should be a separate cause of action for a lawyer's breach of an *ethical* [author's emphasis] duty to conduct himself in accordance with the rules of professional responsibility" (*Suppressed v. Suppressed* 1990). However, the court ruled that it would not judicially create such a cause of action and would leave to the state legislature the role of creating such a duty, with commensurate liability if breached. In fact, the court noted that the Illinois legislature had already acted to criminalize the sexual exploitation of clients by psychotherapists.

In deferring to the legislative branch to *create* law and preserving its role to *interpret* law, the *Suppressed* case followed the traditional, although not universally practiced, role of U.S. courts. In criminalizing sexual contact with clients, state legislatures have not necessarily created a civil action against professionals for sexual misconduct; however, criminalizing such behavior establishes a clear public mandate for the intolerance of sexual misconduct among professionals. These criminal statutes, related law cases, and their meanings for perpetrators, victims, and the clinical social work profession are presented in the following chapters.

The legal profession may reflect the ambiguity of dual relations in its ambivalence in creating ethical standards regarding sexual involvement with clients. The Oregon State Bar Association voted down restrictions on lawyer-client sexual acts as an invasion of privacy. The Oregon bar has ruled that disclosure and consent are required before a divorce lawyer can have sexual relations with a client. The California state bar adopted a rule that presumes the lawyer engaging in sexual relations with a client to be incompetent (DeBenedictus 1992). The California rule is included in appendix C.

This chapter has attempted to set forth the professional background of the law and ethics of sexual misconduct by examining misconduct relations in American culture and among several professional groups. Additionally, legal definitions of conflicts of interest, fiduciary duties, and other terms were presented. The following chapter examines state laws that specifically address sexual misconduct between social workers and their clients.

REFERENCES

Adams, F. (n.d.). *The genuine works of Hippocrates.* New York: William Wood & Co.

Ansen, D., and Springen, K. (1992, April 13). A lot of not so happy endings. *Newsweek,* 58.

Barker, R. (1991). *The social work dictionary.* Silver Spring, MD: National Association of Social Workers.

Berliner, A.K. (1989). "Misconduct in social work practice." *Social Work,* 34(1), 69–72.

Black, H. (1979). *Black's law dictionary.* St. Paul, MN: West Publishing.

Borys, D.S., and Pope, K.S. (1989). "Dual relationships between therapist and client: A national study of psychologists, psychiatrists, and social workers." *Professional Psychology: Research and Practice,* 20(5), 283–93.

DeBenedictus, D.J. (1992). "Sex-with-client ban fails." *ABA Journal,* 78, 24.

DeStefano v. Grabrian, 763 P.2d 275 (Colo. 1988).

Kutchins, H. (1991). "The fiduciary relationship: The legal basis for social workers' responsibility to clients." *Social Work,* 36(2), 106–13.

National Association of Social Workers (1987 and 1990 Supplements). *Encyclopedia of social work.* (18th ed.). Silver Spring, MD: Author.

National Association of Social Workers (1990 revision). *Code of ethics.* Silver Spring, MD: Author.

Pear, R. (1991, August 9). "Study says fees are often higher when doctor has stake in clinic." *New York Times,* A1, A16.

Personal communication (May 29, 1992), Elizabeth DuMez, adjudication associate at the National Association of Social Workers.

Putka, G. (1991, July 21). "Academic barter." *The Wall Street Journal,* A1, A5.

Rich, S. (1991, July 27). "U.S. tightens rules on patient referrals." *The Washington Post,* A4.

Ringle, K. (1990, December 15). "The scandal that rocked Old Virginny." *The Washington Post,* B1, B8.

Suppressed v. Suppressed, 17 F.L.R. 1088 (1990).

Tarasoff v. Regents, University of California, 551 P.2d 334 (Ca. 1976).

Chapter 2

The Criminalization of Clinical Social Worker Sexual Misconduct

The end of chapter 1 described a range of ethical misconduct among a variety of professional groups. These dual relationships were illustrated to highlight two points. The first point is that all professional groups are vulnerable to committing ethical or sexual misconduct. No professional group is immune from personal and/or professional conflicts of interest that harm clients to whom the professional has a fiduciary responsibility.

This chapter will consider, in depth, several state statutes that criminalize psychotherapists' sexual relationships with clients. These statutes define "psychotherapist" very broadly. Beyond clinical social workers, these criminal statutes include all types of mental health professionals (and some professionals you may not think of) in their definition of psychotherapist. Obviously, state legislatures consider sexual relationships with clients to be a problem over a broad spectrum of mental health professionals.

The second point is that society itself is confused and ambivalent regarding the nature of sexual misconduct, the harm that is done to the victim, and the need for sanctions against perpetrators. This confusion and ambivalence often exists among professional groups, as shown by the factual illustrations offered in the previous chapter. Without question, professional groups are moving to address issues of sexual misconduct, though they were reluctant to do so even fifteen years ago (Stone 1976).

The third point of this chapter is that state legislatures and courts have already acted to protect the public. Criminalizing sexual misconduct indicates that sexual relationships are both pervasive and serious enough to warrant criminal prosecution. It is inappropriate to interpret criminal statutes as interfering with the sanctions of professional groups authorizing and licensing clinical social workers. Rather, criminal statutes should be interpreted as sending a message to clients and to potential clients, as well as to authorizing and licensing groups, that states increasingly consider sexual misconduct to be an issue beyond the scope of the licensing bodies and professional groups.

Before directly addressing state statutes criminalizing sexual misconduct among psychotherapists, the following section will describe the legal context of sexual misconduct among professionals. While the previous chapter has examined the *social* context of clinician sexual misconduct, the following section establishes findings in the *legal* context of clinician sexual misconduct. Britton (1988) surveyed 142 law cases involving professional sexual misconduct and found that the problem is widespread and the outcome of the case is predictable by profession.

Britton's first conclusion is that sexual misconduct is widespread among professional groups. Her study included cases involving physicians, psychiatrists, teachers, attorneys, psychologists, chiropractors, judges, dentists, clergy, school counselors, school bus drivers, physician's assistants, hypnotherapists, morticians, and optometrists. In fact, the incidence of cases reported has steadily increased between the 1960s and the 1980s. Figure 2.1 shows these figures.

This figure indicates the general increase of law cases among the professions. Of course, it does not represent the *total* number of sexual misconduct cases, for several reasons. Many incidents of sexual misconduct are never reported. Of those reported, many are never brought to trial because they are handled exclusively by professional organizations or are settled out of court. However, the increase in the volume of *reported* law cases indicates that the volume of the *unreported* incidents probably has increased as well. Britton suggests that while these results are difficult to assess, it seems apparent that those who assert that society is more tolerant of clinician-client sexual contact since the sexual revolution are wrong.

Her second conclusion is that each professional group tends to predictably address sexual misconduct among its membership. For

Figure 2.1
Number of Incidents of Sexual Misconduct by Decade

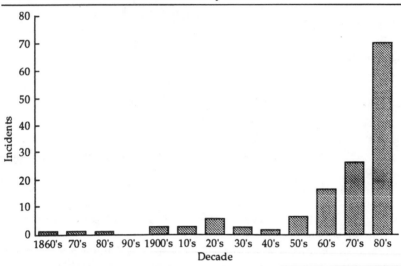

© Hamline Law Review. Used by permission.

example, physicians will likely be convicted on criminal charges or have their licenses revoked, psychiatrists will likely pay monetary damages, teachers will likely be fired, and attorneys and chiropractors will likely have their licenses suspended. Few, if any, clinical social workers have been criminally convicted for sexual misconduct; others have been convicted on civil charges; and far more have been sanctioned by professional organizations such as the National Association of Social Workers. Chapter 3 will discuss these and related issues in more depth.

A third finding was that only 22 percent of the cases surveyed involved criminal actions. At the time of Britton's article, only Wisconsin and Minnesota had enacted statutes criminalizing psychotherapist sexual misconduct. However, Britton points out that other criminal statutes *could* be used to indict and to convict clinicians who have sexual contact with clients (Britton 1988). Among these statutes are: various degrees of rape, various degrees of sexual assault or sexual battery, gross sexual imposition, deviant sexual assault, and various degrees of sexual abuse. Additionally, lesser-used statutes include fraudulent seduction, carnal knowledge, and various "procuring" prostitution laws.

One might well ask why the percentage of professionals criminally indicted is not higher, with such a seemingly wide array of criminal laws. The answer is, essentially, that most of the statutes mentioned above require elements that are inapplicable to the sexual relationship between a clinician and client. For example, rape generally requires the intent to have sex with a victim without his or her consent. The matter of consent is hard to prove or to disprove in a clinician-client sexual relationship. This is because psychotherapy is conducted in a strictly confidential manner—and is often conducted in an informal environment. (This issue is addressed in some detail later in this chapter.) Even among statutes where consent is not a defense (such as statutory rape), many of these statutes have strict age requirements for conviction. Indeed, Virginia requires that the victim in statutory rape be between thirteen and fifteen. Other potential exclusions exist for the other statutes. Clinician-client sexual misconduct requires a new species of criminal statute.

As we will see, states have responded with sophisticated, fairly comprehensive laws, specifically designed to convict sexual misconduct arising out of the clinician-client relationship. Clinical social workers need to understand these statutes for two reasons. The first reason is that virtually every state statute criminalizing clinician-client sexual misconduct includes clinical social workers by name. Second, while only a minority of the states have enacted such statutes, it seems likely that other states will follow.

STATUTES CRIMINALIZING CLINICIAN-CLIENT SEXUAL BEHAVIOR

As of this writing, nine states specifically criminalize clinician-client sexual behavior. Table 2.1 of the relevant statutes is included in this chapter to provide a visual context for the eight statutes. A synopsis of the professionals included in each statute is provided in table 2.2. The complete text of representative statutes is provided in table 2.3.

The Colorado statute (18-3-405.5(1) 1990) can illustrate these new classes of statutes. It reads simply:

> "Any actor who knowingly inflicts sexual penetration or sexual intrusion on a victim commits aggravated sexual assault on a client if:
>
> (I) The actor is a psychotherapist and the victim is a client of the psychotherapist; or
>
> (II) The actor is a psychotherapist and the victim is a client and the sexual penetration or intrusion occurred by means of therapeutic deception."

"Psychotherapist," "sexual assault," and "therapeutic deception" are terms defined in each of the statutes. (The reader is referred to table 2.2 for the specific definitions determined by each state.)

These statutes were created within the past two decades and have several features in common and some differences. The similarities include a broad interpretation of who is considered a psychotherapist for the purpose of the statute, the exclusion of "consent" as an element of the crime, the broad interpretation of the sexual behavior for the purposes of the statute, and the severity of the penalties imposed. The differences include the elements of "therapeutic deception" or "emotional dependency," and whether the crime exclusively covers current clients, or includes former clients as well.

Table 2.1
Statutes Criminalizing Clinical Social Worker-Client Sexual Dual Relations

State	Cite	Elements	Penalties
California	729	sexual contact with current or former client	fines and/or jail
Colorado	18-3-405.5	sexual intrusion or therapeutic deception	felony or misdemeanor
Georgia	16-6-5.1	sexual assault when actual or purported practitioner of psychotherapy engages in sexual contact	1–3 years
Iowa	709.15	sexual abuse with current or former client	misdemeanor
Florida	491.0112(1)	sexual misconduct with client or former client	3rd degree felony
Florida	491.0112(2)	sexual misconduct with client or former client by means of therapeutic deception	2nd degree felony
Maine	17-A Section 253(2)	"gross sexual assault" with patient or client	Class C crime
Minnesota	609.343	"sexual penetration" with or without consent, or therapeutic deception, or if the patient is emotionally dependent upon the clinician, or if false representation of medical purpose	fine and/or prison
Minnesota	609.345	"sexual contact" under same elements as above	fine and/or prison
North Dakota	12.1-20-06.1	sexual contact with client during treatment	felony
Wisconsin	940.22(2)	intentional sexual contact with current client	felony

Table 2.2
Professionals Included in Sexual Misconduct Statutes

State	Professionals Included
California	Psychiatrist; psychologist; clinical social worker; marriage, family, and child counselor and intern; psychological assistant; or associate clinical social worker
Colorado	"any person who performs or purports to perform psychotherapy, whether or not such person is licensed by the state . . ."
Florida	Physician, osteopath, nurse, psychologist, clinical social worker, marriage and family counselor, mental health counselor, "or any other person who provides or purports to provide treatment, diagnosis, assessment, evaluation, or counseling of mental or emotional illness, symptom or condition"
Georgia	"actual or purported practitioner of psychotherapy"
Iowa	Physician, psychologist, nurse, professional counselor, social worker, marriage or family therapist, alcohol or drug counselor, member of the clergy, or any person purporting to provide mental health services
Maine	Psychiatrist, psychologist, or licensed social worker or any other person who purports to be a psychiatrist, psychologist, or licensed social worker
North Dakota	Physician, psychologist, psychiatrist, social worker, nurse, chemical dependency counselor, clergyperson, "or any other person, whether licensed or not by the state, who performs or purports to perform psychotherapy"
Wisconsin	Physician, psychologist, social worker, nurse, chemical dependency counselor, clergy, "or any other person, whether or not licensed by the state, who performs or purports to perform psychotherapy"

The Colorado statute offers a definition of therapeutic deception consistent with that of both Florida and Minnesota. Therapeutic deception means "a representation by a psychotherapist that sexual contact, penetration, or intrusion by the psychotherapist is consistent with or part of the client's treatment" (18-3-405.5(4)(d), 1990 Supp.). In other words, therapeutic deception means that a clinical social worker may convince clients that sexual activity would be good for them, or help lessen their inhibitions, or any other assertion that links sexual behavior with the client to the therapeutic process.

Minnesota, even more than the other states, offers separate statutes to cover separate forms of fraud by clinicians for the purposes of sexual activity. Beyond a separate statute for therapeutic deception, Minnesota offers a statute that criminalizes sexual activity when a clinician engages in sexual activity with a client or former client who is "emotionally dependent" upon the clinician. Minnesota (148A.01,

Figure 2.2
Elements of Sexual Misconduct Statutes in Five States

NORTH DAKOTA 1989 Supp. (Michie, § 12.1-20-06.1)

Sexual exploitation by therapist - Definitions - Penalty. Any person who is or who holds oneself out to be a therapist and who intentionally has sexual contact, as defined in section 12.1-20-02, with a patient or client during any treatment, consultation, interview, or examination is guilty of a class C felony. Consent by the complainant is not a defense under this section. As used in this section, unless the context or subject matter otherwise requires:

   (1)   "Psychotherapy" means the diagnosis or treatment of a mental or emotional condition, including alcohol or drug addiction.

   (2)   "Therapist" means a physician, psychologist, psychiatrist, social worker, nurse, chemical dependency counselor, member of the clergy, or other person, whether licensed or not by the state, who performs or purports to perform psychotherapy.

FLORIDA 1991 Supp. (West, 491.0112)

Sexual misconduct by a psychotherapist; penalties

   (1)   Any psychotherapist who commits sexual misconduct with a client, or former client when the professional relationship was terminated primarily for the purpose of engaging in sexual contact, commits a felony of the third degree, punishable as provided in s.775.082 or s. 775.083; however a second or subsequent offense is a felony of the second degree, punishable as provided in s. 775.082, 775.083, or s. 775.084.

   (2)   Any psychotherapist who violates subsection (1) by means of therapeutic deception commits a felony of the second degree...

   (3)   The giving of consent by the client to any such act shall not be a defense to these offenses.

   (4)   For the purposes of this section:

   (a)   The term "psychotherapist" means any person licensed pursuant to chapter 458 (physician), chapter 459 (osteopath), chapter 464 (nurses), chapter 490 (Psychotherapist), chapter 491 (Clinical social worker, Marriage and Family Therapist, Mental Health Counselor), or any other person who provides or purports to provide treatment, diagnosis, assessment, evaluation, or counseling of mental or emotional illness, symptom, or condition.

   (b)   "Therapeutic deception" means a representation to the client that sexual contact by the psychotherapist is consistent with or part of the treatment of the client.

   (c)   "Sexual misconduct" means the oral, anal, or vaginal penetration of another by, or contact with, the sexual organ or another or the anal or vaginal penetration of another by any object.

   (d)   "Client" means a person to whom the services of a psychotherapist are provided.

Figure 2.2 *(continued)*

COLORADO 1990 Cum Supp (West, § 18-3-405.5)

Sexual assault on a client by a psychotherapist. (1) (a) Any actor who knowingly inflicts sexual penetration or sexual intrusion on a victim commits aggravated sexual assault on a client if:

- (I)   The actor is a psychotherapist and the victim is a client of the psychotherapist; or
- (II)   The actor is a psychotherapist and the victim is a client and the sexual penetration or intrusion occurred by means of therapeutic deception.
- (b)   Aggravated sexual assault on a client is a class 4 felony.
- (2) (a)   Any actor who knowingly subjects a victim to any sexual contact commits sexual assault on a client if:
- (I)   The actor is a psychotherapist and the victim is a client of the psychotherapist; or
- (II)   The actor is a psychotherapist and the victim is a client and the sexual contact occurred by means of therapeutic deception.
- (b)   Sexual assault on a client is a class 1 misdemeanor.
- (3)   Consent by the client to the sexual penetration, intrusion, or contact shall not constitute a defense to such offense.
- (4)   As used in this section, unless the context requires otherwise:
- (a)   "Client" means a person who seeks or receives psychotherapy from a psychotherapist.
- (b)   "Psychotherapist" means any person who performs or purports to perform psychotherapy, whether or not such person is licensed by the state...
- (c)   "Psychotherapy" means the treatment, diagnosis, or counseling in a professional relationship to assist individuals or groups to alleviate mental disorders, understand unconscious or conscious motivation, resolve emotional, relationship, or attitudinal conflicts, or modify behaviors which interfere with effective emotional, social, or intellectual functioning.
- (d)   "Therapeutic deception" means a representation by a psychotherapist that sexual contact, penetration, or intrusion by the psychotherapist is consistent with or part of the client's treatment.

CALIFORNIA 1990 (West, § 729)

Psychotherapist sexual exploitation
(a)   Any psychotherapist, or any person holding himself or herself out to be a psychotherapist, who engages in sexual intercourse, sodomy, oral copulation, or sexual contact with a patient or client, or with a former patient or client when the relationship was terminated primarily for the purpose of engaging in those acts, unless the psychotherapist has referred the patient or client to an independent and objective psychotherapist, recommended by a third-party psychotherapist, for treatment, is guilty of sexual exploitation by a psychotherapist.

Figure 2.2 *(continued)*

(b)   Sexual exploitation by a psychotherapist is a public offense:
   (1)   Violation of subdivision (a) is a misdemeanor.
   (2)   The second and subsequent violation of subdivision (a) shall be
          punishable by imprisonment in the county jail for a period of not more
          than one year, or a fine not exceeding one thousand dollars ($1,000),
          or both, or by imprisonment in the state prison, or a fine not exceeding
          five thousand dollars ($5,000), or both.

          For purposes of subdivision (a), in no instance shall consent of the
          patient or client by a defense. However, physicians and surgeons who
          engage in psychotherapy shall not be guilty of sexual exploitation by
          a psychotherapist for touching any intimate part of a patient or client
          unless the touching is outside the scope of medical examination and
          treatment, or the touching is done for sexual gratification.

(c)   For purposes of this section:
   (1)   "Psychotherapist" has the same meaning as defined in Section 728.
   (2)   "Sexual contact" means the touching of an intimate part of another
          person.
   (3)   "Intimate part" and "touching" have the same meanings as defined in
          [Code sections]

(d)   In the investigation and prosecution of a violation of this section, no person
       shall seek to obtain disclosure of any confidential files of other Patients,
       clients, or former patients or clients of the psychotherapist.

Sexual abuse, misconduct, or relations with a patient
The commission of any act of sexual abuse, misconduct, or relations with a patient,
client, or customer which is substantially related to the qualifications, functions, or
duties of the occupation for which a license was issued constitutes unprofessional
conduct and grounds for disciplinary action for any person licensed under this
division, under any initiative act referred to in this division...

**Prior sexual contact between psychotherapist and patient; psychotherapist or
employer providing and discussing brochure; failure to comply with section;
definitions**

(a)   Any psychotherapist or employer of a psychotherapist who becomes aware
       through a patient that the patient had alleged sexual intercourse or alleged
       sexual contact with a previous psychotherapist during the course of a prior
       treatment, shall provide to the patient a brochure promulgated by the
       department which delineates the rights of, and remedies for, patients who
       have been involved sexually with their psychotherapist. Further, the
       psychotherapist or employer shall discuss with the patient the brochure
       prepared by the department.

(b)   Failure to comply with this section constitutes unprofessional conduct.

Figure 2.2 *(continued)*

(c)   For the purpose of this section, the following definitions apply:
(1)   "Psychotherapist" means a physician specializing in the practice of psychiatry or practicing psychotherapy, a psychologist, a clinical social worker, a marriage, family, and child counselor, a psychological assistant, marriage, family, and child counselor registered intern, or associate clinical social worker.
(2)   "Sexual contact" means the touching of an intimate part of another person.
(3)   "Intimate part" and "touching" have the same meaning as defined in subdivision (d) of Section 243.4 of the Penal Code.
(4)   "The course of a prior treatment" means the period of time during which a patient first commences treatment for services which a psychotherapist is authorized to provide under his or her scope of practice or which the psychotherapist represents to the patient as being within his or her scope of practice until such time as the psychotherapist-patient relationship is terminated.

MINNESOTA Cum Supp 1991 (West, 148A.01)

Criminal sexual conduct in the third degree
Subdivision 1. Crime defined. A person who engages in sexual penetration with another person is guilty of criminal sexual conduct in the third degree if any of the following circumstances exists:
(h)   the actor is a psychotherapist and the complainant is a patient of the psychotherapist and the sexual penetration occurred during the psychotherapy session. Consent by the complainant is not a defense;
(i)   the actor is a psychotherapist and the complainant is a patient or former patient of the psychotherapist and the patient of former patient is emotionally dependent upon the psychotherapist;
(j)   the actor is a psychotherapist and the complainant is a patient or former patient and the sexual penetration occurred by means of therapeutic deception. consent by the complainant is not a defense;

Figure 2.2 *(continued)*

Criminal sexual conduct in the fourth degree
Subdivision 1. Crime defined. A person who engages in sexual contact with another person is guilty of criminal sexual conduct in the fourth degree is any of the following circumstances exists:

    (h)   the actor is a psychotherapist and the complainant is a patient of the psychotherapist and the sexual contact occurred during the psychotherapy session. Consent by the complainant is not a defense;

    (i)   the actor is a psychotherapist and the complainant is a patient or former patient of the psychotherapist and the patient or former patient _is emotionally dependent upon the psychotherapist;

    (j)   the actor is a psychotherapist and the complainant is a patient or former patient and the sexual contact occurred by means of therapeutic deception. Consent by the complainant is not a defense; or

    (k)   the actor accomplishes the sexual contact by means of false representation that the contact is for a bona fide medical purpose by a health care professional. Consent by the complainant is not a defense.

Subd.2.Penalty. A person convicted under subdivision 1 may be sentenced to imprisonment for not more than ten years or to a payment of a fine of not more than $20,000, or both.

1989) defines emotionally dependent as when "the patient's or former patient's emotional condition and the nature of the treatment provided by the psychotherapist are such that the psychotherapist knows or has reason to believe that the patient or former patient is unable to withhold consent to sexual contact by the psychotherapist." The negative consequences of crimes involving emotional dependency are similar to those of crimes involving therapeutic deception.

Similar Elements

In all eight statutes clinical social workers would be considered psychotherapists so as to fall within the purview of these criminal sanctions. The first similarity of all the statutes is the inclusive language used to describe psychotherapists. Table 2.2 shows the professionals that are covered by the statutes.

It seems clear that the statutes seek to encompass a broad range of clinicians—including clinical social workers. The statutes do a fairly complete job in including those professional classes most likely to render mental health services. There are several similarities among these statutes.

The first similarity is that every state *criminalizing* psychotherapist sexual misconduct, except California, includes all who *represent* themselves as counselors or therapists, even if they are not licensed. This definition is significant in broadening the scope of the criminal statute because it narrows the scope of possible defenses. This broadening of the definition of psychotherapist disallows the defense that perpetrators do not fit into the prescribed professional categories. For example, social workers guilty of sexual misconduct cannot claim innocence merely because they are not *licensed, clinical* social workers if they also purport to perform counseling or therapy. Ironically, in California, counselors perpetrating sexual misconduct could escape prosecution by the dubious distinction of having no state license. This broad provision eliminates acquittals based upon such a statutory technicality.

Also, this provision is a deterrent against laypeople who might represent themselves as therapists in order to perpetrate sexual misconduct. Such situations are not unknown. This provision puts laypeople on notice that they will be prosecuted if they fraudulently misrepresent counseling credentials or training for the purposes of perpetrating sexual misconduct.

The second similarity between statutes that criminalize clinical social worker sexual misconduct is the rather broad definition of "sexual contact." The California definition is "the touching of an intimate part of another person" (729(c)(2)). The California Penal Code further defines "touching" to include a host of sexual behaviors. This very broad approach is consistent among the state statutes and is intended to provide the most comprehensive coverage possible of sexual acts toward clients.

The third similarity is the almost universal disregard of "consent" as a defense for psychotherapist sexual misconduct. Only Maine does not specifically disallow such a defense. States explicitly criminalizing sexual misconduct explicitly renounce the defense of "consent." Barring criminal statutes against adultery and other like offenses, when two "consenting" adults have sexual contact, the law is not disturbed. One of the most remarkable elements of these statutes is that consent is *not* a defense of sexual misconduct. This is rightly so. Legal consent is no small issue and it requires more than saying "yes." For a person to give his or her legal consent for something—including sex—the person must be *competent* to consent, know what he or she is consenting to, and know the consequences of his or her decision.

The importance of legal consent can be illustrated by the following examples. Someone who consents to sexual intercourse is not *legally* competent to do so if she or he is considered a minor by the state in which she or he lives. Statutory rape statutes are designed to protect minors from sexual activity. Even if an adult says "yes" to visiting a man in his room, it is not a consent to sexual activity. This is one of the lessons it is hoped we have learned from recent discussions of date rape, although the old saying, "She said no, but she really meant yes" seems to resist its well-deserved death. Finally, even if an adult were to say "yes" to sexual intercourse and really mean it, this does not mean she or he consents to sex with a person infected with HIV. *"Informed consent"* is the same as legal consent and it means understanding all foreseeable risks involved in consenting to an activity. The statutes criminalizing sexual misconduct recognize that informed consent is not possible from a person undergoing psychotherapy. There are many reasons for this; they will be further explained in the chapter discussing the psychodynamics of sexual misconduct. The following is a brief discussion of why clients cannot legally consent to sexual activity with their clinical social workers.

Clients are not on an equal footing with the clinical social workers to whom they have gone for help. The client, simply because he or she is distressed enough to seek counseling in the first place, should enjoy heightened protections similar to those of patients in hospitals. Clients of clinical social workers pay money to enjoy a heightened standard of care—beyond that exercised, say, between two friends exchanging gossip over the backyard fence. In an instance where no professional relationship exists, one neighbor may respond callously, even maliciously, to his or her neighbor without legal consequence. However, when a clinical social worker takes on a client, the *standard of care* changes and the clinician is held to a heightened standard for the client. This *standard of care* is addressed in detail in the next chapter. It is enough to say here that the *criminal* statutes penalizing clinical social workers are consistent with the *civil* statutes penalizing clinicians for behavior below the authorized standard.

Clients cannot legally consent to sexual relations with their therapists due to the psychological dynamics of the client-clinician relationship. Beyond the sense of the clinician's power and the client's vulnerability, the dynamics of personality and other psychiatric disorders (as well as the transference phenomena) conspire to make clients legally unable to appreciate the facts necessary to make a decision to have sex with a clinician or to appreciate the consequences of such a decision. Instead of infantilizing or patronizing clients, these criminal statutes recognize the power relations and psychological dynamics that routinely exist between client and clinical social worker. Other states can be expected to pass similar legislation. A model statute for future legislation is included at the end of this chapter.

The final similar element is the relatively severe sanctions imposed for conviction under these statutes. As table 2.1 indicates, all the states provide for felony charges to be brought against perpetrators. Felony convictions are distinguishable from misdemeanor charges in that felony convictions may involve jail time. Misdemeanors usually involve the payment of a fine and less than a one-year jail sentence. Additionally, a felony conviction may mean the loss of voting rights, the inability to hold public office, the high cost of defending against these more serious charges, and public embarrassment.

While judges usually have some discretion in sentencing a convicted felon, Minnesota illustrates the severity of a possible felony conviction under its clinician-client sexual misconduct statute. There is one sanction for sexual intercourse (not more than fifteen years or not more than $30,000 or both) and another sanction for sexual contact (not more than ten years or not more than $20,000 or both). While *any* criminal conviction is a serious offense, the fact that all the states have *felony* charges that may be brought against the perpetrator is an indication of the severity legislators attach to this problem.

Dissimilar Statutory Elements

Along with similar elements among the statutes, the state statutes also exhibit significant differences. These differences include definitions of what constitutes the practice of counseling or psychotherapy, whether or not sexual relations with former clients are included among the prohibited acts, and whether or not therapeutic deception is an element of the crime.

Of prime importance to the effectiveness of these criminal statutes is the breadth of the clinician's duties that are covered. As we know, clinical social workers perform many duties beyond that of a narrow definition of psychotherapy. For example, could a clinical social worker who *consults* with a group of social work interns be subject to the law if the clinician engages in sexual activity with one of the consultees? States answer this question differently (see figure 2.2). North Dakota seems to offer a comprehensive description of the clinician's duties by covering "any treatment, consultation, interview, or examination." Wisconsin uses precisely the same language. The Florida and Colorado statutes give an inclusive definition to the function of clinicians by defining "client" as "a person to whom the services of a psychotherapist are provided." Wisconsin defines the scope of the clinician-client connection as "any on-going therapist-patient or therapist-client relationship . . .'' While the Wisconsin statute appears somewhat ambiguous, the "any" can be construed to mean the full scope of clinical and consulting services. Such a broad definition would include all the professional activities in which clients are involved.

Other states seem to define more ambiguously the clinical roles that are covered by the statute. California and Minnesota address only a clinician's relationship with a patient or a client. The scope of services remains unaddressed. Unfortunately, this omission may be used as a loophole for clinicians guilty of sexual misconduct who can convince a jury that they were "mere" consultants, supervisors, one-time interviewers or examiners, or conducting psychotherapy. Because criminal statutes can be construed in this fashion, it is necessary to examine this element of the statutes more closely. Indeed, the California and Minnesota legislatures may have intended to prosecute clinicians *only* when they are engaged in psychothera-peutic function when engaging in the prohibited sexual behavior.

The issue is this: should sexual acts between clinicians and consultees, interviewees, and supervisees be criminalized the same way as sexual acts between clinicians engaged in full-blown psycho-therapeutic relationships? On the negative side is the assertion that there is a qualitatively different relationship between a consultee, a supervisee, an interviewee, and a clinician in a short-term, quasi-therapeutic role. For example, a clinician consulting for a department of social services may be less likely to evoke the same emotional dependence, exert the same therapeutic deceptions, or impose his will upon a group of consultees as would a long-term therapeutic counselor. Additionally, consultees are less likely to have the emotional distress and psychic vulnerability, as well as possible psychiatric illness, as do strictly psychotherapeutic clients.

On the affirmative side is the assertion that otherwise guilty clinicians may hide behind the technical terms of "psychotherapeutic clients" versus "consultees" or "supervisees" to avoid prosecution. Such clinicians may claim that sexual relations with consultees or supervisees are not covered by the statute. The work of prosecutors would be easier if they did not have the additional burden of showing that the defendant-clinician was engaged in one particular role at the time of the alleged crime. The argument can be made that an inclusive reading of clinical roles best protects the general public. Additionally, the argument can be made that a broader reading more effectively protects the public. The ultimate resolution of this issue rests, as do most of these issues, in the hands of state legislators. Where state legislators want to criminalize a broad range of behaviors on the part of clinical social workers, the statutes will include a broad range of professional activities or broadly define "client"—which by implication may include all professional acts or relationships.

The second dissimilar element among the criminal statutes is whether the sexual behavior criminalized includes former clients or is confined to current clients. Again, there is a variety of approaches used by various states along a continuum from including past clients to only current clients, with interesting variations in between. One provision of the Minnesota statute includes both current and former clients. The provisions of the Minnesota statutes including therapeutic deception and emotional dependence impose the sanctions for only current clients, as do the Wisconsin, North Dakota, and Colorado statutes. The middle ground is covered by the California and Florida statutes, where former clients are included "when the relationship was terminated primarily for the purpose of engaging in those [prohibited sexual acts]." This provision means that clinical social workers cannot avoid prosecution merely by terminating a professional relationship with a client so that a sexual relationship could ensue. An instance where a clinical social worker intends to begin a sexual relationship with a current client, and terminates therapy simply in order to avoid prosecution, is a cynical ploy. Such a scheme does nothing to undo damage done to the client or protect the "former" client from future emotional trauma. This provision is a significant attempt to close loopholes in the law.

The third dissimilarity among the states' statutes is the provision that therapeutic deception and emotional dependency are elements of the crime. Florida, Colorado, and Minnesota have statutes that make therapeutic deception a separate, more severe offense. Typical of the statutes is Florida's, stating that "any psychotherapist who violates [the sexual misconduct law] by means of therapeutic deception commits a felony of the second degree" (491.0112(2), 1991 Supp.). Not only do these states make therapeutic deception a separate offense in each state, but the punishment for sexual misconduct with the element of therapeutic deception is more severe. For example, the Florida statute considers "mere" sexual misconduct (first offense) a felony in the third degree. With the element of therapeutic deception, the crime is considered a felony in the second degree—a more severe crime. The difference between a third degree and second degree felony can mean thousands more dollars in fines and years more in jail.

The therapeutic deception element of the crime rightly carries a stiffer penalty than sexual misconduct alone. The crimes should be distinguished because the dynamics are different. The following paragraph seeks to distinguish the reasoning behind making sexual misconduct and therapeutic deception two separate offenses (as in Colorado and Minnesota) and viewing therapeutic deception as an aggravating element of sexual misconduct (as in Florida), thereby requiring a more severe penalty. In providing such a discussion the author runs a risk of being misinterpreted as seeming to suggest that crimes without therapeutic deception are less significant than those with the element of therapeutic deception. All crimes against clients are significant; however, those including the element of deception, fraud, or misrepresentation are in a category of severity all their own.

When a client and clinician agree to engage in sexual activity, at least the agreement is based upon *some* consequences or consent. Of course, there is a status coercion on the part of the clinician, as we have previously discussed. And, of course, the acts are unethical if not illegal in all jurisdictions. But it may be the case that the client is not being actively deceived in the process. It may be the case that the client and the clinician are attracted to each other and enter into the sexual activity with what they both perceive as mutual self-interest. In this case, at least both parties know (or have the *potential* of knowing) that they are acting outside the bounds of the therapeutic relationship.

Where deception, fraud, or misrepresentation is perpetrated by the clinician, there is not even the possibility that the client can act in his or her own best interest. It is unfair and perhaps impossible to expect that a client has the knowledge or insight to critique or even question the credentials, the clinical orientation, or the interventions of the clinical social worker. When a clinical social worker says he or she possesses the necessary license to practice in a certain state, or shows papers, licenses, or diplomas to that effect, a client cannot be expected to seek further evidence of accreditation. So too, when a clinician says to a client that sexual activity between them is a necessary or an advisable method of treatment, a client should not be placed in a position to prove that such a treatment option is harmful or dangerous. The client, already distressed enough to seek help in the first place, should not be placed in the position of playing detective with the very person to whom he or she has turned for help. Certainly, clients can be expected to protect themselves to a certain extent, but the statutes criminalizing clinician-client sexual activity are predicated upon this power differential.

The costs of misconduct to the clients, to the public, and to the clinical social work profession are readily deduced. The cost to clients is counted in their mistrust of the profession. If one clinician can deceive them, why should not another? People in need of clinical help may even stop seeking help because they cannot trust the profession as a whole. Professions have developed no foolproof method to uncover fraud. The cost to society is counted in those potential clients turned away from all help by harmful experiences with fraud. The cost to the clinical social work profession is counted in the loss of reputation, standing in the community, and respect in its professional memberships. States that more severely punish sex crimes involving therapeutic deception (and other fraud) appropriately and wisely protect the public.

Thus far in this chapter we have scrutinized statutes criminalizing sexual activity with clients. However, our task is only partially completed. While criminal statutes are legislative efforts in *fashioning* laws, the judicial branch of government has the equally important task of *interpreting* laws. No discussion of the laws of psychotherapist sexual misconduct (or other laws) can be complete without an equally scrupulous discussion of judicial decisions. Judicial decisions give the flesh to the skeleton of statutory law. Judicial decisions establish the course of future cases (precedence) and even guide legislatures to change or modify laws. Additionally, and particularly for our purposes, judicial decisions provide case studies for the legal and ethical consideration of professional groups. Three law cases adjudicated under the "psychotherapist sexual misconduct" laws have already been decided—two in Minnesota and one in Wisconsin.

THE ADJUDICATION OF CRIMINAL STATUTES

Two of the cases to be examined were decided in 1990 and one case was decided in 1991. All cases were appealed to higher state courts. Also, all three cases were tried under the state statutes criminalizing client-clinician sexual misconduct. But this is where the similarities end. Each case was appealed on different grounds. Additionally, each case involved a different class of clinician—neither case involving a clinical social worker. However, clinical social workers need to be aware of these cases for two reasons. First, because clinical social workers as professionals would be treated the same under each statute as the two professionals (generic therapist, minister) involved in the cases. Second, clinical social workers would face similar trial procedures (expert witnesses, the kind of evidence used at such trials, defenses available, etc.) as in the cases cited below. The following sections describe and analyze these relevant cases.

The case of *State v. Dutton* (1990) is considered first, because the case, although appealed, reached the substance of guilt or innocence. The second case considered (*State v. Eichman* 1990) did not reach the legal substance, but was appealed upon procedural grounds. In *State v. Ohrtman* (1991) the state appeals court had to decide if a hug was "sexual contact" for the purpose of the criminal statute. All three cases are significant but for different reasons.

In the *Dutton* case a minister was convicted of four felony counts of psychotherapist-patient criminal sexual conduct. The facts of this case illustrate how the Minnesota statute operates and how legal theories operate in such cases. The client sought help in 1985 for low self-esteem, suicidal thoughts, grief, compulsions, an eating disorder, and premenstrual syndrome. The sessions began with defendant Dutton and the plaintiff-client discussing scriptures and soon led to discussion of sexual issues. The client said that she did not come to Dutton for sexual counseling, but the two hugged at one session and the next session engaged in "hugging and passionate kissing." In April of 1986 Dutton touched the client intimately during her menstrual period, saying that such contact would help her resolve any negative thoughts about her menstruation.

In May of 1986 Dutton had sexual intercourse with the client for the first time, saying that such sexual activity would be good because, while the client's husband was selfish, Dutton was unselfish. Their sexual intercourse continued into August and September of 1986, during which time the client wrote that she had relinquished control of her life to Dutton and had given him thousands of dollars, and that Dutton had intimated that sexual intercourse was therapeutically warranted to lower her sexual inhibitions. He was convicted under the "sexual contact" provisions of the Minnesota law (above) for these acts.

In the second case a Minnesota appeals court further clarified and explained the law against psychotherapist sexual misconduct. A client complained that her male counselor hugged her and pressed her breasts to his chest after removing his shirt and requesting a backrub. The court ruled that a hug does not constitute "sexual contact" within the meaning of the statute (*State v. Ohrtman* 1991).

The court used a dictionary definition of "touch" to distinguish a "hug" that connotes a show of affection from touching for sexual gratification. In dismissing this case, the Minnesota court has also placed significant limits on the scope of this law. The case did not specifically address the backrub or removal of the shirt.

The third case, *State v. Eichman* (1990), illustrates how Wisconsin (and perhaps other states) may construe the term "therapists" to include clinical social work functions. The defendant, a generic therapist employed in a drug and alcohol after-care facility as a house manager, was accused of four counts of sexual exploitation. His duties included conducting group and individual therapy sessions and supervising the treatment goals of the residents. The main issue on appeal was whether or not "expert testimony" could be offered to determine whether the defendant was a psychotherapist under the statute's definition. The trial court refused to allow the expert to testify, but a state appeals court reversed the trial court and allowed the expert to testify. The Supreme Court of Wisconsin, in the *Eichman* case, affirmed the appeals court and ruled that expert testimony would be allowed to help the court determine if the duties of Eichman were psychotherapeutic within the meaning of the statute.

A discussion will follow later in this chapter, detailing the use and importance of "expert witnesses" in criminal cases relating to clinical social worker sexual misconduct. It is enough to say now that the *Eichman* case helped to establish the use of expert witnesses in criminal statutes involving clinical social worker (and other psychotherapist) sexual misconduct. The significance of the *Eichman* ruling lies in the fact that trial courts will have wide discretion in calling expert witnesses to testify as to the meaning of various terms within the sexual misconduct criminal statutes—including "psychotherapist," "emotional dependency," and "therapeutic deception." Expert testimony to help clarify these "terms of art" (professional jargon) is necessary so that judges and juries can render informed decisions. The statute renders a broad reading of both "therapist" and "psychotherapy" and does not require state or professional licensure. Thus, it is likely that this statute will include B.S.W. graduates as well as M.S.W. clinicians who perform a wide range of duties.

ISSUES IN THE CASES

The following sections describe and analyze significant issues raised by these two cases. These issues include the criminal elements necessary to sustain a conviction, the permissible use of expert witnesses at trials, and the defenses available to those criminally charged with sexual misconduct.

Necessary Criminal Elements

Each state establishes the elements for each criminal act. Obviously, whether the defendant actually committed the alleged act is a crucial factor; however, the prosecution must also prove additional elements of the crime. In determining the guilt of Dutton in the Minnesota case, the court reviewed whether Dutton had exploited his client's emotional dependency and used therapeutic deception. An important part of this statute is the elements of emotional dependency and therapeutic deception (Minnesota statute 609.344(i-k), 1991). Unfortunately, a Minnesota case has already had to apply these legal terms to a criminal case (*State v. Dutton* 1990). Emotional dependence means that the plaintiff must prove that he or she is incapable of withholding consent to sexual acts, and therapeutic deception means that the therapist told the client that sexual acts were a legitimate part of the therapeutic process (p. 192).

Under the Minnesota statute, the jury had to find that Dutton committed the sexual acts while the client had an emotional dependency on the therapist and that Dutton used therapeutic deception in his acts. The court found that Dutton's client was unable to effectively withhold sexual consent to Dutton since she had virtually signed away her life to him. The court had evidentiary letters in which the former client stated, "I've relinquished control to you" (p. 191). Additionally, the court found that Dutton misrepresented the nature of the therapy to include sexual contact. This means that the defendant fraudulently induced the client to engage in sexual acts under the false premise that such acts were a legitimate part of therapy. Satisfying these elements in a criminal trial satisfies the *"mens rea"* —the criminal intent—necessary for conviction. American jurisprudence requires that juries find that criminal defendants *intended* the behaviors that causes the convictions. Thus, the jury had to find that Dutton knew, or should have known, that the client was under his power and control when they had sexual relations.

The court heard the testimony of three expert witnesses to help clarify the nature of the relationship between Dutton and his client. Expert witnesses help the judge and jury to understand the nature of psychiatric illness and the resultant client-psychotherapist relationship.

The Use of Expert Witnesses

Increasingly, both civil and criminal courts use the testimony of experts, where allowed by state law, to assist the court's understanding of specialized information. In this case the prosecution called three expert witnesses to help prove its case: a licensed consulting psychologist, a licensed clinical psychologist, and a pastoral counselor of the same religious denomination as the defendant Dutton. The consulting psychologist testified that Dutton's client suffered a dependency personality disorder and was unable to make everyday decisions without excessive reassurance from others. Both the pastoral counselor and the clinical psychologist testified that a gap in power existed between Dutton and the client because the client "idealized" the pastor.

The inclusion of expert witnesses as a part of the criminal justice system is important to clinical social workers for three reasons. First, clinicians may be called upon to testify against other therapists as to the standards of behavior and treatment commonly held by clinical social workers under similar circumstances. Of course, the defendant may offer expert witnesses on his or her own behalf as well.

Second, therapist-defendants need to know that prosecutors can bring to bear a sophisticated array of professionals to testify that any given therapist-client relationship is not only nontherapeutic but also meets criminal standards. Thus, professional judgments and the rationale of therapeutic interventions are no longer beyond the scrutiny of the courts nor beyond the reach of the law.

Third, the advent of expert witnesses at trial undermines the commonly held but erroneous notion that what happens in the confines of a therapy session is strictly confidential (Bullis 1990). Increasingly, courts will scrutinize the therapist's treatment plans, words, actions, meeting times, number of sessions, location of sessions, clinical notes, and related materials. Clinical social workers who proceed upon the assumption that their intentions and conduct in private consultations remain safe from scrutiny operate under an illusion.

The following section illustrates this last point. Mr. Dutton, as a defense, asserted that his therapeutic sessions were protected under the constitutional right of privacy. While this defense was rejected by the court, the court's rationale for dismissing this putative defense illustrates the extent to which clinical social workers' "confidential" sessions with clients will be legally shielded from judicial scrutiny.

The Privacy Defense

In his appeal, defendant Dutton claimed that he had a constitutional right of privacy to engage in consensual, adult sexual activity. The right of privacy has developed over a thirty-year legal history and encompasses some of our most fundamental freedoms. The U.S. Supreme Court held that married persons have a *privacy* right to obtain contraceptives (*Griswold v. Connecticut* 1965) and later extended this right to unmarried persons as well (*Eisenstadt v. Baird* 1972). The limited right to abortion in *Roe v. Wade* (1973) was predicated upon the right of privacy developed in these earlier decisions. The right of privacy has become a significant public protection.

However, the *Dutton* court found that the privacy right is a limited right and is subject to state regulations. The court specifically noted that homosexual behavior between consenting adults may be state regulated (*Bowers v. Hardwick* 1986). The court found that Dutton's private sexual behavior could be regulated by the police power of the state to protect the health and well-being of its citizens. Thus, the Minnesota court ruled that the state law (above) could properly be applied against Dutton.

Additional Criminally-Related Statutes

The following section describes two statutes, placed with the criminal statutes, relating to psychotherapeutic sexual misconduct.

Reporting Requirements. An additional aspect of the Wisconsin law provides that Wisconsin therapists report clients victimized by other therapists (Wisconsin statute 940.(3), 1990). The law requires that a therapist who has a "reasonable cause to suspect" that a client has been the victim of improper sexual behavior by another therapist ask the client if he or she wants the current therapist to report such incidents to the proper licensing board. The county district attorney then decides whether to prosecute. The state law provides for reasonable confidentiality of such reports (940.22(4)) and for the reasonable immunity from liability for those making reports (940.22(5)).

Providing and Discussing Brochure. California law requires that psychotherapists distribute a brochure and discuss it with clients who allege sexual relations with a previous therapist (728, Bus. & Prof. Code). The brochure, developed by the licensing board, delineates the rights and remedies for such clients. As in the related California criminal statute, clinical social workers are included in this statute's requirements.

CONCLUSION

This chapter described and discussed state statutes criminalizing sexual exploitation by psychotherapists. Clinical social workers are included by all the states criminalizing such acts. This chapter analyzed similarities and differences among these statutes. Two important similarities among the statutes, regardless of the state, are that "consent" is no defense for sexual contact with clients and that the crimes for conviction are felonies and high misdemeanors.

These statutes seem to constitute a legal trend. Other states are likely to create similar statutes. Given the general trend toward litigation and professional regulation, these types of statutes can be expected to proliferate.

REFERENCES

Bowers v. Hardwick, 478 U.S. 186 (1986).

Britton, A.H. (1988). Sexual abuse in the professional relationship. *Hamline Law Review*,11, 247–80.

Bullis, R.K. (1990). When confessional walls have ears: The changing clergy privileged communications law. *Pastoral Psychology*, 39(2), 75–84.

Eisenstadt v. Baird, 405 U.S. 438 (1972).

Griswold v. Connecticut, 381 U.S. 479 (1965).

Roe v. Wade, 410 U.S. 113 (1973).

State v. Carpenter, 459 N.W. 2d 121 (Minn. 1990).

State v. Dutton, 450 N.W. 2d 189 (Minn. App. 1990).

State v. Eichman, 456 N.W. 2d 143 (Wis. 1990).

State v. Ohrtman, 466 N.W. 2d 1 (Minn. App. 1991).

Chapter 3

Civil Liability for Sexual Misconduct

INTRODUCTION

The preceding chapter discussed and analyzed criminal actions for sexual abuse by clinical social workers and other therapists. Chapter 3 discusses and analyzes civil actions that can apply against clinical workers who are sexually involved with clients. This chapter will describe and assess the kinds of civil liability possible against clinical social workers who engage in sexual activity with clients, how these liabilities have been applied in cases involving clinical social workers (and other professionals), and defenses available to the accused clinicians. This chapter will also describe other sanctions available against clinicians engaged in sexual misconduct with clients.

Before discussing the theories of liability and how they are applied against social workers, some preliminary issues must be addressed. These issues are the differences between civil and criminal liability and how they are related, the burden of proof, and the advantages and disadvantages of pursuing criminal actions versus civil actions.

CRIMINAL VERSUS CIVIL ACTIONS

The theoretical difference between a civil and a criminal action is that *civil* law resolves disputes between private parties through private attorneys and *criminal* law involves a resolution of public law through public officials. Criminal law involves fines and jail and is tried by public prosecutors. Conversely, civil law involves only fines and is tried by private attorneys. For example, a "slip and fall" case between a customer and a supermarket is a private, civil matter. The customer slips on spilled tomato juice on the floor of the supermarket and is injured. If the customer sues, the customer must obtain a private attorney and try the case against the supermarket, which has obtained its own private attorney. If the supermarket settles the claim out of court, by means of a contract, the contract and negotiations may be kept private.

Conversely, should a thief steal a case of tomato juice from the same supermarket and be caught, the criminal action against the thief is a public affair. The alleged thief is arrested by public officials (the police), carried to the station in public vehicles (squad car), detained in the public safety building, brought to trial by another public officer (district attorney), charged with a public crime established by publicly elected officials (the state legislature), and tried before another public officer (judge) in a courtroom bought and paid for by public funds, in an arena open to the public. Additionally, except in juvenile cases, the trial is open to the public and publicly reported by the press.

Another important difference between civil and criminal cases is *who* must initiate the action. A private party must initiate a civil action. The person who slipped on the tomato juice (or someone connected to the injured party) must initiate and continue the legal action against the supermarket. The police or district attorney cannot get involved unless the supermarket also broke a law. On the other hand, a private citizen cannot charge the tomato juice thief with a criminal violation. That charge must come from the district attorney.

Finally, there can be a connection between civil and criminal cases with the same facts. A clinical social worker's professional misconduct can give rise to both civil and criminal liability. For example, Pennsylvania clinical social work regulations (337.630) provide that the violation of licensing laws carries misdemeanor penalties as well as possible civil and administrative penalties. It is possible that a criminal charge of sexual misconduct could give rise to a civil case as well. It is likely that a prospective plaintiff would allow the criminal case to proceed, with the police gathering and sorting evidence, before beginning a civil case. While a criminal conviction does not require a finding of civil liability, the evidence surrounding such a conviction can be used as evidence of liability. On the other hand, a finding of "not guilty" does not preclude a finding of civil liability. How a judge or jury determines the degree of evidence necessary to determine criminal guilt or civil liability is called the burden of proof.

BURDEN OF PROOF

The differences between civil litigation and a criminal trial also are apparent in how difficult it is to *prove* a criminal offense. In the United States jurisprudence, a criminal charge must be proven "beyond a reasonable doubt." We have all heard the phrase, but few understand its legal context and implications. The burden of proof "beyond a reasonable doubt" is a very high standard of proof. This high standard is by design. American justice has traditionally required proof of a high standard before depriving citizens of their liberty. "Beyond a reasonable doubt" means that if there is a reasonable doubt that the accused did not commit the crime with which he or she is charged, he or she must be set free.

Civil cases do not require such a high standard of proof. The two standards of proof in civil cases are "preponderance of the evidence" or "clear and convincing evidence." Both these burdens of proof for civil cases are easier to prove than the "beyond a reasonable doubt" required in the criminal cases. This difference in the standards of proof required between civil and criminal cases is a reason why injured parties sometimes elect to try the case civilly rather than criminally.

The differences in who may bring a civil or criminal action has important bearings on criminal and civil proceedings. Take, for example, the case in which a clinical social worker behaves sexually toward a client in a state where such behavior is criminalized. The district attorney must bring the criminal charges against the clinician— the injured party cannot do so. This means that, theoretically, charges can be brought against the clinician whether or not the client wants to charge the clinician. The district attorney, in consultation with the police, makes that decision based upon the likelihood of success at trial. The likelihood of success is indicated by how much physical evidence there is (love letters, etc.) and how numerous and credible the prosecution's witnesses are likely to be. The district attorney's decision about bringing a case to trial must always be made in light of the difficulty of proving guilt "beyond a reasonable doubt." The district attorney's pursuit of justice is always related to the ability to prove the case.

Other reasons why a clinician may elect a civil trial over a criminal trial are the availability of money damages in a civil case and the sometimes greater latitude in meeting the requirements of a civil judgment as opposed to a criminal conviction. The criminal law is intended to punish the wrongdoer and to protect society, not to reimburse the victim. While cities and counties increasingly employ "Victim/Witness Coordinators" to assist the victims of crimes and to aid in the witnesses' testimony, the criminal law does not provide for compensation to the victims of crime (Bullis and Bullis 1994). Compensation for the victims is the province of the civil law.

Also, victims of clinician sexual exploitation may opt for a civil trial to avoid the pitfalls of the statute of limitations or the inability to meet the required criminal elements. The statute of limitations sets limits on the length of time that can transpire before a legal action can be brought. If the statute of limitations has passed on a criminal action, the case cannot be brought, even if there is sufficient evidence to prosecute. However, the statute of limitations for a civil action may not have passed; thus, the case could be tried in civil court. By the same token, where the elements necessary for a criminal conviction cannot be proven, the elements for civil liability may be proven. As we have seen in the previous chapter, "emotional dependency" is a criminal element in some statutes. If the prosecutor cannot prove emotional dependence, the jury may not convict the clinician. However, under the rules of a civil trial, the client's attorney may be able to prove the elements necessary to prove liability.

Proving civil liability against social workers is much easier when courts have the authority to do so. There are two ways in which courts obtain the authority to try civil cases. First, legislatures give them the statutory authority. Second, courts decide, from case precedent, that they have the authority.

The following section describes examples of state statutes that confer upon their courts the power to hear cases against social workers *for the specific tort of sexual exploitation*. The word "tort" comes from an old English word for "twisted." Tort law is a generic term for civil liability law.

STATE STATUTES AUTHORIZING A LEGAL ACTION FOR CLIENT SEXUAL EXPLOITATION

This section will examine four state statutes authorizing courts to try cases for psychotherapist sexual exploitation: Illinois (70, Section 801, 1989), California (Bus. & Prof. Code, 726-27, 1990), Wisconsin (895.70,

1991 supp.), and Minnesota (148A.01, 1989). Figure 3.1 reproduces the Illinois civil statute. The statutes will serve as comparisons to illustrate a specific cause of action for psychotherapist sexual misconduct or other similar label. It is important to note that no specific statutes, such as those cited above, are needed to civilly sue social workers for sexual misconduct. Such statutes, however, provide an easier, more defined legal route to impose liability. There are several common points among the statutes.

Both the Minnesota and Illinois statutes specifically name social workers, along with other professionals such as "psychotherapists," as those who can be sued. Both states include *former* patients as well as *current* patients as those with whom the sexual contact gives rise to the liability. This provision means that social workers who have sexual contact with former clients are liable from up to two years (Minnesota) or one year (Illinois). Imposing liability for sexual contact with former clients, as in the criminal statutes, undermines a psychotherapist's excuse of terminating a professional relationship with a client for the purpose of sexual relations.

Both statutes eliminate "consent" on the part of the patient as a defense. Again, this provision follows the criminal statutes. Both statutes also explicitly define the nature of the illicit "sexual contact." In fact, both states use identical language. The language is reproduced below:

> Sexual contact means any of the following . . . sexual intercourse, cunnilingus, fellatio, anal intercourse or any intrusion, however slight, into the genital or anal openings of the patient's or former patient's body or any part of the psychotherapist's body or by any object used by the psychotherapist for this purpose, or any intrusion, however slight, into the genital or anal openings of the psychotherapist's body by any part of the patient's or former patient's body or by any object used by the patient or former patient for this purpose, if agreed to by the psychotherapist;
>
> kissing of, or the intentional touching by the psychotherapist of the patient's or former patient's genital area, groin, inner thigh, buttocks, or breast or of the clothing covering any of these body parts if the psychotherapist agrees to the kissing or intentional touching;
>
> kissing of, or the intentional touching by the patient or former patient of the psychotherapist's genital area, groin, inner thigh, buttocks, or breast or of the clothing covering any of these body parts if the psychotherapist agrees to the kissing or intentional touching.

This explicit definition makes plain that the psychotherapist risks liability even if the patient or former patient initiates the contact and gets agreement from the psychotherapist. Both statutes provide for

EXPLOITATION IN PSYCHOTHERAPY   **740 ILCS 140/1**

ACT 140. SEXUAL EXPLOITATION IN PSYCHOTHERAPY ACT

Section
140/0.01.   Short title.
140/1.   Definitions.
140/2.   Cause of action for sexual exploitation.
140/3.   Liability of employer.
140/4.   Scope of discovery.
140/5.   Admission of evidence.
140/6.   Limitation period.
140/7.   Application.

Library References

I.L.P. Mental Health.

WESTLAW Electronic Research

See WESTLAW Electronic Research Guide following the Preface.

140/0.01. Short title

§ 0.01. Short title. This Act may be cited as the Sexual Exploitation in Psychotherapy Act.

P.A. 85–1254, § 0.01, added by P.A. 86–1324, § 533, eff. Sept. 6, 1990.
Formerly Ill.Rev.Stat.1991, ch. 70, ¶ 800.

Historical and Statutory Notes

Title of Act:
An Act concerning sexual exploitation by psychotherapists. P.A. 85–1254, approved Aug. 30, 1988, eff. Jan. 1, 1989.

140/1. Definitions

§ 1. Definitions. In this Act:

(a) "Emotionally dependent" means that the nature of the patient's or former patient's emotional condition and the nature of the treatment provided by the psychotherapist are such that the psychotherapist knows or has reason to believe that the patient or former patient is unable to withhold consent to sexual contact by the psychotherapist.

(b) "Former patient" means a person who was given psychotherapy within 1 year prior to sexual contact with the psychotherapist.

(c) "Patient" means a person who seeks or obtains psychotherapy.

(d) "Psychotherapist" means a physician, psychologist, nurse, chemical dependency counselor, social worker, or other person, whether or not licensed by the State, who performs or purports to perform psychotherapy.

(e) "Psychotherapy" means the professional treatment, assessment, or counseling of a mental or emotional illness, symptom, or condition. "Psychotherapy" does not include counseling of a spiritual or religious nature, social work, or casual advice given by a friend or family member.

(f) "Sexual contact" means any of the following, whether or not occurring with the consent of a patient or former patient:

(continued on next page)

Figure 3.1 *(continued)*

740 ILCS 140/1   CIVIL LIABILITIES

(1) sexual intercourse, cunnilingus, fellatio, anal intercourse or any intrusion, however slight, into the genital or anal openings of the patient's or former patient's body by any part of the psychotherapist's body or by any object used by the psychotherapist for that purpose, or any intrusion, however slight, into the genital or anal openings of the psychotherapist's body by any part of the patient's or former patient's body or by any object used by the patient or former patient for that purpose, if agreed to by the psychotherapist;

(2) kissing or intentional touching by the psychotherapist of the patient's or former patient's genital area, groin, inner thigh, buttocks, or breast or the clothing covering any of these body parts;

(3) kissing or intentional touching by the patient or former patient of the psychotherapist's genital area, groin, inner thigh, buttocks, or breast or the clothing covering any of these body parts if the psychotherapist agrees to the kissing or intentional touching.

"Sexual contact" includes a request by the psychotherapist for conduct described in paragraphs (1) through (3).

"Sexual contact" does not include conduct described in paragraph (1) or (2) that is a part of standard medical treatment of a patient, casual social contact not intended to be sexual in character, or inadvertent touching.

(g) "Therapeutic deception" means a representation by a psychotherapist that sexual contact with the psychotherapist is consistent with or part of the patient's or former patient's treatment.

P.A. 85–1254, § 1, eff. Jan. 1, 1989.
Formerly Ill.Rev.Stat.1991, ch. 70, ¶ 801.

Library References

Words and Phrases (Perm.Ed.)

140/2. Cause of action for sexual exploitation

§ 2. Cause of action for sexual exploitation. (a) A cause of action against a psychotherapist for sexual exploitation exists for a patient or former patient for injury caused by sexual contact with the psychotherapist, if the sexual contact occurred:

(1) during the period the patient was receiving psychotherapy from the psychotherapist; or

(2) after the period the patient received psychotherapy from the psychotherapist if (i) the former patient was emotionally dependent on the psychotherapist or (ii) the sexual contact occurred by means of therapeutic deception.

(b) The patient or former patient may recover damages from a psychotherapist who is found liable for sexual exploitation. It is not a defense to the action that sexual contact with a patient occurred outside a therapy or treatment session or that it occurred off the premises regularly used by the psychotherapist for therapy or treatment sessions.

P.A. 85–1254, § 1, eff. Jan. 1, 1989.
Formerly Ill.Rev.Stat.1991, ch. 70, ¶ 802.

Figure 3.1 *(continued)*

EXPLOITATION IN PSYCHOTHERAPY   **740 ILCS 140/6**

140/3. Liability of employer

§ 3. Liability of employer. An employer of a psychotherapist may be liable under Section 2 if the employer fails or refuses to take reasonable action when the employer knows or has reason to know that the psychotherapist engaged in sexual contact with the plaintiff or any other patient or former patient of the psychotherapist.

P.A. 85–1254, § 1, eff. Jan. 1, 1989.
Formerly Ill.Rev.Stat.1991, ch. 70, ¶ 803.

140/4. Scope of discovery

§ 4. Scope of discovery. (a) In an action for sexual exploitation, evidence of the plaintiff's sexual history is not subject to discovery except when the plaintiff claims damage to sexual functioning; or

(1) the defendant requests a hearing prior to conducting discovery and makes an offer of proof of the relevancy of the history; and

(2) the court finds that the history is relevant and that the probative value of the history outweighs its prejudicial effect.

(b) The court shall allow the discovery only of specific information or examples of the plaintiff's conduct that are determined by the court to be relevant. The court's order shall detail the information or conduct that is subject to discovery.

P.A. 85–1254, § 1, eff. Jan. 1, 1989.
Formerly Ill.Rev.Stat.1991, ch. 70, ¶ 804.

140/5. Admission of evidence

§ 5. Admission of evidence. (a) In an action for sexual exploitation, evidence of the plaintiff's sexual history is not admissible except when:

(1) the defendant requests a hearing prior to trial and makes an offer of proof of the relevancy of the history; and

(2) the court finds that the history is relevant and that the probative value of the history outweighs its prejudicial effect.

(b) The court shall allow the admission only of specific information or examples of the plaintiff's conduct that are determined by the court to be relevant. The court's order shall detail the information or conduct that is admissible and no other such evidence may be introduced.

(c) Violation of the terms of the order may be grounds for a new trial.

P.A. 85–1254, § 1, eff. Jan. 1, 1989.
Formerly Ill.Rev.Stat.1991, ch. 70, ¶ 805.

140/6. Limitation period

§ 6. Limitation period. An action for sexual exploitation shall be commenced within 2 years after the cause of action arises.

P.A. 85–1254, § 1, eff. Jan. 1, 1989.
Formerly Ill.Rev.Stat.1991, ch. 70, ¶ 806.

(continued on next page)

Figure 3.1 *(continued)*

740 ILCS 140/7   CIVIL LIABILITIES

140/7. Application

§ 7. Application. This Act applies only to causes of action arising on or after its effective date.

P.A. 85–1254, § 1, eff. Jan. 1, 1989.
Formerly Ill.Rev.Stat.1991, ch. 70, ¶ 807.

ACT 145. SLANDER AND LIBEL ACT

Section
145/0.01. Short title.
145/1. False charge of fornication or adultery, slander.
145/2. Charge of false swearing, etc., slander.
145/3. Proof of malice.

Library References

I.L.P. Slander and Libel.
West's Illinois Forms. Civil Practice, Vol. 2
  (1988), Poplett.

WESTLAW Electronic Research

See WESTLAW Electronic Research Guide following the Preface.

145/0.01. Short title

§ 0.01. Short title. This Act may be cited as the Slander and Libel Act.

R.S.1874, p. 992, § 0.01, added by P.A. 86–1324, § 953, eff. Sept. 6, 1990.
Formerly Ill.Rev.Stat.1991, ch. 126, ¶ 0.01.

Historical and Statutory Notes

Title of Act:
  An Act to revise the law in relation to slander and libel. Approved March 23, 1874. R.S. 1874, p. 992.

145/1. False charge of fornication or adultery, slander

§ 1. If any person shall falsely use, utter or publish words, which in their common acceptance, shall amount to charge any person with having been guilty of fornication or adultery, such words so spoken shall be deemed actionable, and he shall be deemed guilty of slander.

R.S.1874, p. 992, § 1.
Formerly Ill.Rev.Stat.1991, ch. 126, ¶ 1.

Historical and Statutory Notes

Prior Laws:
  Laws 1823, p. 82, § 1.
  R.L.1829, p. 163, § 1.

R.L.1833, p. 583, § 1.
R.S.1845, p. 521, § 1.

Law Review Commentaries

The complaint in libel and slander. Joseph E. Wyse, 1955, 33 Chicago-Kent L.Rev. 313.

Essential element of libel is publication by the author. Libert v. Turzynski, 1970, 129 Ill. App.2d 146, 262 N.E.2d 741.

employer liability for acts committed by the psychotherapist. In both statutes the social worker's employer can be liable if the employer fails or refuses to take reasonable action when the "employer knows or has reason to know" that the social worker has engaged in sexual relations with current or former patients.

Minnesota is more rigorous than Illinois in this regard. Minnesota allows employer liability to attach if the employer fails or refuses to make inquiries of a social worker's alternative employer or former employer if allegations of sexual contacts with patients have occurred within the last five years. Additionally, Minnesota allows employer liability if the employer refuses to disclose information about such sexual contact to another or prospective employer if such information is requested. This provision places a burden on employers both to affirmatively disclose information concerning employee sexual contact with a client to potential employers as well as to investigate allegations of sexual misconduct. Minnesota employers cannot turn a blind eye to sexual misconduct when they have evidence to the contrary. Employer liability is discussed at some length later in this chapter.

Courts will hear civil suits for social worker sexual misconduct if they rule that such causes of action are permissible. The theories of civil liability for sexual misconduct are the subject of the next section.

THEORIES OF CIVIL LIABILITY FOR CLINICIAN SEXUAL MISCONDUCT

There are several legal theories or "causes of action" available for the victims of sexual exploitation by clinical social workers. These causes of action include professional negligence (malpractice), *respondeat superior*, negligent supervision of a therapist, intentional infliction of emotional distress, breach of fiduciary duty, and others. Respondeat superior refers to attaching liability to employers for the misdeeds of employees. These theories by no means exhaust the possible theories that could be used in an action for clinical social worker sexual misconduct. It is important to note that, while the standard of proof in civil cases may make them easier to prove than criminal cases, victimized clients (the plaintiffs) must still appropriately plead and prove each element of their cases. The following causes of action must be claimed and substantiated for a civil case to succeed. Each of the causes of action will be illustrated by one or more law cases in which that particular cause of action has been pleaded.

Table 3.1 depicts all the U.S. cases involving clinical social worker sexual misconduct.

Table 3.1
Case-by-Case Description of Successful and Unsuccessful Theories of Liability

Case Name	State	Year	Successful	Unsuccessful
Martino v. Family Services	Illinois	1983	Breach of contract Breach of statute (Confidentiality Act)	Malpractice
Horak v. Biris	Illinois	1985	Malpractice Serious mental distress	
Rowe v. Bennett	Maine	1986	Professional negligence Negligent infliction of emotional distress	
Simmons v. United States	9th Circuit (Federal)	1986	Vicarious employer responsibility Supervisor negligence	
Cosgrove v. Lawrence	New Jersey	1987	Negligent supervision of therapist	Vicarious employer liability
Perkins v. Dean	Alabama	1990		Vicarious employer liability Negligent supervision Tort of outrage

This table, starting from the left, includes the case name, state, date of decision, and both legal theories used successfully and unsuccessfully by the plaintiff to prosecute the case. It offers comparisons and contrasts among the different cases. Table 3.1 also illustrates the varieties of legal theories applied against clinical social workers for sexual misconduct, and the shift within a state to increasingly allow plaintiffs to sue clinical social workers. The following sections more fully discuss each theory of liability.

Social Worker Professional Negligence or "Malpractice"

Social worker professional negligence is also called "social worker malpractice" and has been highly litigated in the past several years. Malpractice actions are legitimized "causes of action" for almost all professionals groups. Lawyers, physicians, psychiatrists, nurses, and a host of other professionals can be held liable when their professional behavior falls below the standard of care required by their profession. "Standard of care" is a term of art that means the level of professional behavior below which harm is created for the client and possible liability is created for the clinician. The standard of care is a legal determination necessary to sustain a malpractice action.

The clinical social worker malpractice cases of *Horak v. Biris* (1985) illustrates the four elements necessary to sustain a cause of action in professional negligence. These elements are:

1. *There is a duty to perform with a minimum standard of care.* This element of a malpractice action is a two-fold requirement. First, this element requires that the clinician have a legal obligation to someone. Courts have no trouble finding that a clinical social worker has a legal duty toward a client. Second, this element requires that the clinician has a duty to perform at a certain level of professional competence toward those to whom the duty is owed. In other words, this first element requires that clinical social workers perform at a minimum standard of competence toward their clients.

2. *The duty is breached.* Simply put, the second element for malpractice is that the clinician fails to perform his or her duties to the client. Obviously, this is a crucial factual matter that must be determined by the judge or jury. Often, this determination is aided by "expert witnesses".

3. *Damages must be proven.* This element means that the plaintiff-client or other person to whom a duty is owed, must plead and prove damage or hurt. Traditionally, courts would compensate plaintiffs only for *physical* damage. Increasingly, however, courts allow emotional or psychic damages to fulfill this element.

4. *The breach of duty must be reasonably related to the injury or harm sustained.* This final element requires an approximate relationship to be made between the clinician's failure to perform his or her duty and the harm done the client. An outlandish illustration of a breach of duty that has *no* relationship to an injury might be where a clinician has sex with a client and the client falls down the steps of the clinician's office and breaks a leg. The injury is clearly provable. Also, the clinician has breached a duty to the client. However, the breach of the clinician's duty is not reasonably related to the injury sustained. Without a reasonable relationship between the injury and the breach of duty, not all the elements of professional negligence have been satisfied and the suit must fail.

We begin a discussion of the elements for a malpractice action against social workers with a recent case, *Perkins v. Dean* (1990). In this case the clients, Roberta and John Perkins, sued social worker Dean and his employer as a result of an alleged sexual relationship between Mrs. Perkins and Mr. Dean. Mr. Dean and Mrs. Perkins engaged in an affair approximately six months after Dean concluded counseling with Mr. and Mrs. Perkins and about four months after Dean resigned from his counseling position. Following Dean's resignation, he socialized with both Mrs. and Mr. Perkins. Mr. and Mrs. Perkins sued Dean under a theory of social worker malpractice and for "outrage." Outrage is a cause of action based upon emotional distress for conduct so extreme as to be regarded as atrocious or intolerable (p. 1219).

The malpractice claim centered upon *when* Dean's duty toward the couple ceased to become professional. Mr. and Mrs. Perkins claimed that the sexual relations, even after treatment, were proof that Dean did not properly treat them. The Supreme Court of Alabama ruled that the sexual relationship was begun after the counseling relationship had ceased, that the sexual relationship was not begun in the furtherance of counseling, and that the sexual relationship did not occur within the "shadow" of a counseling relationship; it concluded that the sexual acts occurred in a strictly social context.

For Dean to be sued for outrage in Alabama required outrageous conduct intended to inflict emotional distress upon Mr. and Mrs. Perkins or that such distress was a likely result of his alleged sexual conduct. The court also dismissed the outrage claim, ruling that a consensual, extramarital sexual relationship, without a professional relationship or a malicious intent to inflict emotional distress, does not constitute outrageous conduct. While the court allowed that society frowns on extramarital relationships, it ruled that such relationships do not rise to the level of legal outrage.

These claims failed on the fourth element of a malpractice action. Even if Mr. and Mrs. Perkins were able to prove that they were harmed by the sexual relations between Mrs. Perkins and Mr. Dean, the court concluded that the alleged harm was unconnected to any duty owed to them by Dean.

In *Rowe v. Bennett* (1986), the court held that a cause of action for social worker malpractice was possible when a clinician continued to counsel a woman after the clinician became involved with the client's companion. The client sued the clinician, alleging that she suffered mental and emotional distress after receiving counseling about her relationship with her companion—and after the clinician from whom she sought counseling began to have a relationship with the very companion about whom the client had sought counseling in the first place. Initially, the trial court (the lowest court) dismissed the case, ruling that there is no such cause of action as social worker malpractice. The plaintiff-client appealed, and the Supreme Judicial Court of

Maine reversed the lower court, ruling that social worker malpractice could be pleaded. This ruling is significant because it establishes the social worker cause of action in Maine, as well as serving as some precedent for cases in other states.

Essentially, the *Rowe* court concluded that the plaintiff-client's allegations sufficiently pleaded the necessary elements for a case of social worker malpractice. The court found that the plaintiff alleged that the clinical social worker undertook to counsel the plaintiff, and as her counselor, was "under a duty to provide care in accordance with the standards of practice applicable to similar professionals engaged in counseling and psychotherapy" (p. 804). The court also heard testimony from the plaintiff's new counselor (a psychiatrist) that the defendant failed to adhere to applicable psychotherapeutic standards when she continued to treat her client after becoming involved with her client's primary companion.

Additionally, and significantly, the *Rowe* court addressed the issue of whether the emotional distress alleged by the plaintiff constituted the proof of injury necessary to sustain a proper malpractice claim. The court recognized that, as a general rule, emotional damages must be accompanied by either a physical injury or an underlying wrongful act. However, the *Rowe* court held that *because of the nature of the psychotherapist-patient relationship*, a client may sue a clinician for damages of serious mental distress under a theory of professional negligence.

The *Rowe* case is significant for three reasons. First, the law litigates sexual misconduct among social workers as it does any other form of professional negligence. Second, law courts increasingly use "expert witnesses" to provide professional opinions as to the nature of professional duties owed to clients and when and how such duties are breached. As we have seen, the *Rowe* court took the testimony of a psychiatrist to help determine the standard of practice among clinicians, whether or not the clinician breached her professional duties, and the nature of the harm that the alleged breach may have produced. Thus, the standard imposed upon clinicians is a legal determination based upon evidence from other clinicians. Third, the *Rowe* decision provides legal precedent for future cases. Legal precedent refers to the body of prior decisions upon which to establish future decisions. The *Rowe* case, while ruling precedent with the state of Maine, can be used by other states to build a case both for social work malpractice and for the inclusion of "serious mental trauma" (or other words) to allow psychic injury to fulfill the "injury" or "damage" requirement for professional negligence. Other states have already moved to allow sufferers of such psychic injuries to receive compensation.

The following case examples further demonstrate the elements of clinical social worker malpractice in the context of clinical social worker sexual misconduct with clients. While these cases arose and were decided in Illinois and addressed the issue of social worker malpractice, each case was decided differently. Chronologically, the first case decided involved allegations that the director of a county family services agency engaged in sexual relations with the husband of a client (*Martino v. Family Service Agency of Adams County* 1982). The client, the wife, sued both the agency and the clinical social worker, claiming that the clinician used information derived from the clinical relationship against the client, revealed this information to others, fell in love with the client's spouse, and engaged in intimacies with the client's spouse. The allegations conclude with the claim that after this conflict of interest developed, the clinician neither informed the client nor terminated the counseling relationship. The wife claimed that the social worker breached both the contract between the clinician and client and the state Confidentiality Act. The court found that the plaintiffs would be allowed to prove that the counseling center breached its contract to furnish competent counseling in the client's best interest. Additionally, the plaintiffs would be allowed to prove, by specifying exactly what information was disclosed to whom, that the clinician violated the state Confidentiality Act.

The wife-plaintiff also alleged that the clinician's actions amounted to social worker malpractice. The court indicated that the allegations might state a cause of action by fulfilling three of the necessary elements, but ruled that no claim for social worker malpractice could be brought because such claims fail to provide the fourth element. The court had no trouble finding that the clinician's actions were improper and did not dispute that the clinician owed a duty to the client-wife and that a breach of such a duty could cause an injury to her. However, the court disputed that an injury caused by a social worker fit the proper criteria for compensable damages. The court ruled, "The damages a client might receive from the improper practice of social work are unlikely to be pecuniary in nature and extremely unlikely to be physical in nature." Thus, the court declined to assess mental damages without a physical injury (unlike the *Rowe* court); thus, the malpractice claim failed because the damage element remained unproven. It took only three years for another Illinois court of equivalent jurisdiction to allow a malpractice action against a social worker under similar factual circumstances.

In 1985, another Illinois Appellate Court determined that a malpractice action could, indeed, be lodged against a social worker. Ironically, this case, too, involved allegations of sexual misconduct (*Horak v. Biris* 1985). A husband sued a clinical worker, alleging that the clinician had sexual relations with his wife during the course of her marital therapy. The allegations stated that the clinician discovered sensitive information about the wife and her relationship to her husband. The counts also alleged that the clinician-defendant "appeased" his own self-interest at the therapeutic expense of the plaintiff, allowed the wife's condition to deteriorate, and continued a course of treatment compounding the plaintiff's harm.

In allowing the husband to sue the social worker for malpractice, the court found that the social worker represented himself as a licensed clinician able to render marital therapy, that the clinician mishandled the transference phenomena in the treatment, and that the clinician owed a fiduciary duty to the client to do nothing that was not in her best interest. Because of such findings, the court ruled that the social worker was legally required to exercise the same degree of skill and knowledge exercised by other social workers under similar circumstances. In other words, the law required that the clinician render a standard of care equivalent to that of the profession to which the clinician belongs.

The *Horak* case also serves to illustrate the necessary elements in a malpractice action founded upon sexual misconduct. While the Supreme Judicial Court did not determine guilt or innocence, it did rule upon the sufficiency of pleadings to state a claim for malpractice. The court found that the plaintiff alleged the facts necessary to prove that a duty existed between the clinician and the plaintiff. The court heard evidence that the defendant was a licensed clinical social worker who undertook to counsel the plaintiff—thus establishing the clinician-client relationship as well as the clinician-client duty. The court also found that this duty placed him in a position of trust with respect to the client. This duty extended to rendering only services or conduct "calculated to improve the patient's mental or emotional well-being" (p.17).

The court also properly noted that, because the defendant represented himself as a *clinician*, he would be held to the standard of knowing and handling "fundamental psychological principles which routinely come into play during marriage and family counseling" (p. 18). Such fundamental principles, concluded the court, include the proper responses to the "transference" and "countertransference" phenomena. Significantly, the *Horak* court found considerable precedence that the mishandling of transferences "which generally results in sexual relations or involvement between the . . . therapist and the patient, has uniformly been considered as malpractice in other jurisdictions . . ." (p. 18). The court concluded that the plaintiff in *Horak* would be given the chance to plead his case under a theory of social worker malpractice. It seems likely that malpractice actions will be used increasingly to attach liability to clinical social workers for misconduct, particularly sexual misconduct.

Respondeat Superior

Respondeat superior ("Let the master answer") is a species of theories of legal liability that holds the employer legally responsible for the negligent acts of employees (Black 1979). This species of liability, also known as "vicarious employer liability," has increased in recent years as courts have allowed this theory of liability to be argued. The general test for this theory is whether the employee accomplished his or her wrongful act "within the scope of employment." Plaintiffs have the "deep pockets" incentive to use the theory of *respondeat superior*. The "deep pockets" incentive means that plaintiffs seek judgments against those most able to pay. Victory in civil court is empty without the ability to *collect* the award of damages.

Each state can establish the criteria to determine whether an employer can be held liable for the negligent acts of its employees. Some states have legal criteria making it easier to apply *respondeat superior*, while other states more strictly apply the criteria. An example of a stricter application of this rule is the *Perkins v. Dean* case. The court ruled that because the extramarital affair between the former client and the social worker began after counseling ceased, the alleged sexual misconduct was not within the line or scope of employment. Thus, the employer could not be held liable.

An example of the more accommodating rule follows from the facts of a case decided in federal court under the state law of Washington (*Simmons v. U.S.* 1986). A clinical social worker for the Indian Health Service, an agency of the federal government, was sued by a former client, a female member of the Chehalis nation. The social worker saw his client from 1973 until 1981. She came to him divorced and pregnant with her fourth child, and with a history of sexual and emotional abuse as a child. In 1978 the clinician initiated a romantic relationship with his client after she professed romantic feelings toward him. In January 1980 the head of the nation relayed her concerns about the relationship between the clinician and client to the social worker's supervisor. The supervisor neither relieved the clinician of his duties nor acted to correct his actions.

Later in 1980, the plaintiff moved to Seattle, Washington, and began to experience a series of emotional problems culminating in a suicide attempt. She was told, upon psychiatric consultation, that her problems were essentially due to the social worker's inappropriate handling of normal transference phenomena. She sued under the Federal Tort Claims Act and was awarded $150,000.

The crux of the judgment was whether the social worker's sexual relationship was within the "scope" of his employment. If his actions were outside the scope of employment, the government would not be responsible for his actions. If the clinician's actions were within the scope of employment, the government would be liable. The court of appeals affirmed the judgment against the government for the wrongful acts of the social worker. The court based its ruling on Washington state's specific test for scope of employment. This test is whether he was engaged in *furthering the employer's interests at the time of the alleged wrongdoing*. The court ruled that the sexual relationship between the client and clinician was within the scope of employment because the sexual contact "occurred in conjunction with his legitimate counseling activities" (p. 1369).

A California court reached the same result when a client claimed that her psychiatrist had sexual relations with her. The court ruled that the client stated a proper cause of action for vicarious employer liability because the psychiatrist was acting within his scope of employment and scope of authority as the head of a psychiatry department to provide services on behalf of himself and the hospital (*Richard H. v. Larry D.* 1988)

Even though the court specifically noted that the clinical social worker's actions were a breach of duty constituting malpractice under Washington law, the sexual relationship was within the scope of employment for the purposes of determining the employer's liability. States using "furthering the employer's interest" as a test for determining whether to hold an employer vicariously liable make it easier for plaintiffs to sue the employers.

However, not all states employ such a lenient standard for *respondeat superior* in cases of sexual misconduct. A lower state court in New Jersey refused to allow a former client to sue a clinical social worker's employer. The clinician was accused of having sexual relations with the client several times over a one-year period of therapy. The court ruled that sexual liaisons were not the kind of conduct for which the clinician was employed. A lower court in New York state reached the same conclusion and refused to allow a client to sue a therapist's employing hospital when she claimed drug dependency, an abortion, and emotional damages after an affair with her psychiatrist (*Noto* 1988). The *Noto* court found that the psychiatrist did *not* further the interests of the hospital in having sex with a client.

A brief survey of cases addressing the issue of *respondeat superior* among other professional groups indicates that states differ on the "test" they use to determine how strictly they will construe "scope of employment." What is undisputed, however, is that plaintiffs increasingly will try to hold employers vicariously liable for their employees' wrongful acts. It is also likely that they will increasingly succeed.

Negligent Supervision of Therapist

The negligent supervision or hiring of a therapist is a type of vicarious liability increasingly used to hold employers liable when *respondeat superior* is unavailable. When the alleged wrongful activity is unlikely to be determined "in the scope of employment" by courts, a plaintiff may sue the employer under a theory of negligent hiring or supervision.

In *Perkins v. Dean*, Mr. and Mrs. Perkins sued Dean's employer under a theory of negligent supervision. The test for negligent supervision in Alabama was whether Dean's alleged negligence was actually known by the employer or discoverable with due diligence. The court summarily held Dean's employer owed no duty to Mr. and Mrs. Perkins.

The plaintiff in *Simmons*, discussed above, sued under both a theory of *respondeat superior* and the theory of negligent supervision. Under Washington law the test for supervisory negligence is whether the supervisor knew or should have known that the employee posed a danger to clients. Given the fact that a tribal leader informed the supervisor about the clinician-client relationship and the supervisor failed to pursue the matter, the court allowed the judgment against the government to stand. Had the supervisor either discovered the illicit acts sooner and corrected them, or corrected the situation when so informed, the outcome might have been different.

Similarly, another couple sued through the Federal Tort Claims Act for sexual misconduct under a theory of negligent supervision. A husband and wife sued the federal government, claiming that a therapist (physician's assistant) seduced the wife into sexual relations with the proposition that such acts would best treat her depression. In *Andrews v. U.S.* (1984), the court found that the physician's assistant was *not* acting within his scope of employment when he manipulated the woman to have sex with him. However, the court concluded that the *supervisor* was clearly acting within his own scope of employment when he failed to adequately supervise the therapist.

The implied test of negligent supervision was, like the *Simmons* case above, whether the supervisor knew or should have known that the employee posed a danger, and failed to take adequate protections against such potential harm. The court accepted testimony from the trial court that a patient informed the supervisor of the therapist's misconduct. The therapist denied any wrongdoing when the supervisor confronted him with these allegations and the supervisor declined to pursue the matter further.

Intentional Infliction of Emotional Distress

Clinical social workers are also exposed to liability under the legal theory of intentional infliction of emotional distress. While the following case examples do not include clinical social workers, this theory would apply equally to them, as well as to psychiatrists and psychologists. The *Noto* case, involving sexual relations between psychiatrist and client, sets forth the elements for a successful cause of action under this theory—"intentional or reckless conduct so shocking and outrageous that it exceeds all reasonable bounds of decency, and causes severe emotional distress" (p. 448). The *Noto* court found that the client pleaded a proper cause of action under intentional infliction of emotional distress because she claimed that the psychiatrist coerced her with alcohol and marijuana to have sex with her, even though he knew she had a drug dependency.

Additionally, the pregnancy and subsequent abortion resulting from the sexual activity exacerbated her mental condition. A similar result was reached in a Maryland court when a licensed psychologist counseled, jointly and individually, a married couple. The husband later sued the psychologist under a theory of intentional infliction of emotional distress, claiming that the psychologist advised the husband to be "distant" from his wife and to ultimately leave her. Allegedly, the psychologist told the husband that he was a "codfish" and that his wife deserved a "fillet" (p. 1186). At the same time, the psychologist allegedly entered into a romantic relationship with the wife, eventually causing the marriage to break up. The court held that the husband properly pleaded a cause of action against the psychologist for intentional infliction of emotional distress (*Figueiredo-Torres v. Nickel* 1991).

The court held that "a jury may find extreme and outrageous conduct where a psychologist who is retained to improve a marital relationship implements a course of extreme conduct that is injurious to the patient and designed to facilitate a romantic, sexual relationship between the therapist and the patient's spouse" (p. 1186). This court, even while allowing the plaintiff to prove intentional infliction on the psychologist's part, was careful to notice that intentional infliction of emotional distress is not available to any client dissatisfied with his or her therapy. However, the court was satisfied that the psychologist acted out of his own self-gratification and recklessly disregarded his patient's interest.

Negligent Infliction of Emotional Distress

Akin to the legal theory of *intentional* infliction of emotional distress is *negligent* infliction of emotional distress. "Negligent" infliction of emotional distress differs from "intentional infliction" only in that the elements of "negligence" must be pleaded and proved.

The Supreme Court of California allowed a cause of action for negligent infliction of emotional distress against a psychologist who allegedly molested children. The psychologist counseled both a mother and her children. The court allowed the claim where the mother claimed that the psychologist knew or should have known that his alleged molestation would directly injure and cause severe emotional distress to the mother as well as to the parent-child relationship also under his care (*Marlene F. v. Affiliated Psychiatric Medical Clinic, Inc.* 1989).

Fraud

A civil action for fraud has also been successfully used in therapist sexual misconduct cases. Again, different states may require different elements for a successful case of fraud, but there are fundamental elements. The California case of *Richard H.* offers one such interpretation. The court held that a psychiatrist who induces a patient into sexual acts under the guise that it is therapeutically necessary is liable under fraud.

Other states may use the terms "seduction" or "deceit" to attain the same results. *Richard H.* held that those who engage in sexual relations, misrepresenting that they are disease-free or sterile, can be held liable as well, if their actions harm the plaintiff.

Liability Based upon Breach of Statute

Civil liability can also be premised upon the breach of statutory obligations. Where clinical social workers, committing sexual misconduct or dual relations violations, fail to fulfill statutory obligations, civil liability may also be imposed.

A surprising array of statutory violations, indirectly or directly related to sexual misconduct, are reported. For example, the clinical social worker in the *Martino* case was sued for breach of the Illinois

Confidentiality Act. Illinois provides that breach of confidentiality under the act allows the injured party to sue for damages and attorney's fees. The court concluded that the defendant social worker could be sued under the provisions of the Confidentiality Act.

Another plaintiff made an interesting, although vain, attempt to impose liability under the RICO (Racketeering Influenced and Corrupt Organizations Act) laws. A woman brought suit in federal court alleging that her divorce attorney coerced her into having sex with him as payment for his legal fees. Among other things, RICO laws protect citizens against unlawful extortion of property. The court conceded that the attorney's threatening letters and phone calls constituted a scheme to defraud her of money and fell within the RICO provisions. The court, however, concluded that the lawyer did not collect more money than owed him; thus, her damages were to her person, not her property. While the RICO action involved an attorney, not a social worker, increasingly creative attempts to impose liability against social workers who engage in dual relations can be expected.

The Use of the NASW Code of Ethics

Another issue raised in some of these cases is the role of the National Association of Social Workers Code of Ethics. As stated earlier, codes of ethics are different than civil or criminal statutes. Codes of ethics of professional organizations do not carry the weight or power of law. However, courts have addressed the NASW Code of Ethics directly— with some surprising results.

In *Cosgrove v. Lawrence* (1987) the court cited the NASW code of Ethics' prohibition against sexual activity in its decision to void a finding of employer liability. The court reasoned that if the social worker violated his or her Code of Ethics, sexual activity could not be an activity acceptable by employers. While other courts may not take the same view, it is clear that courts look to the NASW Code for definitions of appropriate and inappropriate behavior.

The *Martino* case also addressed the NASW Code of Ethics. The plaintiff used the code to argue for a finding of malpractice against the social worker. While the court declined to make such a ruling, the court seemed to agree that, under the code, a violation had taken place. A determination of a duty to clients and a determination of a breach of that duty, at least, satisfy the first two elements for a malpractice action described earlier in this chapter.

Yet, the *Martino* court determined that no *damage* was done to the client that could be legally cognizable. The court ruled, "The damages a client might receive from the improper practice of social work are unlikely to be monetary in nature and extremely unlikely to be physical in nature" (p. 9). The decision seems not to take the role of social work seriously. A serious view of social work practice would conclude that dual relations, especially sexual exploitation, can have extremely harmful consequences. As will be shown in the next chapter, the emotional damage to a client is pecuniary in that treatment is long and costly and the inability to work and provide for family is also costly. The emotional damage also can become physical as the body registers and interprets the trauma. Given court trends toward allowing provable emotional damages, and medical and social sciences' ability to recognize and treat sexual exploitation, it is unlikely that such reasoning will stand.

Sexual Harassment

Sexual harassment is outlawed by federal statute as part of the 1964 Civil Rights Act prohibiting sexual discrimination. Sexual harassment, as defined by the Equal Employment Opportunity Commission, is unwanted sexual contact when:

1. Submission is made either explicitly or implicitly a term or condition of employment.
2. Submission or rejection is used as the basis for employment decisions affecting such individuals.
3. Such conduct has the purpose or effect of unreasonably interfering with an individual's work performance or of creating an intimidating, hostile or offensive working environment (Code of Federal Regulations 1980).

Sexual harassment claims may be used against social workers who sexually exploit employees, trainees, or others under employment or supervisory control by social workers. Social workers who contribute, by sexual misconduct, to a hostile work environment are liable for civil money damages under harassment laws.

The starting point of defining unacceptable sexual behavior begins with discussing the legal definitions of "hostile work environment." While the final chapters on sexual harassment have not yet been written, enough court cases have now been decided to paint a legal portrait of a successful sexual harassment suit. It is clear that sexual favors for employment, promotion, or continued employment are actionable. Beyond this, a "hostile work environment" can include sexually oriented words, pictures, and gestures that are designed to humiliate or intimidate. For example, in a national survey of female lawyers, researchers found the following percentages reported "yes" as to whether they received uninvited and unwanted attention from a superior, colleague, or client: sexual teasing, jokes, remarks, or questions (60 percent); unwanted pressure for dates (20 percent); deliberate touching, leaning over, cornering, or pinching (24 percent); or pressure for sex (11 percent) (Torry 1989).

Court decisions do not present a unified picture of all that sexual harassment may entail. The mixed bag of decisions on sexual harassment has been noted (Goldbert 1991), including no harassment found when a country club manager joked that a secretary should perform oral sex on prospective members and hang a red light over her desk (*Fox v. Ravinia Club, Inc.* 1990), but found harassment in a work environment of sexual remarks, jokes, and pornographic displays (*Robinson v. Jacksonville Shipyards, Inc.* 1991). The primary significance of these cases for the purpose of this study is to show the variety of the complaints under sexual harassment as well as the divergence in court opinions. However diverse the decisions or complaints of sexual harassment, one thing is clear—sexual harassment complaints are now a permanent part of the repertoire of legal responses to sexual exploitation by social workers.

DEFENSES

Defenses are legal excuses used to relieve culpability for wrongdoing. The defenses enumerated below are exclusively "affirmative" defenses. Affirmative defenses deny the legal sufficiency of the claims leveled against them. They do not specifically deny the facts alleged.

Defenses illustrate one of the ways that social workers differ from their helping professional counterparts. Because social workers often work in government agencies, they can defend against lawsuits by a system of immunities afforded to government agencies. The first of the defenses discussed here is that of sovereign immunities, or immunities for government officials and government workers.

Sovereign Immunity

Immunities are statutory freedoms from prosecution or liability. These freedoms are granted to specific classes of persons under certain circumstances. Both federal and state legislators are granted broad immunities for libel and slander when making speeches in the legislative chambers. They can, and sometimes do, call each other names and accuse each other of crimes and misdemeanors that would land private citizens in court. However, because of a "sovereign" immunity granted to legislators, they can accuse each other of unseemly things and suffer no civil or criminal penalties.

"Sovereign immunity" is derived from the concept of "the king can do no harm." This does not mean that it is legally impossible for the king to do harm, or that the king can do whatever he wants. The saying means that the king *should* do no harm. Because the king is ascribed with such righteousness, he and his court are granted immunity for their official acts. American law incorporated sovereign immunity from the English common law.

Sovereign immunity can apply to clinical social workers if they work for governmental agencies, must exercise their independent judgment in making decisions, and are acting within the scope of their employment. For example, social workers and their employers who initiated dependency proceedings in a case of alleged child abuse were both sued. The child's father claimed that the social worker and the social services department were maliciously and erroneously trying to separate him from his child (*Meyers v. Contra Costa County Department of Social Services* 1987).

The court ruled that the social worker has absolute sovereign and quasi-absolute prosecutorial immunities because he or she must exercise independent, discretionary judgment in deciding when and against whom to bring dependency hearings. The court also concluded that such decisions are often based upon incomplete information. The court held that granting such immunity from prosecution for social workers helps ensure that such decisions are not accompanied by fears of prosecution and lawsuits.

While absolute sovereign immunity provides a blanket of protection, this blanket has some holes. Courts will scrutinize the acts of a social worker closely to determine whether the activity from which the allegations arise requires discretionary judgment or is ministerial in nature. The federal Court of Appeals has held that a social worker's obligation to place and supervise children in foster care is a ministerial function—one that does not require independence or discretion—and refused to grant the immunity to social workers sued personally for failure to properly supervise, inspect, and ensure the safety of children in foster care (*National Bank of South Dakota v. Leir* 1982). While governmental immunity may provide some protection for discretionary judgments by social workers, such immunities are unlikely to provide defenses for job requirements that are clearly within a clinical social worker's professional duties and competencies.

Statute of Limitations

The statute of limitations imposes a statutory time limit within which a suit or other legal action must be filed. In most cases, if legal actions are not commenced within that time frame, the suit cannot be brought at all—regardless of the merits of the case.

Usually, state statutes establish the statute of limitations. Statutes of limitations are of two types. The first type places a time limit between the time the alleged misconduct took place and the time the complaint was filed. The Illinois statute (70, section 806) states: "An action for sexual exploitation shall be commenced within two years after the cause of action arises."

A different approach is taken by the Wisconsin statute of limitations (893.585, 1991 supp.). While it imposes a three-year statute of limitations, it also provides:

> If a person entitled to bring a [civil suit for sexual misconduct] due to the effects of the sexual contact or due to any threats, instructions or statements from the therapist, the period of inability is not part of the time limited for the commencement of the action, except that this subsection shall not extend the time limitation by more than 15 years.

Thus, the Wisconsin statute of limitations takes into account the dynamics between the victim and the perpetrator. These dynamics are more fully described in chapter 4. As already seen from the cases cited in chapters 1 and 2, instructions or threats to keep the abuse silent are intimidating. The Wisconsin statute of limitations also stops ("tolls") the normal three-year period if abuse syndromes (fear of disclosure, guilt, etc.) prevent the victim from filing a complaint.

An example of the statute of limitations in case law is the *Simmons* case. In that case the defendant asserted that the plaintiff did not bring the action within the two-year "window of opportunity" required by the Federal Tort Claims Act. Thus, the defendant claimed that the action could not be brought against him at all. Upon a close examination of the nature of therapist misconduct, the court disagreed with the defendant and ruled that the plaintiff-client filed the suit within the required two-year period.

The crucial matter in any statute of limitations question is *when* the statute of limitations begins to run; that is, at what juncture in time the two-year period begins. In federal tort actions, the law has determined that the limitations begin to run *when the plaintiff discovers both the existence and cause of injury*. This definition is both legally and clinically significant. Therapist sexual misconduct involves a qualitatively different injury from a broken leg. The *Simmons* court recognized that negative consequences of therapist sexual misconduct cannot always be readily recognized, nor can the cause be readily attributed to actions by the therapist.

The court cited precedent (*Greenberg v. McCabe* 1978) to describe factors that explain this delay: (1) dependence by the client upon the therapist impedes such discovery; (2) so do assurances by the therapist that such behavior is "therapy"; and (3) continuation of therapy disguises such discovery. The *Simmons* court examined the record, including the testimony of Ms. Simmons' emotional dependence and transference toward her therapist, and concluded that Ms. Simmons brought suit as soon as she identified both that she sustained injury, and the nature of her injury. Given these facts, the court held that the plaintiff lodged her complaint within the statute of limitations.

A more recent example of the ambiguity of statutes of limitations and how courts resolve them is provided by *Riley v. Presnell* (1991). Plaintiff Riley claimed that his therapist, Dr. Presnell, persuaded him in 1975 to engage in sexual acts as a way of resolving unresolved issues with Riley's father. After two or three of these sexual incidents, Riley refused to participate further. In 1979, Presnell terminated Riley's treatment without benefit of referral and a year later Riley began treatment with another therapist. Subsequently, Riley filed a complaint against Presnell claiming negligence, breach of contract, infliction of emotional distress, and invasion of privacy. The trial court summarily dismissed all counts because they were time-barred by the three-year statute of limitations.

On appeal, the court reversed the trial court and held that the jury should decide whether or not "a reasonable person" knew or should have known that he or she had a cause of action and filed the suit within the limitation period. The court allowed that an "injury of the mind" could interfere with the plaintiff's discovery of the cause of action. The court ordered a new jury trial to determine whether a "reasonable" person, claiming similar abuse, should have filed a claim within the statutory period. Thus, courts have held that the statute of limitations can be extended due to the unique dynamics of client sexual abuse.

The *Riley* case is suggestive of the kind of therapeutic "threats, instructions or statements" that reinforce client dependency and undermine client disclosures and complaints as discussed in the above statute from Wisconsin. The court record discloses that Riley wondered whether Dr. Presnell was "God" and that Presnell told Riley to keep their sexual relationship secret because it was "special" and no one would understand or approve (p. 783). Dependency and intimidation are classic *modus operandi* of psychotherapists who sexually abuse their clients. They are an indication of the extent to which abusers go to maintain their secrets. A fuller discussion of dependency and other dual relations dynamics is the subject of the next chapter.

REFERENCES

Andrews v. U.S., 732 F.2d 366 (4th Cir. 1984).

Black, H. (1979). *Black's law dictionary.* Minneapolis: West Publishing.

Bullis, R., and Bullis, A. (1994). Cooperation between professional counselors and Virginia Victim Witness Programs. *Virginia Counselors Journal*, 22(1), 65–71.

Code of Federal Regulations (1980)

Cosgrove v. Lawrence, 522 A. 2d 483 (N.J. Super. A.D. 1987).

Doe v. Roe, 17 F.L.R. 1188 (1991).

Figueiredo-Torres v. Nickel, 17 F.L.R. (1991).

Fox v. Ravinia Club, Inc., 761 F. Supp. 797 (1990). 29 Code of Federal Regulations, Part 1604, 1980.

Goldberg, S.B. (1991). Hostile environments. *ABA Journal*, 77, 90–92.

Greenberg v. McCabe, 453 F. Supp. 765 (E.D. Pa. 1977), *cert. den'd.* 444 U.S. 840 (1979).

Horak v. Biris, 474 N.E. 2d 13 (Ill. App. 2 Dist. 1985).

Marlene F. v. Affiliated Psychiatric Medical Clinic, Inc., 770 P.2d 278 (1989).

Martino v. Family Service Agency of Adams County, 445 N.E. 2d 6 (Ill. App. 1982).

Meyers v. Contra Costa Co. Dept. Social Services, 812 F. 2d 1154 (9th Cir. 1987).

National Bank of South Dakota v. Leir, 325 N.W. 2d 845 (S.D. 1982).

Noto v. St. Vincent's Hospital and Medical Ctr. of N.Y., 537 N.Y.S. 2d 446 (Sup. 1988).

Perkins v. Dean, 570 So. 2d 1217 (Ala. 1990).

Richard H. v. Larry D., 243 Cal. Rprt. 807 (Cal. App. 1 Dist. 1988).

Riley v. Presnell, 565 N.E. 2d 780 (Mass. 1991).

Robinson v. Jacksonville Shipyards, Inc., 769 F. Supp. 1486 (1991).

Rowe v. Bennett, 514 A. 2d 802 (Maine, 1986).

Simmons v. United States, 805 F. 2d 1363 (9th Cir. 1986).

Torry, S. (1992, August 5). Study finds sexual harassment prevalent in western U.S. courts. *Washington Post*, A2.

Chapter 4

▶ ·························· ◀

The Dynamics
of Sexual Misconduct:
A Holistic Approach

▶ ·························· ◀

INTRODUCTION

Attempts to understand and describe the psychodynamics of social worker sexual misconduct and other dual relations are necessary to effective discipline and prevention. Without understanding the underlying causes of such behavior, possible cures and remediations are limited. This chapter reviews assessments from the social sciences. Metaphors from theology are used to explain sexual misconduct and other professional misconduct. The Supreme Court case of *DeShaney v. Winnebago County Department of Social Services* (1989) is used to illustrate such issues. Additionally, a new metaphor for healthy social work relationships is asserted and explained.

The following section addresses these dynamics from the client's perspective. This is not an exercise in "blaming the victim," but rather an attempt to provide a starting point for discussing sexual and other ethical vulnerabilities in the client-social worker relationship.

WHY AND HOW CLIENTS TRY TO SEDUCE CLINICIANS

The motivations and the means of clients who try to seduce helping professionals have been described (Edelwich and Brodsky 1991).

They include: to gratify sexual desire, to divert attention from treatment issues, to manipulate, to compromise the therapist's function, to gain status among one's peers, to gain strength from bonding with the clinician, and to gain power through using accustomed strategies. These motivations may be applied specifically to social workers, and may be categorized as malicious or benign in intent.

The benign intent might be understood in two ways. First, it can be emphasized that it is the *client* who seeks help from the social worker, and the duty of professional care runs from the social worker to the client. The client may feel he or she is already in a vulnerable, possibly powerless state. The client may be a victim of sexual abuse and may be acting toward the therapist in the same manner as he or she has been acted upon, thus recapitulating his or her previous history. Indeed, this may be exactly why the client is seeking help in the first place. To blame the client for the choice to seek help is inappropriate.

Second, the client may be trying to equalize the power differential between him or herself and the social worker. Seeking to sexually stimulate or divert attention from the treatment issues at hand may be ways in which clients seek to be seen on a par with the "healthy" therapist. This acting out also may be a way in which clients seek to "forget" temporarily that they are the clients—the ones in need of help. Thought of in this way, such client actions can be seen as ways to avoid being infantilized or patronized due to their need for help.

Client actions with these purposes may not be only sexual. Attempting to buy the social worker things (dinner, gifts, etc.) or entering into business relations with the social worker are other ways that clients can attempt to place themselves on a power par with social workers. "I'm just as smart (as wise, as healthy, as "together," as educated, as wealthy) as the social worker," may be what such client actions express. Social workers who want to normalize their clients to an extreme may actually invite such client reactions.

On the more malicious side, clients may intend to harm the social worker. Social workers can expect to work with those who, for whatever reason, may delight in harming others. Manipulating social workers for their own ends, placing social workers in jeopardy with the law or with a licensing board, or placing them at risk in a civil lawsuit are troubles some clients may intend to inflict on their social workers. Social workers who seek to protect themselves from the machinations of clients do not do clients harm. An empathetic social worker does not have to succumb to liability or to unethical behavior. Unconditional acceptance of clients or a nonjudgmental attitude toward clients does not mean that social workers collude with clients in their manipulative behavior. Nor do these ethical principles mean that social workers accept self-destructive or anti-therapeutic behavior that places the social worker in legal or ethical jeopardy. Social workers who place legitimate limits on client behavior do not jeopardize the ethical principles of nonjudgment or unconditional acceptance. The social worker's therapeutic interventions should not be dependent upon the client's intentions. Another issue, transference, is discussed at some length later in this chapter.

It bears repeating that this discussion in no way blames the client. Explaining client dynamics does not create blame. At all times during the relationship between the social worker and the client and beyond, it is the social worker who holds the professional power. This power obliges the social worker to accept the responsibility for his or her behavior with the client—despite the intensity of transference or the amount of persuasion employed by the client.

SPIRITUAL-PSYCHOSOCIAL CONSEQUENCES FOR THERAPIST-ABUSED VICTIMS

Pope (1988) has provided a helpful summation of the characteristics of the "therapist-patient sex syndrome." He asserts that this syndrome is similar to other analogous syndromes including the Battered Spouse Syndrome and the Rape Response Syndrome. The client may experience guilt, emptiness and isolation, impaired ability to trust, emotional liability, suppressed rage, and cognitive dysfunction. Each characteristic will be discussed specifically in relation to social workers.

Guilt is nearly always present and can be pervasive and persistent. The client may feel that if he or she had been smarter, more cautious, or more assertive, such sexual behavior could have been avoided. Clients sometimes blame themselves for their therapist's mistakes. The resulting guilt often is not resolved. Too often the client does not discuss the incidents or his or her feelings about the incidents. Such guilt is compounded by the client's having sought help from the social worker in the first place. This guilt must be expressed, explained, and addressed before it can be released.

Bringing charges against the social worker—either through licensing boards, professional organizations, or courts—is a way to address these guilt feelings. Additionally, finding others with the same experiences can be a way to express and resolve guilt feelings.

Emptiness, isolation, and feelings of worthlessness can accompany sexual relations with social workers. The emotional logic can run in many directions. First, clients may feel "used" by the very professional they sought out to validate them. Second, clients may feel isolated from others because of their sexual experience. Some clients are embarrassed just to seek out the services of social workers. Sexual relations only compound the sense of isolation.

Isolation and guilt feed each other. Guilt inhibits freely discussing sexual relations with peers and other professionals—which, in turn, reinforces isolation. Isolation inhibits finding the legal, regulatory, and social redress for the social worker's actions, making resolution of guilt that much more difficult.

Impaired ability to trust operates at two levels. First, the client may mistrust himself or herself for trusting the social worker. This mistrust may exacerbate feelings of low self-esteem and inability to cope that are already present. Second, the client may learn to mistrust social workers. This mistrust can be generalized to include other helping professionals. Ironically, this mistrust can inhibit the client from seeking the help needed to overcome difficulties associated with the sexual misconduct as well as the presenting problem.

Suppressed rage is an understandable response to sexual misconduct. This rage, however, is usually not expressed because of the guilt, the lingering effects of influence by the offending social worker, and the paralysis of ambivalence many clients feel. This paralysis stems from the ambivalence of wanting to protect the social worker from the victim's own rage and fearing that the social worker will involuntarily commit or otherwise harm the client if the sexual behavior is exposed.

Cognitive dysfunctions, including intrusive, frightening images, nightmares, and flashbacks form part of the syndrome. Such cognitive consequences intrude from the past suddenly and unexpectedly to haunt the client's present and future.

Three points emerge from the above discussions. First, social workers have particular access to client vulnerabilities, and therefore, particular access to client sexuality. Social workers, almost alone among professionals, make house calls on clients and service clients in nontraditional settings. Nontraditional settings such as homes offer fewer restrictions and fewer possibilities of discovery than regular visits in an office setting. Second, these consequences (guilt, suppressed rage, mistrust, etc.) distort and intensify the client's original problem. Unfounded guilt, inability to trust, rage, and other difficulties distort the client's ability to analyze problems, consider options, assess responsibility, and persevere with decisions. Third, these consequences inhibit their ability to get other professional help. Given the characteristics of mistrust and emotional paralysis, among others, it seem unlikely that clients would turn again to social workers or other professionals for help. The result is a silent suffering, with the victims' mouths closed by combinations of clinical consequences.

WHY AND HOW
SOCIAL WORKERS TRY TO SEDUCE CLIENTS

This section addresses more directly social worker vulnerability to sexual and other misconduct. A colorful, if not quite clinical, description of sexual misconduct is found in *The Lecherous Professor* (Dziech and Weiner 1990). The authors describe sexual behavior by roles the professional assumes, including: the counselor-helper, the confidante, the intellectual seducer, the opportunist, and the power broker. No large amount of imagination is needed to translate the roles below into social worker situations.

The counselor-helper seduces others by seeming to act as an agent or benefactor for the one he or she is trying to seduce. Such "counseling" may take the form of acting as the go-between between two students who are attracted to one another. The "counselor" then plays one off the other to insinuate him or herself into the student's affections.

The confidante takes a "buddy-buddy" approach to seduction. By intentionally becoming friendly with students, the seducer steals caresses when using students in class demonstrations or moving instructional equipment, or by indebting the student by some personal favor conferred by the confidante.

The intellectual seducer uses mind games as a mode of "intellectual intercourse." He or she uses shared interests in art, movies, books, or other disciplines as a pretext for seduction. Intellectual discussions become a foreplay of sorts, designed to ingratiate the seducer to the student. One version of intellectual seduction is to request students to take "personality inventories," engage in hypnosis, model nude, and other charades. Of course, these and other activities have legitimate educational purposes, absent seductive intent. However, it is the nature of sexual misconduct that legitimate activities are twisted to serve the illegitimate ends of the seducer.

The opportunist uses situations and the crises of others for his or her own advantage, taking advantage of close physical proximity to caress or hold others. Field trips, private advising sessions or private instructional time, conventions, and other quasi-institutional settings provide the opportunities to achieve sexual ends behind the facade of professional tasks.

The Lecherous Professor asserts that the power broker is the most familiar persona of the abuser. The power broker uses grades, credentials, references, job opportunities, or other media of control to gain power over his or her conquest. With subtle or not-so-subtle threats, intimidation, or coercion, the power broker exerts economic or social influence over the student. Power is the prime dynamic of all the above roles. In fact, the English word "power" comes from the Greek work (transliterated "dunamis") meaning "dynamics." Given the power differential between many social workers and their clients, "dynamics" are probably at play in most clinical sessions.

In this regard alone, there are many similarities between the illegitimate roles played by professors and the illegitimate roles that social workers can assume. Despite notions of the "empowerment" of clients, social workers, by virtue of their education, credentials, and expertise, have an enormous power to direct the perceptions and purposes of their clients. Such a power differential is not lost upon clients and it is a double-edged sword. On the one hand, clinicians can use their power to influence clients therapeutically. On the other hand, they can use their power to control and dominate clients.

Second, social workers act in capacities similar to professors. Many social workers are, in fact, professors in professional educational programs. Social workers, like others in the social services, directly deal with clients' values and vulnerabilities. Thus, the dynamics of sexual misconduct in higher education cited above cannot be disregarded by the social work profession.

CLINICAL DESCRIPTIONS

Descriptions of a more clinical nature fall into five broad categories: countertransference, sexual addiction, sexual narcissism, personality disorders, and previous sexual abuse. While other power issues are at work in dual relations, these elements constitute the broadest and most serious threats. Along with these psychosocial dynamics, spiritual dynamics of misconduct are also discussed.

Figure 4.1 represents these dynamics in relationship to social worker seduction. The dynamics are represented by squares and arrows, which represent client vulnerability for seduction. These dynamics are analogous for the entire spectrum of misconduct.

Transference and Countertransference

Countertransference has been described as the clinician's *total response* to the client (Brockett and Gleckman 1991). This response shifts

Figure 4.1
The Cycle of Social Worker Seduction

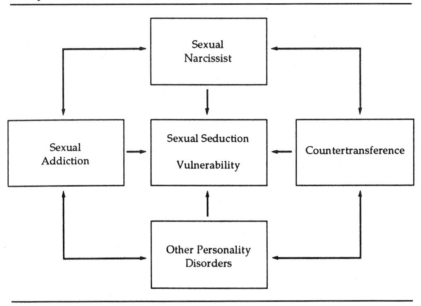

feelings and thoughts onto the persona of the clinician or the client. If the clinician happens to remind the client of a first love, a lost love, or an unresolved love, the clinician may be in danger of sustaining the client's transference. Countertransference is the twin of this process—where the client sustains the feelings and thoughts of the social worker.

Transference and countertransference provide almost infinite possibilities for misconduct. The past feelings that are transferred onto another will almost inevitably include feelings of action, trust, tenderness, and solicitude. Such feelings, if mishandled, can lead to self-delusion and seduction on the part of the social worker and client.

Almost all of the courts that have considered social worker sexual misconduct in any depth have inculpated the transference or countertransference phenomena. The *Horak v. Biris* (1985) court recognized that "[t]he mishandling of this phenomena, which generally results in sexual relations or involvement between the . . . therapist and the patient, has uniformly been considered as malpractice or gross negligence . . ." (p. 18). The *Horak* court also held that an allegation of the transference-countertransference phenomena alleges a breach of the therapist's duty.

Sexual Addiction

Sexual addiction may also play a role in sexual misconduct. The sexual addict acts compulsively in his or her professional and personal relationships. For clinicians afflicted with symptoms of sexual addiction, a pool of clients may serve as an unwitting but fruitful source of objects to relieve sexual tension. While the extent of sexual addiction is unknown and the diagnosis itself is controversial (Moser 1993), the addiction cycle and symptoms have been described (Earle and Crow 1990; Goodman 1993). Sexual addiction fits the pattern of: stress and emotional strain, followed by acting out impulses, followed by a period of remorse and promises of reform, followed by what may pass for reform, inevitably followed by acting out again. This cycle seems to be fairly consistent among addictive behavioral patterns.

The symptoms of the sexual addict include efficiency lapses and rapid, unexplainable mood changes, as well as changes in sexual behavior marked by extremes of hyposexuality and hypersexuality. Sexual addiction can be joined with other compulsive behaviors (eating, smoking, drinking). Additionally, sexual addiction can run in families. The current generation of addictive personalities act out learned behaviors from their parents or other caretakers.

The attributes of addictive behaviors, sexual addiction in particular, also have been described. These attributes include the tendency to hold unrealistic and distorted opinions of oneself, other people, and one's circumstances, a desire to repress or suppress unpleasant or uncomfortable emotions, an extremely powerful memory of a "high" at least once in one's lifetime, and a finely-honed ability to deny one has a problem.

Given the pervasive strength of this denial, it is fair to say that an exclusive regimen of self-help is insufficient for recovery. For the purposes of sexual misconduct, a person suffering from sexual addiction is unlikely to "cure" himself or herself without the requisite help from other professionals.

Sexual Narcissism

Two researchers have posited a counter-explanation for what might be described as sexual addiction or sexual compulsion. Researchers Hulbert and Apt postulate that such sexual behavior can be characterized as "sexual narcissism" (1992). Sexual narcissism is analogous to the DSM-IV classification of narcissism, but with the sexual element. While the narcissist harbors illusions of personal grandeur, the sexual narcissist harbors illusions of grand sexual prowess. Prime characteristics of the sexual narcissist also include the use of sex to medicate low self-esteem, a self-centered view of sexual pleasure and gratification, and the view that sex is an achievement and partners are conquests.

If such a description holds under continued study, the sexual narcissist may be a prime candidate for sexual misconduct. Social workers suffering from such an illness are in prime positions to act out their deluded prowess, self-esteem, and search for sexual achievement among those who might already look up to the social worker for help and guidance. Sometimes clients with low or unsteady self-esteem cannot defend themselves from the glib and smooth seductions of a sexual narcissist. As we have seen before, a social worker who imposes his or her own illness upon clients is like the proverbial fox guarding the chicken coop.

Borderline Personality Disorder

Borderline personality disorder has been recognized as a fertile clinical dynamic of sexual dual relations (Gutheil 1989). Essential features of borderline personality disorder are an unstable self-image, dependency, need, difficulty in maintaining interpersonal relationships, and chronic boredom or emptiness. This disorder appears to be fairly widespread and is commonly diagnosed among females (American Psychological Association 1987). Given these data on this disorder, those who are entering early adulthood can be sexually vulnerable by virtue of the very qualities for which they seek help.

Gutheil (1989) describes several features of borderline personality disorder that can help "set up" clients with this type of presenting problem. These features include borderline rage, neediness and dependency, boundary confusion, and manipulation/entitlement.

In borderline rage the therapist is confronted with sudden eruptions of anger and antagonism. The therapist can become intimidated by or fearful of this anger. The therapist may be intimidated into giving in to the borderline client's demands, including sexual demands. Because of the intensity of the anger, even seasoned therapists might be tempted to agree to sexual relations simply to mollify the client. Giving into the demands of those with personality disorder, however, does not put an end to the demands.

Persons with borderline personality disorder may exhibit an extreme sense of helplessness. The client may play the role of the street urchin or pathetic orphan. These behaviors are designed to elicit the social worker's sympathy. However, the social worker must make clear distinctions between an empathetic pose to these clients and a sympathetic reaction. An empathetic pose will maintain the professional balance and demeanor toward these clients, while a sympathetic pose may open the social worker to overindulgent and "savior"-like behavior that may lead to sexual misconduct. Without such distinctions a social worker's nurturing response may become negligent.

Personality disordered boundary confusion is marked by the client's severely diffused distinctions between themselves and others. This diffusion is particularly relevant with respect to the roles of social worker and client. The social worker may ask, "Who is the client here and who the social worker?" In boundary confusion the personality disordered client may attempt to reverse the roles. Such reversal can be a form of "psychodynamic seduction." Social workers must be vigilant and persistent (and sometimes downright unpleasant) in maintaining strict professional boundaries.

Less invasive than borderline rage, but no less dangerous, is manipulation. While any client can be manipulative, borderline disordered individuals may try to convince others, covertly or overtly, that their needs are special and that they require special treatment. This "entitlement" argument can gather great force when coupled with other borderline features, especially borderline rage. Social workers may think they have successfully worked through rage or boundary confusion, only to succumb to a more subtle intimidation.

The preceding paragraphs have applied *client* personality disorder to the prospect of sexual misconduct. This is not to preclude *social worker* personality disorder from the prospect of misconduct. It is tempting to simply say that the processes work the same, but in a reversed way. However, little theoretical work has been published on this issue. Obviously, practitioners with personality disorders pose considerable risk to their clients in any event. Screening and treating personality disordered practitioners involves additional ethical dilemmas and must be addressed elsewhere.

Previous Sexual Abuse

Previous sexual abuse on the part of the social worker or client can promote or encourage the initiation of or collusion in sexual misconduct from either party. While the role of previous sexual abuse in misconduct may lack current empirical support (Gutheil 1989), such untreated trauma has been linked to problems in other areas of life. Incest survivors, for example, may believe that sex is the only way to receive love and affection (Woititz 1985). It seems unlikely that sexual misconduct would be the exclusive exception.

The tragedy of untreated sexual abuse has been stated (Woititz 1989). Some of the consequences have a direct bearing on sexual misconduct. These include guilt and shame, confused role boundaries, and a sense of powerlessness. Long-term effects include compulsive behaviors and lack of role models.

Once again we see the recurrent theme of boundary confusion, wherein no proper boundaries are established in childhood, or, if boundaries *are* created, they establish the child as an object of sexual gratification or in inappropriate roles as an adult or surrogate parent. Improperly treating childhood sexual trauma, such as with sexual misconduct, repeats abusive sexual patterns. When the social worker harbors untreated memories of sexual abuse, he or she may use authority and power to initiate illicit alliances based upon his or her own needs—not those of the client.

A client whose self-image is distorted or truncated by sexual abuse can be an easy target for the social worker. Such clients may succumb to the professional's attentions, even sexual advances, hungering for authentic affection. Instead of bread, some clients get only stones. Having a damaged self-image often means having a damaged *sexual* self-image as well. Clients may acquiesce to sexual advances, thinking that since they are only worthy as sex objects, a social worker could not possibly want, respect, or value them for anything else.

The symptoms of prior sexual abuse can be seen singularly in clients or in combination with other symptoms. A client's vulnerability can be tied directly to the combination and intensity of these symptoms. The complete symptoms of untreated sexual trauma sometimes are far greater than the sum of the parts. For example, client guilt and shame over prior, untreated sexual abuse, coupled with a feeling of powerlessness in his or her personal and professional life, can combine to make the client succumb to a social worker's advances.

This tendency toward vulnerability is especially true for clients with compulsive behaviors. Compulsive behaviors are often associated with increased stress. Entering counseling is a stressor, and compulsive sexual behaviors may act as an outlet for stress, particularly if accompanied by damaged self-esteem and boundary confusion. Acting compulsively with a lack of role models can also exponentially increase a client's vulnerability. Lack of healthy role models may mean that clients cannot distinguish between affection and exploitation, and in severe cases, will actually seek destructive relationships.

It may be reiterated that regardless of the subtlety or intensity of the borderline personality disordered person's expressed desire for sexual relations, the burden is always upon the social worker to recognize and address these characteristics professionally. The client comes to the social worker for help in solving problems—it is not for the social worker to use client problems as an opportunity for meeting the needs of the social worker. The legal and ethical duties *always* run from the social worker to the client. Simply because a client may be vulnerable to other illicit dual relations does not give the social worker the right to exploit that vulnerability.

Ignorance, Naivete, or Mild Neurosis

Researchers have also posited that the ignorant, the naive, and the mildly neurotic also pose misconduct dangers to clients (Schoener and Gonsiorek 1988). Those who are ignorant of the harm caused by sexual or other misconduct, those who have trouble distinguishing between personal and professional relations, and those who act out inappropriately under stress are potential offenders. This class of persons seems most likely to benefit from training designed to prevent misconduct, intense coursework, peer support, and counseling.

It may be appropriate to distinguish this type of offender from those with more serious characteristics for the purpose of examining disciplinary actions by state boards and criminal misconduct. The punishment should fit the crime. Currently, state laws make no such distinctions, either in class of crime or in penalty. State licensing boards and professional organizations can take the lead in making such clinical distinctions part of the rehabilitation process.

Gender-Based Psychodynamics in Dual Relations

Only preliminary and tentative remarks can be made on the potential differences between males and females in sexual and other misconduct. Researchers have uncovered some percentage differences between the incidence of male and female therapist sexual involvement with clients. The 1986 survey conducted by Gartrell (cited in Beck, Springen, and Foote 1992) found that 7 percent of male psychiatrists and 3 percent of female psychiatrists admitted having sexual relations with their clients. Additionally, research indicates that male therapists tend to have nonsexual relations more with female clients than with male clients (Borys and Pope 1989).

Reasons that professional females become sexually involved with clients have been identified (Laury 1992). They include material gratification coupled with client sexual advances, and a "Good Samaritan" attitude toward client care. Material gratification in concert with client advances means that some clients, particularly clients of high social or economic status, may make sexual advances toward female therapists or caregivers. As Laury puts it, "The usual social barrier is lowered" (p. 12). With the lowering of the social barrier, the professional barriers may also be lowered. The client may feel diminished by virtue of his being a client; the female therapist may feel more powerful as a therapist. Seducing the client may seem a challenge to the female therapist, or she may interpret a male client's need for help as a seduction signal.

The "Good Samaritan" syndrome means that the female therapist feels that her devotion to a male client's needs will cure him, even where others have failed. Where the female social worker harbors either "rescue" fantasies or the need to "save" others, a dependent or clinging male client may encourage such salvation. Similar dynamics for male therapists seem plausible, although research has not yet specifically addressed this theme. Same-sex exploitation is an area that is under-researched and under-addressed. Certainly, same-sex exploitation is likely to occur. The specific dynamics, frequency, and consequences need to be studied.

Religious-Spiritual Dynamics of Misconduct

Hurting others is always a moral concern. Social work often attaches moral values to both individual and social actions (Goldstein 1987; Leiby 1985; Siporin 1982). The harm done to others is also the proper province of religion and spirituality. Spiritual terms for engaging in coercive activities with clients, including sexual exploitation, are numerous. While the dynamics of sin no doubt can properly be applied to clients, this section is specifically designed to apply to social workers who sexually exploit their clients.

Peck (1978), Menninger (1973), Lapsley (1972), and Jung (1958) have enriched and integrated theology's concept of "sin" with psychodynamic insights. Hiltner (1972) examines both the traditional concept of the seven deadly sins and other metaphors for sin as psychological and social sickness. The seven deadly sins are: pride (hubris), covetousness, lechery, anger, envy, gluttony, and accidie (a form of depression). These categories of sin might be considered theological equivalents of the DSM-IV. Most misconduct can be typed in these categories. (It is instructive to note that *The Lecherous Professor* incorporates the third deadly sin.)

Hiltner also employs three principle metaphors: rebellion, "missing the mark," and isolation and alienation. These metaphors are the theological equivalent of social work assessment. Each of these metaphors can be understood as a dysfunction and can be applied to dual relations, particularly sexual misconduct.

Rebellion means more than disobedience; it means a rebellion against proper human limits. Rebellion, understood in this way, is hubris—a Greek word meaning human pride that contests the jurisdiction of the gods. The metaphor of rebellion suggests much more than just "disobedience" of a rule or order. Rebellion literally means "to make war again." In the context of professional misconduct, it means to make war against the rightful limits of human relations. Rebellion, the opposite of humility, suggests that professional misconduct stems partly from an exaggerated sense of one's own power, authority, or control over another.

The analogy of missing the mark comes from the biblical phrase "Avoid the godless chatter and contradictions of what is falsely called knowledge, for by professing it some have missed the mark as regards the faith" (1 Timothy 6:20–21 RSV). This analogy refers to knowledge that is used only for one's own purposes or knowledge used to gain advantage. Missing the mark, in professional misconduct relations, refers to using knowledge to insinuate oneself into another's confidence or trust for ulterior motives. This analogy of sin can serve as a warning against those who would pervert knowledge or loyalty as a means of control, coercion, or seduction.

Isolation or alienation also offers rich metaphors for professional misconduct. They refer to being disconnected—like a flower from its root. If the root cannot feed the flower, the flower dies. Isolation from one's true source or purpose causes one to lose the necessary connection to others and to one's own spiritual roots. If this spiritual umbilical cord is cut, the abuser does not have the necessary apparatus (call it "conscience") to act humanely.

The alienation and isolation metaphor for misconduct sheds light on the nature of dual relations in two ways. First, this metaphor sheds light on *when* the true "sin" of misconduct begins. Alienation precedes misconduct. The disconnection from the client precedes the act of entering a relationship that undermines the connection (and duty) of care between the social worker and the client. This means that social workers do not first sin with an act of misconduct, but sin first with an essential mental, emotional, and spiritual betrayal of the client and of themselves. Second, the alienation metaphor suggests how misconduct may be prevented. If alienation describes the cause of some illicit actions, then the social work profession has a vested interest in establishing the ethical underpinnings and means for a strong, professional connection between social workers and clients.

Part of the contribution of religion and spirituality is in creating metaphors to describe and to analyze this relationship.

A Religious-Spiritual Analysis of the DeShaney Case

The bulk of this book addresses social work sexual misconduct. This section addresses another form of misconduct. While sexual misconduct is described as *intentional* misconduct, misconduct can often be *negligent* misconduct. This distinction embodies crucial differences between law and social work practice. Intentional misconduct refers to conduct that is deliberate, even premeditated. Negligent misconduct, on the other hand, imposes liability for carelessness or inattention to dangers for others that falls below an established level of care. In sexual misconduct, the social worker intends to touch or to fondle the victim. The law considers these acts that the social worker knows to be wrong. Negligent acts do not carry the same degree of intentionality nor the same degree of culpability.

The most frequent population about which social workers are sued is the juvenile population (Snyder 1985). These suits most often involve wrongful placement in adoption or wrongful removal of children from their parents' custody. Social workers sued for negligence in adoption and custody cases are held liable for *negligent* acts. Their liability stems from careless acts conducted below the accepted standard of care owed to the parents or to the children themselves.

The leading case in social worker liability with juveniles is the Supreme Court decision in *DeShaney v. Winnebago County Department of Social Services* (1989). This case is unusual for two reasons. First, it is unusual that a case of alleged social worker misconduct should reach the U.S. Supreme Court. Most such cases are adjudicated at the trial levels, or at most, an appellate court. Second, the facts of this case are unusually painful.

Randy DeShaney, upon his first divorce in 1980, was granted custody of his one-year-old son Joshua. Randy and Joshua then moved from Wyoming to Winnebago County, Wisconsin. There, Randy remarried. Winnebago County Department of Social Services (DSS) first suspected that Randy was abusing Joshua in January of 1982 when Randy's second wife complained to the police that Randy "hit the boy causing marks." Randy and his second wife also divorced. DSS interviewed Randy, who denied hitting Joshua, and did not pursue accusations further.

In January of 1983 Joshua was admitted to the hospital with multiple bruises and abrasions. The attending physician notified DSS, which obtained a court order placing Joshua in temporary custody of the hospital. A child protection team, including DSS caseworkers, determined there was insufficient evidence of abuse to take Joshua away from his father. The team, however, recommended that Randy enroll Joshua in a preschool program, get counseling, and ask his girlfriend to move out of the home. Joshua was returned to Randy.

One month later, emergency room personnel told Joshua's caseworker that Joshua had once again been treated for suspicious injuries. The caseworker concluded that there was no basis for action against Randy. During the six months the caseworker made several visits to Randy and Joshua's home, where she observed suspicious injuries to Joshua's head, that he was not enrolled in a preschool program, and that the girlfriend had not moved out of the home.

In November 1984 the emergency room once again notified DSS that Joshua had been treated for injuries they believed to be caused by child abuse. On the next two visits to Joshua's home, the caseworker was told that Joshua was too ill to be seen. Finally, in March of 1984, Randy beat Joshua so severely that Joshua fell into a life-threatening coma. Joshua awoke from the coma, but his brain had hemorrhaged so badly that he is expected to remain confined to an institution for the rest of his life. Randy was convicted of child abuse.

Joshua and his mother brought suit against DSS and individual employees of DSS in federal court under a novel theory of liability. They claimed that the defendants had deprived Joshua of his liberty without due process of law, in violation of the due process clause of the Fourteenth Amendment. This clause states that the state shall not ". . . deprive any person of life, liberty, or property, without due process of law." Joshua and his mother argued that DSS, in failing to protect Joshua from the risk of violence that Randy posed, sentenced Joshua to permanent confinement.

The Supreme Court, although clearly sympathetic to Joshua's case, ruled that the due process clause guards private citizens against unconstitutional intrusion by government employees. The court held that the due process clause does not obligate the government to protect private citizens from the acts of other private citizens. Thus, the court ruled that it would not expand the liberty right to impose an affirmative duty for government to protect citizens.

Joshua and his mother also argued that "liberty interests" were created when the county DSS created a "special relationship" with Joshua. While the Supreme Court allowed that where convicts are imprisoned against their will, the state has a corresponding duty to provide for their general well-being, the court ruled that the state cannot be responsible for the mistreatment of Joshua when he was not in state custody.

The court called the facts of this case an "undeniable tragedy." There are several tragedies here. The first tragedy, of course, is Joshua. His damages are physically permanent and legally incompensable. The second tragedy is that social workers, whose efforts often go unnoticed and unheralded for years, have received a lifetime's worth of adverse publicity. The third tragedy is that the religious, spiritual, and ethical consequences of *DeShaney* have yet to be explored. The following paragraphs attempt to do just that.

This case brings together the elements of social worker liability and the moral nature of social work practice. Marion Wright Edelman, Director of the Children's Defense Fund, writes of the spiritual and moral obligations society owes to children in her book *The Measure of Our Success: A Letter to Your Children and Mine* (1993). She writes that not protecting children from poverty and violence, or viewing children as commodities, is the mark of a "spiritually impoverished," a "morally lost," and an "ethically confused" nation. What Wright says on the macro level can be said on the micro level.

The *DeShaney* case illustrates missing the mark with clients, isolation, and alienation. The first religious or spiritual aspect of *DeShaney* is that just because Joshua and his mother lost their case does not mean that Winnebago DSS "hit the mark." The absence of liability does not mean the absence of responsibility. It is obvious that Joshua's life, at critical points, was dangerously unprotected. Joshua's story is a reminder that the state or county DSS and individual social workers are often the last, best chance for protecting society's most vulnerable citizens. This protection is not just a legal duty, but a moral one as well. Put positively, "hitting the mark" with clients means not only providing a minimum, legal standard of care, but a standard of care that preserves the client's spiritual, physical, and emotional dignity.

DeShaney also illustrates alienation. Whether Joshua got lost between the cracks of DSS, or professional judgments were made that left Joshua vulnerable, it is clear that Joshua was alienated from the help, personnel, and services he needed. When suits involving the most helpless citizens against the very people hired to protect them, are the single most prevalent kind of lawsuit, such suits involve spiritual and religious as well as legal and psychosocial issues. The final section of this chapter suggests holistic models for healthy social worker relations with clients.

SPIRITUAL-PSYCHOSOCIAL DYNAMICS
OF HEALTHY PROFESSIONAL RELATIONS

This chapter has described how dysfunctional social worker-client relationships can occur. No one can dispute the importance of knowing the causes and qualities of dysfunctional professional relationships. Assessing the roots of sexual misconduct and other professional misconduct, however, does not provide the entire means of addressing these problems. A model of healthy, functional professional relationships is also necessary. Such a model is lacking in the professional literature. Naming the problem is only half the answer. Describing and utilizing models and metaphors for healthy professional relations furthers both the prevention of misconduct and client health. While chapter 7 specifically addresses prevention issues, this chapter would be incomplete without raising prevention issues directly. A series of considerations follows:

1. *Use metaphors to describe ethical social worker-client relationships.* If a metaphor can describe a cause for a sick professional relationship, then a metaphor can describe a cure. The proposed metaphor is that of a "covenant"—a covenant between social workers and their clients. This word has a rich history. "Covenant" comes from an Old English and Old French word ("covenir") meaning to agree or come to an agreement. In law, covenant means an agreement or promise to do something or *not* to do something, or to stipulate to the truth of certain fact (Black 1979). A covenant is a sacred bond between the social worker and the client or clients. The utility of a covenant comes from its connection to legal, professional, and theological spheres.

Covenants can be traced back at least to the Hittite kingdoms in the Near East (1450–1200 B.C.) and began in the form of a relationship between the Hebrews and the Lord of the Old Testament (Mendenhall 1954). The covenant relationship was a trusting, respectful, yet demanding one. The duty of loyalty was a prime element.

A covenant means more than a contract; it is more than a *quid pro quo* for professional services rendered. A covenant implies a relationship between the social worker and the client based upon more than an economic, legal, or psychological connection. The covenant relationship recognizes and values the essential, spiritual link that binds persons together. As Jesus of Nazareth said, "Truly, I tell you just as you did it to one of the least of these, who are members of my family, you did it to me" (Matthew 25:40 NRSV). This saying epitomizes the covenant relationship, one that will respect, safeguard, even cherish, the dignity of clients.

The covenant relationship is the ethical equivalent of "starting where the client is." Starting where the client is has become a hallmark practice principle that assures the client's values and needs are respected (Goldstein 1983). The covenant professional relationship operationalizes client-centeredness.

Investing the social worker-client relationship with spiritual, legal, and ethical as well as professional components establishes a true ecology of professional relations. The covenant metaphor places the proper worth upon values inherent in the social worker-client relationship.

2. *Define the value-based nature of the professional relationship.*Social workers, social work educators, and social work professional organizations can define the professional value base relative to sexual and other misconduct. A strong, clear, and consistent stand is necessary to inform clients and social work practitioners what acts constitute misconduct and what sanctions will be imposed. A strong, consistent value base relative to misconduct is both practical and imperative for two reasons.

First, social work is a value-laden profession. From the Jewish tradition, social work values include *tzedakah*, meaning "charity" or "righteousness" (Linzer 1979); from the Buddhist tradition, social work values include *karuna* and *metta*, meaning "compassion" and "loving-kindness" respectively (Canda and Phaobtong 1992); from the Islamic tradition, such values include *al hayat al tayyibah* ("the good life") and *sa 'adah* ("the good") (Ansari 1990). Altruism, responsibility, and social interdependence are other values affirmed by the social work profession (Siporin 1982). By whatever name, from whatever traditions, social work recognizes its history as a value-driven profession. Values proceed to a concern for dispossessed groups, for the alienated, the forgotten, and the vulnerable. Speaking about values is second nature to social workers.

Second, if social workers, professional organizations, and the social work profession do not provide values and accompanying training for their practitioners or memberships, others will. In fact, as we have seen in the first two chapters, laws and lawsuits have brought social worker misconduct into state and federal courts. Recent articles in *Newsweek* (April 13, 1992) and other popular magazines have brought this issue to the court of popular opinion. If all groups connected to credentialing, licensing, training, and supervising social workers do not speak plainly and convincingly about the values associated with misconduct, states will step in with increased regulation.

3. Recognize and accept social worker vulnerability. The helping professions are particularly vulnerable for several reasons. There is the tendency for a client to relate in an ambivalent way to the one giving help. This may be described as the "idolize-despise" syndrome. On one hand, the client may want to identify with the social worker, with what he or she sees as a role model. On the other hand, a client may secretly (or not so secretly) resent an unwanted or embarrassing intrusion into his or her private pain or need. The tension of these feelings or the tension of the "idolize-despise" syndrome may generate sexual energy.

Ambivalent, contradictory, and other mixed feelings may also flow from the social worker to the client. The social worker may over-identify with the client. This identification may take the form of envying a client's lifestyle, looks, or liberties. Conversely, the social worker may resent a client's mannerisms, lifestyle, or imposition upon his or her time or emotions.

4. Recognize and resist the lie of invincibility. Social workers are not immune from the passions and pitfalls from which case law develops. Vulnerability is no excuse for misconduct. Recognizing and acknowledging such vulnerability, however, is a first defense against arrogance and indifference to ethical and legal lessons. The model of social worker as superman or superwoman is hubris that no professional, and no profession, can afford. While acting on destructive desires or unresolved conflicts is a sign of clinical negligence and incompetence, recognizing vulnerability is a sign of health.

5. Conduct regular self-examination (Brockett and Gleckman 1991; Vasquez 1988). Of course, the problem with this suggestion is that self-knowledge is unclear and subjective. After misconduct has begun, a social worker may find objective reflection increasingly difficult, if not altogether impossible. The key is ongoing professional assessment. When social workers are themselves their own judge and jury, it is hard for them to render a fair verdict. Self-examination requires a model and the honest motivation of self-reflection. Reading a book on professional ethics does not, in itself, promote honest self-appraisals. However, this book provides a tool for such self-examination in chapter 5.

If a social worker lacks the desire and capacity for self-examination, others are required to do the job. Prosecutors, courts, and professional ethics committees can do the job, but no profession can long stand scrutiny at the hands of other professional groups. Social workers and social work organizations that cannot or will not scrutinize themselves will face increasing public regulation, public opprobrium, and ultimately, public renunciation.

6. Model morality, not moralism. Morality is the practice of values arising from authentic self-examination, while moralism is the imposition of external rules by another. Morality is characterized by authenticity and honesty; moralism is characterized by external conformity. No one professional group has a corner on the morality market. Clinical diagnoses, if used arbitrarily and without compassion, can be just another mode of moralism.

To the extent that social workers model morality, they encourage their clients to confront the social worker's own prejudices and presumptions. To the extent that social workers model moralism, they control, dominate, and manipulate discussions of values and judgments of right and wrong. Modeling morality requires that the social worker disclose professional ethics to the client and invite the client to scrutinize the worker's own behavior.

7. Promote healthy dispassion, not passion for clients. Most social workers have a healthy, mature regard for both their professions and themselves. They know that they cannot, and should not, place upon themselves the dubious burden of "saving the world." Enthusiasm, even vigor, for personal and political healing for individuals and groups is a proud hallmark of the social work profession. Where enthusiasm, however, borders on the evangelistic, the client is in danger of being converted into a sexual, social, or economic disciple of the social worker. Social workers who have a controlling passion for their clients are in danger of perverting the social worker-client relationship.

The religious language of "conversion" used here is deliberate. Social workers, as well as clergy and other professionals, have the persuasive tools to influence clients in their own image. Whether the rationale is God's demands or therapeutic intervention (backed up with the imprimatur of scientific data), the results are the same. The client's autonomy and "personhood" are sacrificed on the altar of idolatry.

Passion can easily be misplaced into patronizing the client, a desire to take personal control of the client, and even a desire to dominate the client. Dispassion towards a client is closer to the principle of self-determination. Self-determination means that clients have the knowledge and opportunity to make independent decisions. If there is passion in the professional relationship, it should be directed toward the *professional relationship*, not the client. It is an easy leap from patronizing the client, to taking personal control over the client, to sexually dominating the client.

8. Cultivate other interests. To put the matter in its most negative light, a social worker who must have control over others should cultivate interests outside his or her professional life. He or she can dominate in sports, or in political or civil affairs, but should not dominate clients.

To put the matter in a more positive light, social workers can use outside interests to enrich and to provide diversity in their lives. Such enrichment and diversity can lend much needed perspective and distance for social workers. Social workers need times of release and refreshment in order to work with greater purpose and pride.

9. Protecting clients sometimes means being humble. Everyone wants to be honored and recognized. However, honors may exaggerate the client's tendency to idolize and the social worker's misplaced feelings of self-importance. Other professionals have addressed this issue. Newman (1963) relates the story of an honored rabbi traveling by carriage to the city. A throng of followers come to meet him. The rabbi, seeing the crowd approaching, leaps from his carriage and runs to meet the crowd, saying that he wants to join them in paying honor to such a learned man and asking, "Where is this rabbi?"

This is not just a quaint old story. Learned rabbis and other professionals do not want disciples or followers at the expense of the disciples' own growth. The same should be true for social workers and their clients. Perhaps the ultimate way that social workers can release their clients to their own autonomy and self-determination is to encourage clients to place honors in perspective. Clients may first find health through social workers, then find health despite them. Regardless of the operative theory of practice, the ultimate goal is for the client to bear responsibility for his or her own behavior.

Social workers engaging in sexual misconduct encourage "hero worship" on the part of their clients (Pope 1988). Discouraging sexual relations can mean the insistence that clients ultimately value their autonomy over clinical expertise. The social worker's practice can uphold, support, and sustain a client during times of difficulty. In this professional capacity the social worker provides clinical help for the client's benefit. This help, however, is not intended to last forever. Limitations in both time and resources always prevail—and they should. Clients who have symbolically "dis-honored" their social workers are less likely to engage in sexual relations with them. Social workers who foster client dependence help neither themselves nor their clients. Those workers who provide clients with the tools with which to "dis-honor" their clinicians, also provide their clients with the means to improve their own health.

REFERENCES

American Psychological Association (1987). *Diagnostic and statistical manual of mental disorders*. Washington, DC: Authors.

Ansari, A.H. (1990). Islamic ethics: Concept and prospect. *American Journal of Islamic Social Science*, 6(1), 81–91.

Beck, M., Springen, K., and Foote, D. (1992, April 12). Sex and psychotherapy. *Newsweek*, 52–57.

Black, H.C. (1979). *Black's law dictionary*. St. Paul, MN: West Publishing.

Borys, D.S., and Pope, K.S. (1989). Dual relationships between therapist and client: A national study of psychologists, psychiatrists, and social workers. *Professional Psychology: Research and Practice*, 20(5), 283–93.

Brockett, D.R., and Gleckman, A.D. (1991). Countertransference with the older adult: The importance of mental health counselor awareness and strategies for effective management. *Journal of Mental Health Counseling*, 13(3), 343–55.

Canda, E.R., and Phaobtong, T. (1992). Buddhism as a support system for Southeast Asian refugees. *Social Work*, 37(1), 61–67.

DeShaney v. Winnebago County Department of Social Services, 489 U.S. 189 (1989).

Dziech, B.W., and Weiner, L. (1990). *The lecherous professor: Sexual harassment on campus*. Chicago: University of Illinois Press.

Earle, R.H., and Crow, G.M. (1990). Sexual addiction: Understanding and treating the phenomenon. *Contemporary Family Therapy*, 12(2), 89–104.

Edelman, M. (1993, July 18). America's children: They need our help. *Richmond Times-Dispatch*, F4.

Edelwich, J., and Brodsky, A. (1991). *Sexual dilemmas for the helping professional*. New York: Brunner/Mazel, Publishers.

Goldstein, H. (1983). The neglected moral link in social work practice. *Social Work*, 18, 180–86.

Goodman, A. (1993). Diagnosis and treatment of sexual addiction. *Journal of Sex and Marital Therapy*, 19(3), 225–51.

Gutheil, T. (1989). Borderline personality disorder, boundary violations, and patient-therapist sex: Medicolegal pitfalls. *American Journal of Psychiatry*, 146(5), 597–602.

Hiltner, S. (1972). *Theological dynamics*. Nashville, TN: Abingdon.

Horak v. Biris, 474 N.E. 2d 13 (Ill. App. 2 Dist. 1985).

Hulbert, D. and Apt, C. (1992) Sex addict or sexual narcissist? *Contemporary Sexuality*, 26(4), 1–2.

Jung, C.G. (1958). *The undiscovered self*. New York: The New American Library.

Lapsley, J.N. (1972). *Salvation and health*. Philadelphia: The Westminster Press.

Laury, G.V. (1992). When women sexually abuse male psychiatric patients under their care. *Journal of Sex Education and Therapy*, 18(1), 11–16.

Leiby, J. (1985). Moral foundations of social welfare and social work: A historical view. *Social Work*, 30(4), 323–30.

Linzer, N. (1979). A Jewish philosophy of social work practice. *Journal of Jewish Communal Service,* 60(3), 309–17.

Mendenhall, G.E. (1954). Covenant forms in Israelite tradition. *The Biblical Archaeologist,* 17(3), 50–76.

Menninger, K. (1973). *Whatever became of sin?* New York: Hawthorne Press.

Moser, C. (1993). A response to Aviel Goodman's "Sexual addiction: Designation and treatment." *Journal of Sex and Marital Therapy,* 19(3), 220–24.

Newman, L.I. (1963). *The Hasidic anthology.* Northvale, NJ: Jason Aronson, Inc.

Peck, F.S. (1978). *The road less traveled.* New York: Simon and Schuster.

Pope, K.S. (1988). How clients are harmed by sexual contact with mental health professionals: The syndrome and its prevalence. *Journal of Counseling and Development,* 67(4), 222–26.

Schoener, G.R., and Gonsiorek, J. (1988). Assessment and development rehabilitation plans for counselors who have sexually exploited their clients. *Journal of Counseling and Development,* 67(4), 227–32.

Siporin, M. (1982). Moral philosophy in social work today. *Social Service Review,* 56(4), 516–38.

Snyder, F. (1985). Legal liability: The social worker and juveniles. *Journal of Juvenile Law,* 9, 36–52.

Vasquez, M.J.T. (1988). Counselor-client sexual contact: Implications for ethics training. *Journal of Counseling and Development,* 67(4), 238–41.

Woititz, J.G. (1989). *Healing your sexual self.* Deerfield Beach, FL: Health Communications, Inc.

Woititz, J.G. (1985). *Struggle for intimacy.* Deerfield Beach, FL: Health Communications, Inc.

Chapter 5

▶ ·························· ◀

An Ethical Ecology of Sexual Misconduct

▶ ·························· ◀

We now address the relationships between law and ethics, and law and justice, as well as addressing ethics as a subject of philosophic inquiry versus the practice of professional ethics. Of course, law and ethics are not the same. Law is the body of statutes, case law (judicial decisions), and regulations that govern our society. Chapters 2 and 3 have detailed the *law* surrounding ethical misconduct, especially sexual misconduct of clinical social workers. As we have seen, the statutes and case law among the states can be vague, inconclusive, and even contradictory. This chapter distinguishes between types of ethics and the law, and proposes an "ethical ecology" as a model to understand misconduct in professional ethics.

The distinctions between law, ethics, and professional ethics are made clear for two reasons. First, it is improper and inaccurate to confuse ethics, professional ethics, and law. They are not interchangeable concepts and using them interchangeably further complicates an already complex topic. Second, confusing these terms can be professionally harmful. To say that avoiding sexual relations is only an *ethical* duty is inaccurate, and can create legal vulnerabilities on the part of the social worker.

Ethical considerations serve the interests of all, serve consistent purposes, and help form conclusive assumptions about the nature of human beings and of assertions about behavior. Ethics is the determination of good and bad behavior. Entire branches of philosophy and theology are devoted to this important study. Certainly, the argument can be made that law should be ethical and that ethics should be codified into law. However, this is not always the case. Because the United States is a democratic republic, laws are necessarily made in the rough and tumble—the "realpolitik"—of the political process. It is no secret that laws are made with the expertise and care of some, the indifference of many, the weight of special interests, and legislative horse-trading among politicians.

It is important to make the necessary distinctions between *ethics* and *professional ethics*. Bayles (1989) defines professional ethics "as a system of norms" (p. 17). Professional ethics, as used in this book, means ethical determinations and guidelines *specifically determined by or specifically determined for* a professional group. These professional ethics or "norms" are not vague assertions about the behavior expected from professionals. Professional ethics establish specific professional norms of behavior. Professional norms can be operationalized by the codes of ethics promulgated by professional groups or by state professional licensing boards. This, of course, is the case for the clinical social work profession. State licensing boards establish codes of ethics for licensed social workers (clinical and otherwise), and organizations, such as the National Association of Social Workers also promulgate ethical codes.

The difference between ethics as a theological or philosophical discipline and professional ethics is the difference between role and function. The purpose of ethics as a discipline of theological or philosophical inquiry is to establish principles of normative or moral behavior. While such principles often form the bases for professional codes of ethics, such principles rarely provide the specificity necessary for a professional code of ethics.

Conversely, professional codes of ethics are public, operational, and enforceable. This means that professional ethics must specifically guide professionals both by defining unethical behavior and defining ethical behavior. These codes are established in public (by committees) and are published and circulated to members within the profession and the public at large. The codes are operational in that they apply to specific situations likely to occur. The NASW Code of Ethics is much more specific than a series of philosophic principles or moral admonitions. The NASW Code is designed to be readily applicable to a number of practice situations. Lastly, the professional codes are enforceable because they have the backing of a professional organization that establishes procedures to take complaints, investigate complaints, adjudicate claims, and punish breaches of the code.

Additionally, the results of such claims of unethical behavior are publicized.

Social workers are responsible for behaving within the confines of their *professional* codes, not general philosophic or moral codes. While moral philosophy, religious codes, and philosophies of ethics contribute significantly to the discipline of professional ethics, social workers are not required either by law or by their profession to abide by them. These various ethical considerations can be contradictory. There are almost as many opinions on ethical matters as there are ethicists.

PROFESSIONAL CODES OF ETHICS AND THE LAW

Clinical social workers may have professional ethics codified by a number of professional groups. Because such groups are so numerous, only two groups can be discussed here. Both the National Association of Social Workers and the National Federation of Societies for Clinical Social Workers have promulgated codes of ethics. These codes were chosen to be addressed here because of their availability and widespread distribution among clinical social workers.

The promulgation of ethical codes is significant for the professional and the public. Codes of ethics place the clinical social worker and the public on notice that a certain standard of behavior is expected; behavior deemed below that standard will be punished. The punishment and the means of punishment are open to the public, even if the trials are confidential. Usually, the names of offenders and the punishments meted out are highly publicized through professional newsletters, journals and other media.

Laws that determine professional social work behavior can be similar to social work codes of ethics. For example, the NASW Code of Ethics specifies that client confidentiality and privacy is a norm and expectation (II,H). Most state laws that license social workers also provide for a "privileged communication" statute (Bullis and Biggerstaff, in press). Privileged communication statutes provide laws that determine how, when, and where social workers may divulge client confidences in court.

However, the differences between law and codes of ethics are worth distinguishing. First, the processes of promulgating and prosecuting laws and social worker codes of ethics are different. The legislatures of each state promulgate laws and the courts sitting in each state interpret these laws. State legislators do not sit as representatives of any one profession. They pass laws to protect the general public safety and welfare.

Second, the prosecution of laws is different from the prosecution of ethical violations. The state criminal prosecution of a social worker who violates the privileged communications law uses investigators and prosecutors engaged by the state, and sanctions are imposed by the state. Additionally, even in a civil case against a social worker who violates confidentiality, public courts are used. On the other hand, the NASW will use its own, private resources and staff to take complaints, investigate complaints, adjudicate claims, and sanction violations of confidentiality.

It bears repeating that a violation of ethical codes can be independently a source of criminal, civil, and professional investigation, and possible sanction. In other words, social workers can be fined, be imprisoned, have money damages assessed against them, have their licenses revoked, and be denied membership in NASW for the same violation.

Table 5.1 illustrates state statutes that list ethical breaches that can result in sanctions. The sanctions include suspending and revoking clinical licenses of social workers. Table 5.1 indicates that a broad range of ethical breaches is covered, including sexual misconduct; it also indicates that some statutes are very general in requiring "good standing" as determined by the licensing board, while other states specifically denote the offensive behaviors.

Table 5.1
Current Statutes Illustrating Grounds for Suspension, Rule-Making Authority, or Other Sanctions for Clinical Social Workers

State	Cite	Ethic
Alabama	34-30-4	Felony conviction as provided by Board
Alaska	08.95.110	In good standing as determined by Board
Arkansas	17-39-305	Gross negligence, unprofessional conduct, federal or state felony
California	Ch. 14, 4992.3 (Business and Professional Code)	"Engaging in sexual relations with a client, or committing an act of sexual abuse, or sexual conduct with a client, or committing an act punishable as a sexually related crime, if that act or solicitation is substantially related to the qualifications, functions, or duties of a clinical social worker."
		"Paying, accepting, or soliciting any consideration, compensation, or remuneration, whether monetary or otherwise, for the referral of professional clients."

(continued)

Table 5.1 (continued)

State	Cite	Ethic
Delaware	Ch. 24, 3915	Crime involving moral turpitude ". . . knowingly engaged in an act of consumer fraud or deception, or participated in price-fixing activities."
District of Columbia	2-3305.14	Pays for, or splits a fee for bringing or referring a client to another; engages in sexual harassment of a patient or client.
Florida	491.009	Committing any act upon a patient or client which would constitute sexual misconduct defined in 491.0111.
Georgia	43-10A-17	". . . unprofessional, immoral, unethical, deceptive, or deleterious conduct or practice harmful to the public, which conduct or practice materially affects the fitness of the licensee or applicant to practice the specialty, or of a nature likely to jeopardize the interest of the public, which conduct or practice need not have resulted in actual injury to any person or be directly related to the practice of the specialty but shows that the licensee or applicant has committed any act or omission which is indicative of bad moral character or untrustworthiness; unprofessional conduct shall also include any departure from, or the failure to conform to, the minimal standards of acceptable and prevailing practice of the specialty"
Hawaii	467D-6	"Engaging in sexual conduct in connection with professional services or activities"; "Engaging in dishonorable, unethical, or unprofessional conduct of a character likely to deceive, defraud, or harm an individual or the public in the course of professional services or activities"
Idaho	54-3210 54-3211	Establishment of a code of ethics Conviction of any offense involving moral turpitude; fraud or deceit in connection with professional services
Illinois	Ch. 111, 6369	Conviction of any crime "directly related" to the practice of clinical social work; malpractice; professional incompetence
Indiana	25-23.6-5-7	Prior disciplinary action; Board may determine whether violation has direct bearing on practice ability
Iowa	154C.4	Standards of professional conduct

Table 5.1 (continued)

State	Cite	Ethic
Kansas	65-6311	Felony conviction, unprofessional conduct; negligence
Kentucky	335.150	Board may revoke, deny, or suspend any license
Louisiana	37:2713	Final conviction of any felony; "gross" negligence
Maine	32, Sect. 7059	Fraud or deceit in practice; gross negligence, incompetency or misconduct in practice
Massachusetts	Ch. 112, Sect. 137	"conviction of felony involving moral turpitude"
Minnesota	148B.44(M)	Engaging in sexual contact with a client or former client as defined in 148A.01
Mississippi	73-53-17	lewd conduct in practice, false or misleading advertising, gross negligence, dishonorable, unethical, or unprofessional conduct likely to deceive, defraud, or harm the public
Missouri	337.630(5)(13)	Incompetency, misconduct, fraud, misrepresentation or dishonesty in the performance of functions; violation of any professional trust or confidence, guilty of unethical conduct as defined in the ethical standards for clinical social workers adopted by state committees
Montana	37-22-311	Sexual relations with a client, solicitation of sexual relations with a client, sexual misconduct, or a sex offense, or solicitation is substantially related to the qualifications, functions, or duties of the licensee, committed a felony, gross negligence, incompetency, or misconduct in practice, violation of rules established by Board
New Mexico	61-31-17	Unprofessional, unethical, "grossly" negligent, or incompetent service
New York	Art. 154, 7704	Be of good moral character
North Carolina	90B-11	Gross unprofessional misconduct; dishonest practice or incompetence; any fraudulent or dishonest conduct
Ohio	4757.13	Accepted a commission or rebate for referrals; convicted of "misdemeanor" in course of professional work
Oregon	675.540	Federal or state felony conviction, gross negligence

(continued)

Table 5.1 *(continued)*

State	Cite	Ethic
Pennsylvania	Ch. 32, 1266	Felony conviction and, after investigation, the determination that the offender is not sufficiently rehabilitated to merit the public trust; found guilty of unprofessional conduct as defined by Board rule
Puerto Rico	T. 20, 822	Powers to issue and revoke licenses
Rhode Island	5-39-16	". . . convicted of any crime which has a substantial relationship to the activities and services of the person certified or an essential element which is misstatement, fraud, or dishonesty"; gross negligence
South Carolina	40-63-110	fraudulent, false, or misleading statements connected with receiving a license or conducting practice
South Dakota	36-26-32	fraud or deceit in connecting with receiving a license; violating the NASW Code of Ethics
Tennessee	63-23-106	fraud, deceit, or misrepresentation in connection with social work practice, unethical or unprofessional behavior as prescribed by licensing board
Texas	Human Services 50.021	violate ethical principles established by licensing board
Utah	58-35-11	conviction of fraud or deceit in practice; found guilty of unprofessional conduct of licensing board or of NASW Code of Ethics
Virgin Islands	T.27, 540	Felony conviction, gross negligence
Washington	18.130.180	Abuse of a client or patient or sexual contact with a patient or client
Wyoming	33-38-110	Crimes of moral turpitude; unprofessional or unethical behavior; gross incompetence or malpractice

THE ETHICAL ECOLOGY OF SEXUAL MISCONDUCT

The ethical ecology is a model designed to describe and interpret interrelated components of ethical decision making regarding sexual misconduct (see figure 5.1). These components influence each other, and constitute a system—an open system, much like an ecology of a river or an ocean. In an ocean ecosystem, every environmental component is important. Recent events such as the Exxon Valdez oil

Figure 5.1
The Ethical Ecology of Sexual Misconduct

The Ethical Ecology
of
Sexual Misconduct

Actions
1. Client contacts
2. Record behaviors

Code of Ethics
1. Code provisions

Professional Values
1. Preamble to NASW Code of Ethics

U.S. Law
1. Statutes (State & Federal)
2. Case law decisions
3. Stare decisis

Social Values
1. U.S. Charter
2. U.S. Declaration of Independence
3. U.S. Constitution

Mythic Values
1. Bible
2. Aesop

Reflection
1. Describe behavior
2. Compare behavior with ethical norms
3. Compare behavior with law, social norms, and mythic values
4. Evaluate behavior difference between ethics and action

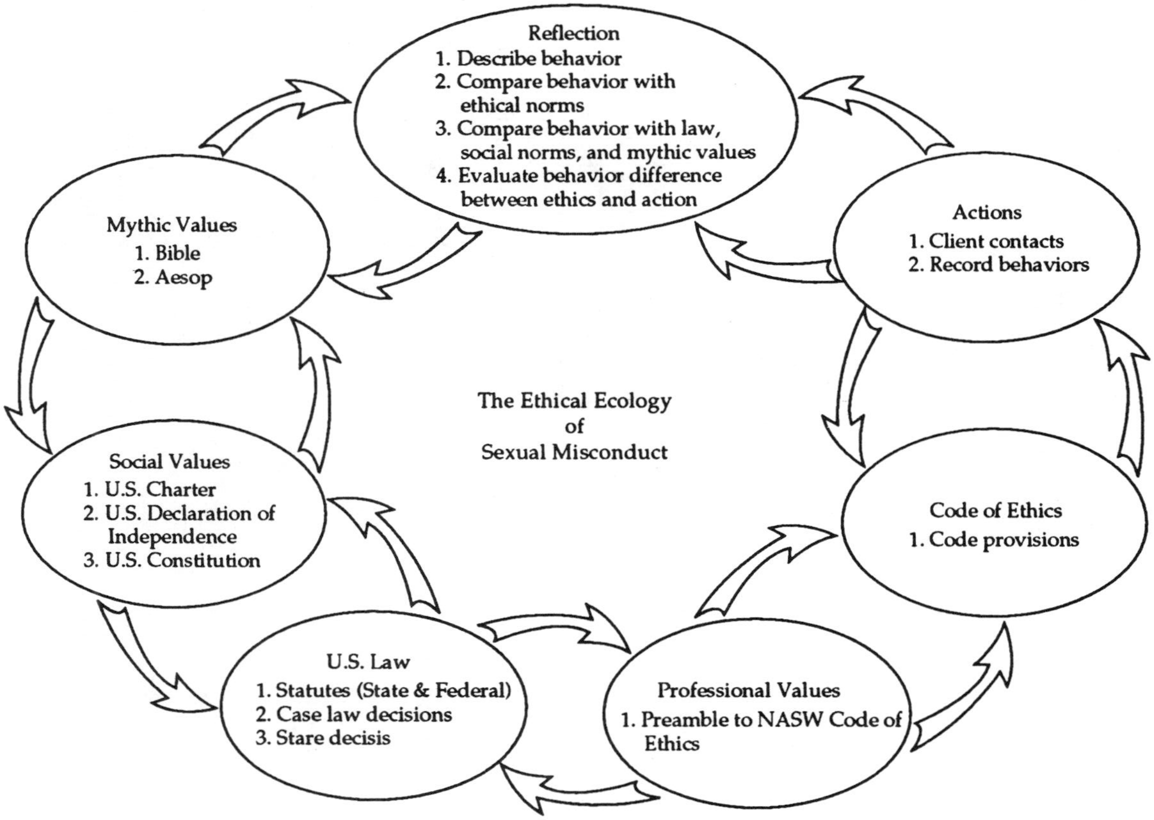

spill in Alaska dramatically illustrate how an environmental disaster in one component (the sea) can affect the land, birds, animals, and other components of the system. The ethical ecology of sexual misconduct operates in much the same way. Each of the elements makes up a component of a whole by which U.S. clinical social workers operate under social and legal forces and values.

An ethical ecology is important to the ethics and law of sexual misconduct because professional ethics does not arise full-grown, like Athena out of the head of Zeus. Ethical principles and professional ethics are promulgated and prosecuted in a cultural milieu. To understand the ethical admonitions against inappropriate dual relations, permissible dual relations, and trends in the ethical considerations, it is necessary to understand the cultural principles from which they grew. The components of this ethical ecology are discussed next.

Mythic Values

Mythic or cultural values are the integral principles of a cultural group. Such values often arise from or are associated with divine or religious figures. Myths are psychic and cultural structures that determine the nature and form of culture (Campbell 1972). Mythic values can extend beyond the borders of one country or they can be bounded within one particular country.

To illustrate Western mythic values, it is reasonable to look at both the Bible and Aesop's fables. Aesop's fables are brief stories with a single moral point. It is said that Aesop lived from 600–520 B.C. Some say that he was a slave of Iadmon of Samos (Greece) and was freed because of his wisdom. Legend has it that Aesop once lived at the court of King Croesus, where he met the philosopher Solon and the Seven Sages of Greece. Aesop's fables both reflected and formed Western moral and ethical behavior.

The influence of the Bible remains remarkably consistent and persistent. Recent polls indicate that four out of five Americans believe that the Bible is inspired by God. Even many of those who do not believe that the Bible should be taken literally regard it as the basis for moral values and the rule of law. Of the 81 percent of Americans who occasionally feel depressed, more read the Bible (48 percent) than seek help from a doctor or professional counselor (14 percent). Additionally, Bible reading is viewed as more effective in relieving depression (Gallup & Castelli 1989). This evidence indicates that many Americans consider the Bible to be of mythic importance.

While mythic values often transcend narrow cultural boundaries, this book relates mythic values to American law as it is found in statutes and case law. The scope of this book cannot include discussion of comparative myth or comparative law. Thus, diverse non-Western sources remain unaddressed not because they are unimportant, but because U.S. law has its roots in the West.

The Bargain of Personal Freedom

Aesop wrote a wonderful fable about the cost and value of personal freedom, titled "The Dog and the Wolf." A starving wolf meets a well-fed dog. The wolf asks the dog how it is that the wolf is always hungry and has no home, while the dog always has enough to eat. The dog tells the wolf that he would gladly show the wolf how he too could have plenty to eat. However, on the way to the dog's home, the wolf notices something unusual about the dog.

"Why is all the fur around your neck gone?" asks the wolf. The dog replies that it is the place where the master puts on the collar. "It chafes a bit, but you get used to it," says the dog. The wolf leaves, preferring his freedom to an easy slavery (Junior Great Books 1963).

The bargain of personal freedom is succinctly told. Freedom costs time, energy, risks, vulnerability, and pain. However, the story clearly favors personal freedom. It is not too broad an assertion that this fable reflects, and perhaps helped form, the Western value of individual freedom. Individual freedom is an essential element in the social work principles of nonjudgmentalism and individual client self-determination. In American jurisprudence, the promulgation and protection of individual rights is paramount. The U.S. Bill of Rights, including the due process rights of criminal defendants and the right of assembly and speech, addresses individual rights that can be adjudicated in courts of law designed for individual defendant and plaintiff contests.

Responsibility for Others

A central parable in the New Testament relative to responsibility for others is that of the Good Samaritan. Parables are ancient stories that have a single, unifying message or point. Jesus of Nazareth tells the story in response to a lawyer's question, "What is the most important law?"

The story is that a man is left wounded and robbed by a roadside. First, a religious leader walks by and does nothing. Second, a rich man walks by and does nothing. Finally, a Samaritan comes by, gives the man aid, helps him walk into town, and gives an innkeeper money to house and care for him. The point of the story is intensified by the knowledge that Samaritans, at the time when Jesus told this parable, were considered second class citizens. So, the single point of the parable is that the most important law is the law of compassion.

It is significant that Jesus tells this famous parable as a response to a question of law. Jesus is essentially asked to describe the animating values of his culture. He responds with a story illustrating the law of kindness in dramatic terms. Jesus demonstrates a case of responsibility for others as the epitome of his culture's law.

Personal Choice

The Old Testament offers a striking illustration of the theme of personal choice. The scene unfolds as Joshua, the successor to Moses, leads the Israelites into the proximity of the promised land. Joshua is a warrior as well as a politician and urges the Israelites to fight against the Moabites and the Amorites. He presses the Israelites into the fight for a land of their own with a stirring soliloquy. Joshua also seeks to bind his people to the salvation history of the liberation from slavery in Egypt and the Red Sea crossing—he urges them to be true to their tradition.

> Now therefore fear the Lord, and serve him in sincerity and in faithfulness; put away the gods which your fathers served beyond the River, and in Egypt, and serve the Lord. And if you are unwilling to serve the Lord, choose this day whom you will serve, whether the gods your fathers served in the region beyond the River, or the gods of the Amorites in whose land you dwell, but as for me and my house, we will serve the Lord. (Joshua 24:14–15, RSV)

A choice was required on the part of the Israelites. The choice was a clear one—serve the God of the Israelites or the gods of the Amorites. Additionally, the choice had to be made immediately. Joshua's call required both an individual and a community choice.

The people of Israel chose to serve the God of the Israelites. Joshua sought to impress upon the people the seriousness and consequences of their decision. Joshua said, "You are witnesses against yourselves that you have chosen the Lord, to serve him" (Joshua 24:27). The term "witnesses against yourselves" may mean that once an oath—a choice—has been made, a rejection of that choice can have serious consequences.

Significantly, once the choice was made, a covenant was struck between the people and their God, mediated by Joshua. "So Joshua made a covenant with the people that day, and made statutes and ordinances for them at Sheckem. And Joshua wrote these words in the book of the law of God; and he took a great stone, and set it up under the oak in the sanctuary of the Lord" (Joshua 24:25). The covenant was an agreement—a divine contract. The covenant was memorialized in the three most permanent forms: wood, stone, and the book.

In this story the movement from mythic or cultural values to national values is illustrated. The oath to God (a mythic value) by the Israelites became a set of laws and ordinances under which the Israelites began to form the legal structure of a people—and a nation.

Social Values

Social values refer to values or principles integral to a country's or a society's identity. One document that both embodies Western social values and enjoys increased recognition is the Charter of the United Nations. Beyond organizing nations to promote peace and international cooperation, the Charter reads:

> To develop friendly relations among nations based on respect for the principle of equal rights and self-determination of peoples, and to take other appropriate measures to strengthen universal peace. (Article I, 2)

The principles of equal rights and self-determination are significant Western ideologies. Western civilization, at least since the time of the Enlightenment, has upheld equal rights and personal self-determination as basic human freedoms.

Another document embodying American social values is the Declaration of Independence. The Declaration states the ethical rationale for independence in the language of inherent, natural human rights. It concludes:

> We hold these truths to be self-evident, that all men are created equal, that they have been endowed by their creator with unalienable rights, that among them are life, liberty and the pursuit of happiness.

The Declaration of Independence, written by educated men of the Enlightenment, illustrates two central social values—self-determination and the importance of personal acquisition.

Self-Determination

Self-determination is the right to control one's life. This control includes having access to pertinent information with which to make decisions. An uninformed act of self-determination is not self-determination at all.

Self-determination is an expression of the individualism of Western culture. The individual chooses the terms of his or her role in actions and their consequences. The Aesop fable of the dog and the wolf illustrates the primacy of the individual's right both to *have* choices and to freely act upon them.

But this self-determination is not without boundaries. The law and professional ethics hedge the individual social worker and client with rules intended to protect the health and safety of society. Later, this chapter will discuss the specific practice limitation of the *Tarasoff* decision. Child and vulnerable adult reporting laws also place significant legal parameters around professional social work practice.

Pursuit of Happiness

The "pursuit of happiness" is another term for property. At the time the Declaration was written, property was a prerequisite for personal freedom. Without property, one could not vote. Without property, there was no personal freedom. The above rights were considered "unalienable" (part of human nature) because they were "natural." "Unalienable" means that they cannot be taken away and natural means that they are part of the human condition.

Interest in natural rights has experienced a revival of sorts with the appointment of Judge Clarence Thomas to the U.S. Supreme Court in the summer of 1991. However, there is little question that the drafters of the U.S. Constitution considered the rights and freedoms they proposed to be unalienable. While these unalienable rights do not in and of themselves possess the force of law, they undergird much of American statutory and case law.

Laws

Chapters 1 and 2 discussed the criminal and civil law surrounding misconduct, particularly of sexual dual relations. Even this body of law, however, does not exhaust statutes surrounding such misconduct. A third source of law applicable to social worker misconduct is statutes that govern the licensing of social workers, particularly clinical social workers. Table 5.1 outlines state statutes that impose sanctions against sexual misconduct and related infractions.

As one can see from table 5.1, states impose license suspension or revocation for a broad range of offenses, including conflict of interest, disloyalty, and the breach of fiduciary duty to clients.

Laws have several important functions relative to the ecology of ethical behavior. First, laws publicly announce the intentions of the legislature. These intentions, embodied in statute, can be described as both a source of and a reflection of public ethical choices. Second, many state laws reflect social work professional ethics. It should come as no surprise that many of the sanctions described in the state codes are similar to, if not the same as, the ethical requirements of social work organizations. Professional organizations lobby for statutes that protect their membership, and, it is hoped, the general public. Professional licensing laws often reflect the ethical codes of the given profession—licensing laws of the social work profession are no different.

Some states are not represented because they do not specifically license social workers or because their regulations are codified in department regulations, not the state law codes. For example, Virginia's regulation against licensed social clinical worker sexual misconduct is codified in Department of Health Professions regulations (VR620-01-2, Section 6.1 (10)), not in the law code itself. The regulation forbids conduct:

> . . . with clients that might compromise the client's well-being or impair the social worker's objectivity and professional judgment (to include such activities as counseling close friends or relatives, engaging in sexual intimacies with a client).

These laws, used in conjunction with the criminal and civil laws discussed in the first two chapters, impose penalties for infractions. Rules adopted by the licensing boards carry penalties ranging from permanent revocation of license to temporary suspension to reprimand. Given the general language of the regulation and its undefined terms (e.g., "close friends," the client's "well being," "objectivity"), even regulations that specifically mention sexual misconduct require ethical reflection for specific practice application.

Professional Values

Professional values are the guiding principles of a profession. These values are expressed in the preambles of the Codes of Ethics that regulate the clinical social work professions. There are primarily two professional organizations that promulgate ethical codes for clinical social workers: the National Association of Social Workers and the National Federation for the Societies of Clinical Social Workers. The NASW code preamble clearly expresses the values underlying its provisions:

> This code is based on the fundamental values of the social work profession that include the worth, dignity, and uniqueness of all persons as well as their rights and opportunities. It is also based on the nature of social work, which fosters conditions that promote these values.

It seems clear that the NASW preamble emphasizes the rights of the individual. This theme is consistent with the principles of the Declaration of Independence and the preamble to the U.S. Constitution. The theme of individual rights is repeated expressly in the preamble to the NFSCSW Code (1985), stating, "The principal objective of the profession of clinical social work is to enhance the dignity and well-being of each individual who seeks its services." Thus, these professional values are consistent with both American national values and law.

Ethical Code Provisions

Codes of ethics are documents describing the ethical norms of professional groups. Sometimes these codes of ethics are vague and broad, sometimes they are defined and explicit. The NFSCSW Code (II,c, 2-3) provides pointed provisions on sexual relations:

> Clinical social workers do not engage in or condone sexual activities with clients.
>
> Clinical social workers do not initiate, and should avoid when possible, personal relationships or dual roles with current clients, or with any former clients whose feelings toward them may still be derived from or influenced by the former professional relationship.

This provision reinforces the statutes, discussed in chapter 2, that criminalize sex with *former* clients. This code restates the rationale that emotional dependency effectively eliminates the client's capacity for independent and autonomous decision making.

As we have seen in the previous chapter, sexual misconduct represents an interference with professional discretionary judgment. Another pertinent section in the NASW Code addresses conflicts of interest more directly. The specific provisions (II,F) read:

> Primacy of Clients' Interests—The social worker's primary responsibility is to clients.
>
> 2. The social worker should not exploit relationships with clients for personal advantage.
>
> 4. The social worker should avoid relationships or commitments that conflict with the interests of clients.

NASW has also promulgated Standards of Practice for Social Work Mediators (1991). The introduction to this document states that the "Standards" are designed to complement the NASW Code of Ethics. Thus, social work mediators work under two ethical standards: the NASW Code of Ethics and the mediation standards.

Mediation Standard 11 directly addresses conflict of interest. It reads:

> The mediator shall not use any information obtained during the mediation process for personal benefit or for the benefit of any group or organization with which the mediator is associated.

While a paragraph of "interpretation" is added to this and all other standards, the interpretation is essentially a restatement of the standards, and gives no additional guidance. The interpretation reads:

> Mediators are often given access to information that could be used for personal or organizational benefit. It is inappropriate for the mediator to compromise the mediation process by using this information outside the mediation process.

The interpretation refers to information that compromises the mediation process. How and in what way this information compromises the mediation process is unclear. It is also unclear how the social worker is to determine when, and to what degree, information divulged in mediation cannot be used outside the mediation process. These NASW standards are more thoroughly discussed in chapter 6.

A "complementary" use of the standards and the NASW code is one in which they carry equal weight in making ethical decisions. In interpreting Standard 11 the mediator needs also to figure the "Integrity" section of the code (I,D) into the calculus of potential conflicts of interest. Each provision must be synchronized with the other. Alternatively, a method must be devised to prioritize them. For example, proscribed information of Standard 11 may be information that undermines "professional discretion" or "impartial judgment." Applying the "Integrity" section to Standard 11 broadens the proscribed information beyond the mere "benefit" proscription specified in Standard 11. A fuller examination of inconsistencies inherent in applying codes of conduct and the ethical ecology is the subject of the next chapter.

Behaviors

The behavior component of this ethical ecology means the actions of clinical social workers. In terms of dual relations, this behavioral component means all the actions that may undermine or compromise the social worker's fiduciary duty or duty of loyalty, or that may present a conflict of interest with respect to a client or clients. In the ethical ecology, the social worker needs to record and document those suspect behaviors without judgment. The figures below help focus and clarify such behaviors. Figure 5.2 is a "Potential Misconduct Window." This window has four panes, each pane revealing personal and/or professional relationships between the social worker and the client.

Pane 1 (top left) indicates personal relationships on the part of both the social worker and the client. Potential for misconduct may be where the social worker and the client interact as members of the same social club or the same school. Pane 2 (top right) indicates a professional relationship on the part of the social worker and a

Figure 5.2
The Potential Misconduct Window

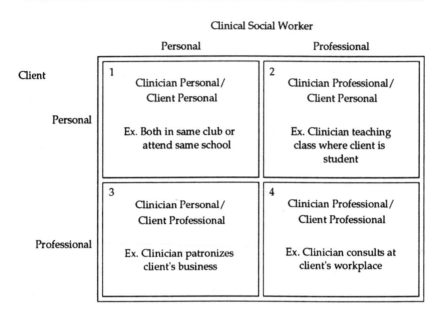

personal relationship on the part of the client. Potential misconduct might occur where the social worker teaches and the client is a student. Pane 3 (bottom left) indicates a personal relationship on the part of the social worker and a professional relationship on the part of the client. Misconduct might occur where the social worker patronizes a client's business. Pane 4 (bottom right) indicates professional relationships on the parts of both the social worker and the client. Potential misconduct here might occur where the social worker consults at the client's place of business.

Figure 5.3 is the worksheet for the "Potential Misconduct Window." Social workers fill in the relationships that correspond to each pane. This exercise may help operationalize the mix of personal and professional relationships. Revealing these relationships is a necessary prerequisite for serious reflection upon them.

Self-Reflection

The final link in our ethical ecology is self-reflection related to possible misconduct. This reflection cannot hope to be objective once misconduct has been initiated. Thus, it is important to conduct self-reflection

Figure 5.3
Worksheet for the Potential Misconduct Window

DUAL RELATIONSHIPS WINDOW
Clinical Social Worker

	Personal	Professional
Client Personal	**1** Clinician Personal/ Client Personal 1. 2. 3.	**2** Clinician Professional/ Client Personal 1. 2. 3.
Professional	**3** Clinician Personal/ Client Professional 1. 2. 3.	**4** Clinician Professional/ Client Professional 1. 2. 3.

habitually—even when there is no reason to suspect a compromised relationship. Steps of such self-reflection follow:

1. Is the possibility of misconduct revealed upon completing the worksheet for Potential Misconduct Window (see figure 5.3)?
2. If the Window reveals potential misconduct, does this offend laws or ethical codes pertinent to the social work profession?
3. If no laws or ethical violations are broken, does the misconduct harm society or the client? This final question should be addressed in light of the psychodynamics of misconduct (chapter 4) and in light of mythic and social norms discussed in this chapter.

USING THE ETHICAL ECOLOGY MODEL

There are three principles upon which the use of the ethical ecology model is predicated. These principles are only guidelines and are discussed below.

1. Each element does not carry equal weight at all times. The intense interrelatedness of the ethical ecology does not always mean that all ethical components stake equal claims. An ethical ecology does not mean an ethical democracy. Sometimes one component partially eclipses or conflicts with another.

A prime example of such ethical discontinuity is the California decision *Tarasoff v. Regents, University of California* (1976), requiring protection of third parties by psychotherapists. This decision, codified now by statutory law in some states, is still being debated and misunderstood by some social workers (Weil and Sanchez 1983). On one hand, the *Tarasoff* ruling sought to safeguard the interests of possible victims of violent crimes by persons undergoing mental health treatment. On the other hand, the decision placed limits on the confidentiality that can be guaranteed to clients. In the *Tarasoff* decision the court linked two ethical conflicts to each other in an uneasy embrace.

2. Specific ethical codes or laws often conflict with broader, more general national or mythic values. Generally, the codes that closely detail specific behaviors will command more serious consideration than less specific or less detailed codes. This might be called the "Rule of Specificity." Often, the more specific the rule or law, the more weight in ethical decision making it carries.

For example, the statutes or codes that specify which relationships are considered unethical or unlawful usually prevail over general admonitions against some general behavior. On a superficial level, it is obviously easier to adhere to clearer statutes. If no one is aware of a prohibition, it is hard to enforce. On a deeper level, if sanctions are not specifically expressed, social workers cannot be expected to create sanctions on their own.

For example, a heroic personal characteristic in the United States is the "rugged individualism" traditionally illustrated by the characters played by John Wayne—more recent varieties of the same character are the personas of Rocky, Dirty Harry, and Rambo. While these characters are all male, female "rugged individualists" also have been part of the American cultural heritage.

Both men and women have carved their niche in our cultural mythology. Actresses like Mary Pickford, who co-founded United Artists, Mae West, Marlene Dietrich, and Ava Gardner, as well as adventurers Amelia Earhart and Amy Johnson (first to fly from England to Australia) symbolize risk-takers. The recent movie *Thelma and Louise* creates an updated version of these personalities. The popularity of such movies attests to the enduring quality of rugged, self-made, action-oriented, self-directed characters.

In many ways such characters are sympathetic. They strike a refreshing chord in our cultural consciousness. Americans have often favored the underdog who follows his or her vision, standing up against what is often perceived as our overly mechanized, highly industrialized society. It may be that private practitioners are the social work equivalents of entrepreneurs. Certainly, it can be argued that the motivation to enter private practice is the freedom to be one's own boss and to achieve the satisfaction of "making it or breaking it" on one's own. In an increasingly regulated mental health field, however, even private practitioners are not free from legal or ethical restraints on their trade.

3. *There need not be total consistency among all elements in the ethical ecology.* Interrelatedness means neither uniformity nor conformity. An increasingly important example of how ethical demands can be inconsistent is that of social workers who are employed by a governmental agency. In that capacity, social workers must serve two masters. They are obligated to adhere to the social work code of ethics. If they are licensed social workers, they must adhere to the ethical codes of the state licensing board. They must also adhere to the standards and procedures established by the government agency. Government standards, it is not unreasonable to say, often serve the efficiency of the bureaucracy more than they serve clients.

The issues of informed consent and confidentiality are just two issues that illustrate this conflict. It is clear that a major social work principle is confidentiality. In private practice, the records of clients can be closely kept. Consultants and others may see the records for legitimate purposes, but the control is usually under the direct authority of the social worker. In public agencies and other government agencies, client records are often examined for quality control and for statistical purposes. In such situations, the determinative ethical consideration may be accountability to the public rather than the primacy of client confidentiality. In *Belmont v. California State Personnel Board* (1974), the court upheld the suspensions of social workers who refused to release client information so that such information could be computerized.

Addressing the differences between public and private social work practice must be continued in the next chapter. Additionally, chapter 6 presents several types of ethical dilemmas discussed in terms of the three steps of self-reflection above noted. Chapter 6 also examines specific issues of misconduct from an ethical perspective.

REFERENCES

Bayles, M. (1989). *Professional ethics*. Belmont, CA: Wadsworth Publishing Co.

Belmont v. California State Personnel Board, 36 Cal. App. 3d 518, 111 Cal. Rptr. 607 (App. 1974).

Bullis, R., and Biggerstaff, M. (in press). Communication in social work practice: Confidentiality and privilege. In M. Biggerstaff (Ed.). *The legal regulation of social work practice*.

Campbell, J. (1972). *Myths to live by*. New York: Bantam Books.

Gallup, G., and Castelli, J. (1989). *The people's religion*. Macmillan: New York.

Junior Great Books (1963). *Aesop: fables, medieval tales*. Great Books Foundation: Chicago.

National Association of Social Workers. (1990). *Code of ethics*. Washington, DC: Author.

National Association of Social Workers. (1991). *Standards of practice for social work mediators*. Washington, DC: Author.

National Federation of Societies for Clinical Social Workers. (1985). *Code of ethics*. Author.

Tarasoff v. Regents, University of California, 551 P.2d 334 (ca. 1976).

Weil, M., and Sanchez, E. (1983). The impact of the *Tarasoff* decision on clinical social work practice. *Social Service Review*, 57(1), 112–24.

Chapter 6

▶ ·························◀

Specific Ethical Conflicts and Contradictions

▶ ·························◀

This chapter considers specific ethical dilemmas and circumstances, expanding the content of the previous chapters to broaden the range of ethical issues examined. The purpose of this chapter is to consider specific ethical problems from the perspective of the previous chapters. This chapter does not attempt to solve these issues, but to offer suggestions and guidelines. To accomplish these ends, ethical problems and situations are grouped into categories consistent with the ethical principles involved. These issues are conceptualized through a series of dichotomous relationships as follows: autonomy versus community responsibility; professional discretion versus professional discipline; empathy versus professional distance; private licensure versus public service; self-examination versus clinical assessment; and professional non-judgmentalism versus professional analysis. These relationships are considered serially.

Before considering these dichotomous tensions, however, two factors must be recognized. Social work is a heterogeneous profession. Some social workers have private practices, some practice in public agencies, and still others practice in public policy areas. In some ways ethical considerations, embodied in social work ethical codes, apply to all without regard to the work setting. The essential function of codes of ethics, in this sense, applies to the *professional practice* and not merely the *place* of practice.

113

On the other hand, professional ethics are not like some clothing, where one size fits all. Some ethical bounds are easier to maintain in some professional settings than in others. For example, social workers who are residential counselors eat with, work with, and in some instances recreate with their clients. In these situations, the professional boundaries are more blurred than in a strictly office practice.

The individual social worker and the social work profession must find ways to preserve the integrity of the code of ethics, be sensitive to the variety of social work practices, and remain practical in the variety of social work settings. Codes of ethics that are impersonal, impractical, and inscrutable are of little use to the practitioner or to the profession—and the public will soon discover that the code is of little protection to them.

AUTONOMY VERSUS COMMUNITY RESPONSIBILITY

This dichotomy pits ethical principals from myths and social values against the demands of state law. Mythic and social values of autonomy contrast with the community responsibilities mandated in state law. The ethical issues considered are confidentiality, particularly in light of AIDS, and professional relationships with close friends and relatives.

Confidentiality and the Duty to Protect

Confidentiality goes to the root of the ethical conflict of keeping client confidences while conforming to the demands of law. Confidentiality and the duty to warn are primary ethical issues and place the social worker in the roles of both client advocate and protector of society—particularly that of third parties. It is common professional knowledge that the "right" of confidentiality has eroded in recent years. With the 1976 decision by the California Supreme Court (*Tarasoff v. Regents of California*) allowing liability against psychotherapists who do not properly protect third parties from dangerous clients, confidentiality was dealt a major blow. This rule has now been expanded to other jurisdictions by both judicial decision and statutory law (Fulero 1988). The *Tarasoff* ruling exists in some form or other in at least a dozen states by judicial decision. Other states have adopted the "duty to protect" principle by statute.

This rule, however, has not been universally adopted by social workers. A 1983 study (Weil and Sanchez 1983) revealed that a significant portion of social workers surveyed knew about the ruling but did not abide by it. This suggests profound value conflict because the price for not adhering to the *Tarasoff* rule can be severe civil liability.

Confidentiality favors the welfare of the individual client over the welfare of society. The *amicus curiae* ("friend of the court") briefs of psychotherapeutic organizations in the *Tarasoff* decision argued that the therapy of individual clients might be damaged if patients did not trust their counselors to keep their secrets. The court addressed this concern head-on, saying that the health and safety of others must sometimes take precedence over the right of confidentiality. Clearly, the social worker is placed on the horns of an ethical and legal dilemma.

Luckily, statutes provide guidelines as to when and under what circumstances prudent and law-abiding social workers should keep silent and when they should speak. Such guidance is given by the Michigan "Duty to Warn" statute (330.1946, 1991), which reads:

> If a patient communicates to a mental health practitioner who is treating the patient a threat of physical violence against a reasonably identifiable third person and the patient has the apparent intent and ability to carry out that threat in the foreseeable future, the mental health practitioner has a duty to [warn or protect].

The statute lists the ways in which that duty to protect is discharged, including hospitalization of the client; a reasonable attempt to warn the threatened person; an attempt to warn the local sheriff or police in the area where the potential victim lives; and, if the potential victim is a minor, an attempt to communicate the threat to the minor and to the applicable department of social services. Social workers and state certified social work technicians fall under the provisions of this law.

The NASW Code (II, H) also provides the following guidance:

1. The social worker should share with others confidences revealed by clients, without their consent, only for compelling professional reasons.
2. The social worker should inform clients fully about the limits of confidentiality in a given situation, the purpose for which information is obtained, and how it may be used.

These provisions place a premium on client confidentiality and privacy. There is no further definition of disclosure for "compelling" reasons. The provisions provide the basis for informed consent as well. Informed consent is a legal and ethical requirement for ethical and lawful social work practice and plays a central role in confidential communications. Informed consent is consent given with both adequate knowledge and understanding of the consequences of the actions for which consent was given. It is discussed in this chapter and is defined in the glossary in chapter 8. The NFSCSW Code (V, a) makes this connection explicit:

> Clinical social workers reveal confidential information to others only with the informed consent of the client, except in those circumstances in which not to do so would violate the law or would result in the clear and imminent danger to the client or to others.

AIDS, the Duty to Protect, and Confidentiality

HIV and AIDS focus the conflict between confidentiality and the duty to protect with increasing urgency (Reamer 1991; Cohen 1990). Perhaps no issue in American society and the world poses more urgent ethical dilemmas for society and health professionals than the eradication of HIV and the symptoms of AIDS. If, when, and to what extent a social worker should protect or warn the sex partner of an HIV-infected client—these are the ethical conflicts.

These conflicts revolve around the conflicting imperatives of protecting third-party sex partners from HIV-infection by clients and maintaining the privacy of HIV-infected persons. Information about HIV is limited, but it is clear that HIV is currently incurable and takes time to diagnose. For the HIV-infected person, it exacts a tremendous social, economic, and emotional toll beyond the symptoms themselves. The social stigma, fear, isolation, and alienation often accompanying this disease are additional "secondary, social symptoms" that can cause loss of job, medical insurance, and social support. While states and the federal government have moved to protect the "disabilities" of HIV victims and others with legislation such as the *Americans with Disabilities Act,* and similar state legislation, the secondary, social symptoms amplify the conflict between confidentiality and the duty to protect. These imperatives are not easily reconciled and constitute an illustration of using the "Ethical Ecology of Dual Relationships." It could be argued that given the enormity and seriousness of the HIV epidemic, community survival is the compelling ethical consideration. Indeed, the argument is not so much over how to protect the integrity of individuals, but how to promote responsible, *individual* behavior to protect the survival of society itself.

U.S. law and professional codes of ethics seem to offer only contradictory answers on this issue. Noted above is the Michigan "Duty to Warn" law. This law, however, does not specify whether a sexually active HIV-infected client threatens "physical violence" to the sexual partner or whether having sex with a partner constitutes an "apparent intent" to carry out the threat. To date, there is no case law specifying that an HIV-infected person is a *Tarasoff* threat to third parties. Criminal indictments have been issued against HIV-infected persons who have had sexual relations without informing their partners about their condition (Blum 1993). Additionally, in claims for "negligent sex," plaintiffs seek damages for sexually transmitted diseases from sexual partners (Reidinger 1987).

It is part of the conflict and confusion of this ethical dilemma that HIV has now seemed to place the consent to sexual intercourse in the realm of a life-threatening activity. Additionally, civil courts have held that clinicians can be sued both for inappropriately disclosing client information and for inappropriately withholding client information (Reamer 1991).

Noted above is the NASW provision that allows disclosure of otherwise confidential information only for "professionally compelling" reasons. The code is silent on whether HIV infection constitutes such a compelling reason. It is clear that the code favors confidentiality and the "burden of proof" is upon the discloser to show that the disclosure is necessary. The NFSCSW code is more explicit in allowing the social worker to follow applicable law. Indeed, the NFSCSW code (V, a) explicitly states the necessity for informed consent in confidentiality:

> Unless specifically contraindicated by such situations, clients should be informed in advance of any limitations of confidentiality, and informed and written consent should be obtained from the client before confidential information is revealed. Such consent includes telling the client about the purposes for which the information is obtained and how it may be used.

Other considerations with respect to confidentiality, and the duty to warn the HIV-infected clients, begin *prior* to any disclosure of illness by the client.

A case for "qualified disclosure" can be made with the following considerations: where the threat is not known by the third-party sex partner, where sexual activity is unprotected, and where there is at least some legally compelling authority to do so. Obviously, such decisions can only be made when the social worker has a working knowledge of applicable state and federal law on this issue (Reamer 1991). Additionally, the bare fact of HIV-infection of a client is insufficient reason to disclose the confidence. Fairly detailed information about his or her sexual practices, the likelihood of infection, and knowledge of or reason to know about the infection on the part of the sex partner can only be obtained after many discussions. The following are four guidelines applicable to confidentiality, especially in light of HIV-positive clients and *Tarasoff* warnings.

1. *Keep current with new laws.* Limitations and exceptions to confidentiality have increased recently. The social worker should be thoroughly familiar with the law of privileged communications in the jurisdiction where he or she practices. By statute and by case law, the once-impermeable wall of client confidentiality is now eminently porous.

   Many of these limitations include information about HIV and other public health and safety information. Laws of privileged communications and of confidentiality change each year. Such laws are likely to keep changing so long as the medical, social, and legal environments of HIV change. Regular in-service training should be conducted, or seminar time and travel provided, for understanding the statutory and case law.

2. *State, in written form, limits and exceptions to confidentiality at the very beginning of the professional relationship.* Clarify the limits and exceptions to confidentiality throughout the therapeutic process—especially where clients divulge possibly criminal issues such as past or current child abuse, elder abuse, threats against another (including property), or threats to hurt themselves.

3. *All such conversations should be documented as to the time, place, and nature of the discussions of confidentiality.* As part of the intake process, the client should be asked to sign a document indicating that he or she has read *and understands* the limits and exceptions to confidentiality. Such an informed consent form should be a prerequisite for services. This document should include any agency, department, state or federal regulation, or administrative policy statement regarding disclosure or non-disclosure of HIV-infected clients. Additionally, any further discussions related to confidentiality should be recorded and kept as a regular part of the client's file.

4. *If no policy or provision is stated in the intake consent form, update the form to do so.* Individual clinicians cannot be expected to make up their own rules, particularly where they may be in violation of the law or leave the employing agency open to civil or criminal suit. At the very least, social workers allowed to create individual rules on HIV confidentiality will be arbitrary and inconsistent.

Counseling Friends and Relatives

The other ethical issue related to the autonomy and community responsibility requirements is counseling friends and relatives. The NFSCSW Code (1985) (II, 1) places counseling friends and relatives squarely within the rubric of dual relations. It reads:

> Clinical social workers avoid entering treatment relationships in which their professional judgment will be compromised by prior association with or knowledge of a client. Examples might include treatment of one's family members, close friends, associates, employees, or others whose welfare could be jeopardized by such a relationship.

The information a clinician gains in counseling clients might prove harmful to an employee or others in a subordinate relationship. Thus, not only friends and relatives are included, but also *all* other persons who might divulge information that the counselor could use to their detriment. For example, the Virginia state Standards of Practice for Licensed, Clinical Social Workers (VR620-01-2. (6.1), prohibits "counseling close friends and relatives."

As we have seen, the illustrative Virginia regulation of licensed clinical social workers prohibits all conduct that undermines the "objectivity" of the social worker. Beyond sexual relations, the only other example is the prohibition against counseling "close" friends and relatives. There is no statutory definition for "close." An ethical examination, however, can reveal some guidelines. As in ethical issues of confidentiality, counseling friends and family pits social workers' cultural and social values against regulatory prohibitions. Cultural and social values can place priorities of family and friend integrity and welfare over that of regulatory schemes. When regulations take priority over family and friends, conflicts can arise.

Counseling friends and family can be an attractive idea. After all, the social worker may be the only help these people will seek or accept. Additionally, the social worker probably knows friends and family as well as anyone, and can save time and effort getting to know the client's situation.

On the other hand, counseling friends and family can be exhausting, demeaning, and destructive to the friend or family. Emotional conflict between being helpful and being confrontational will arise. Friends and family may patronize the social worker because they knew the worker before he or she became a professional. Friends and family may be tempted to tell the social worker embarrassing stories in an attempt to undermine the worker's power, authority, independence, and professional judgment.

"Close" friends or family can be operationally defined as those who refuse to pay for services. If friends or family are uncomfortable about paying for services or if the social worker is uncomfortable about *asking* for payment, the individuals are too "close" to receive treatment. The payment criterion provides a test to determine whether the social worker has the emotional, social, and financial distance for his or her professional judgment and discretion to remain intact. If the social worker has trouble in asserting the payment issue, he or she may well have trouble asserting other clinical issues as well.

Disclosure can be a second test for maintaining professional integrity. Disclosing dual relations to a supervisor, licensing board, peer supervisor, or other colleague helps protect the integrity of the professional from "secret" clients and is a source of self-examination. If a social worker fears disclosure about *any* client, red flags of dual relations should be raised.

On the other hand, if the social worker freely discloses a professional relationship with close friends or relatives, the power to undermine professional judgments is greatly reduced. At the very least, colleagues can offer their insights into the therapeutic and ethical advantages or liabilities. The above two tests are objective in that they utilize observable facts. Either social workers take money from friends and relatives, or they do not; either social workers disclose dual relations, or they do not. Disclosure is a useful test in the next section as well.

PROFESSIONAL FREEDOM VERSUS PROFESSIONAL DISCIPLINE

In this section we examine two ethical issues concerned with the discretion of professionals: the method of reimbursement for professional services and the duty to protect independent professional judgment. The specific issues considered are fee splitting and bartering for services. They place professional freedom against professional discipline.

Fee Splitting

Fee splitting is a form of gratuity where charges for professional services are divided or shared among two or more professionals. The problem of fee splitting is that such divided fees can cover up a form of kickback for referral where clinicians collude with one another to charge a client for duplication of services, to charge a client for unnecessary services, or to provide a kind of finder's fee for clients shared among clinicians. The NFSCSW Code (1985) (IV, b) states:

"Clinical social workers do not give or receive any fee or other consideration to or from a third party for the referral of a client."

The code does not expressly prohibit fee splitting, but does reinforce prohibitions against rewarding others for referrals or receiving fees for referrals. But restriction of fee splitting conflicts with free enterprise and the freedom to enter into contractual relationships. American capitalism and courts usually allow considerable latitude to enter into contracts unless prohibited by public policy. The freedom to discount fees in response to the market economy, for example, illustrates the freedom of practitioners to respond to changes in the economy and to independently market their services. The freedom to use referral services can be justified, assuming those referring do not profit from those to whom they refer. Should the referring agency have a financial or other interest either in the outcome of the therapy of in the clinician to whom the client is referred, the agency engages in questionable ethical conduct.

A type of fee splitting involves paying (rewarding) other clinicians for referrals. This form of fee splitting is dangerous because of the collusion among clinicians to refer to each other regardless of the competence of either. The NFSCSW Code (III, c) states:

> In referring clients to allied professionals, clinical social workers ensure that those to whom they refer clients are recognized members of their own disciplines and are competent to carry out the professional services required.

The code stresses that regard must be paid to the competency of the professionals to whom the referral is made. Referrals made to friends in order to pay back or to curry favors are inappropriate. In illegal and unethical fee-splitting arrangements, assessment-centered competence takes a backseat to profit-taking. Thus, fee splitting does clients substantial therapeutic and financial harm. The general social and legal norms are insufficient to control unethical fee splitting and are sometimes antithetical to this limitation upon the economic dynamics of practice. The NASW Code concisely adds another consideration, stating: "The social worker should not accept anything of value for making referrals."

Two questions arise even with these prohibitions. When does a gift become a bribe? NASW's prohibition against accepting a gift of "value" is unclear; however, the intent of the prohibition can govern the amount. A relatively clear answer is not to accept any gift likely to incur a debt, or feeling of debt, on the receiver's part. Where an actual or perceived sense of debt is inculcated, the receiver is tempted to repay the debt with further referrals. In ethical and emotional terms, it is not the actual cost of the gift that counts; it is the cost to the client that counts.

Another way to handle gifts is to disclose the nature and the amount of gifts to supervisors. This is often mandated in public-sector social service employment and in some private agencies, for the very reasons stated in this section. Members of Congress and other state and federal government officials are obliged routinely to disclose the nature and cost of gifts given to them. Private businesspeople are often obligated to report similar gifts received in the course of business.

Respect for a colleague's clinical competence versus the desire to refer clients for social or financial reasons constitutes another ethical dilemma not easily resolved by any ethical formula. Dispassionately considering a colleague's qualifications for a certain referral often cannot be isolated from the friendship established through attending seminars and classes together, and from other quite legitimate activities. Two considerations might be applied. The first one is to consider whether the referring professional is gaining, in any way, from the referral. The "Potential Misconduct Window" exercise might help to clarify these relationships. If there is a gain, then is the gain the primary reason for the referral or is the gain incidental to the referral? An incidental gain is one that is gratifying (a card or a phone call), but does not, in itself, prompt the referral. If the gain is incidental, it may be innocent.

The second consideration requires some imagination. Imagine you are sued for a referral you made to a colleague that you knew, or should have known, was incompetent for the case, and the client was harmed. Imagine further that the prosecuting attorney uncovers the fact that you have enjoyed complimentary dinners, theater tickets, and other amenities following such referrals. Now imagine that you must defend your actions to a judge or jury. How would your defense sound? Would you believe your own defense? If not, or if the *appearance* seems awkward or embarrassing, chances are that the relationship violates the spirit, if not the letter, of ethical codes.

Bartering for Services

Bartering is another issue that involves professional freedom and professional discipline (St. Germaine 1993). Bartering is trading one service for another without currency changing hands. For example, a social worker trades one hour of clinical work for a client who is a dentist for one hour of dental services. Such an arrangement may be given some impetus because of its purported tax advantages.

Bartering for services, of course, allows the social worker the professional freedom to set a fee schedule and a manner of collecting payment. It can be argued that this freedom is a function of professional services. On the other hand, bartering is at least one step removed from a disinterested, independent manner of collecting for services rendered. It is likely that a special relationship will be developed through negotiating the bartering arrangement. After all, it is unlikely that a client and social worker without a prior relationship will discuss bartering for services. Bartering for services pries the dual relations door open just a little further.

Social Functions

Social relations with clients is another example of the tensions between professional freedom and professional discipline. Borys (1988), cited in Herlihy and Corey (1992), indicates that therapists rarely (92 percent against) consider inviting clients to a personal party to be an ethical practice. Similarly, going out to eat with clients after a session is rarely ethical (81 percent against). Therapists also reported (33 percent) that it is unethical for them to accept a client's invitation to a special event. Indeed, clinicians honored such views in practice (92 percent).

There are two components to such social engagements that relate to ethical considerations. First is the extent to which the social engagement confuses the legitimate role of the social worker. For example, if the social engagement occasions disclosures that the social worker or the client finds embarrassing or inaccurate, the social engagement may undermine the trust and care for which both have worked.

Second, the social engagement may provide a state for the improper imposition of a power dynamic onto the therapeutic relationship. This imposition of power can be exercised in such subtle ways as who becomes indebted to whom in paying the check, in returning a hosting responsibility, or in taking on social roles that conflict with therapeutic goals.

EMPATHY VERSUS PROFESSIONAL DISTANCE

While this book mainly addresses erotic touch, social workers also need to address "nonerotic" touch with clients. When, if ever, is nonerotic touch therapeutically valid? Under what circumstances, if ever, is nonerotic touch ethically permissible? Touching clients non-erotically is open to considerable professional variation and debate.

For example, researchers have revealed that psychologists differ widely on their practice of nonerotic touch (Pope, Tabachnick, and Keith-Spiegel 1987, cited in Holub and Lee 1990). While about half the psychologists reported that kissing a client is unethical, another 23.5 percent "rarely" kissed them, 5 percent kissed them more often than "rarely," and 36.6 percent believed it largely unethical.

Even more significant from an ethicist's perspective is that researchers found that nonerotic touch may be at least partially influenced by the therapist's theoretical orientation. For example, Holroyd and Brodsky (1977), cited in Holub and Lee (1990), found that 30 percent of humanistic therapists thought that nonerotic hugging, kissing, and affectionate touching serves valid therapeutic purposes, while only 6 percent of psychodynamic therapists felt the same way. If these data suggest an ethical point, it is that the ethics of nonerotic touch should not be determined by therapeutic orientation. No professional social work organization makes differentiations in its provisions according to therapeutic orientation. No organization could afford to make such distinctions. Social workers' codes of ethics must apply to all, whatever their theoretical orientation.

The line between erotic and nonerotic touch is often a fine one. Few courts and no social work ethical codes define that line. One court that waded in those murky waters was the Court of Appeals of Minnesota—which had to decide whether a hug given by a psycho-therapist was "sexual contact" as defined by the Minnesota psycho-therapist sexual exploitation statute. (The Minnesota statute is set forth in the appendix.) The defendant's (J) complaint stated that Mr. Ohrtman, in their third counseling session, requested a beer, re-quested and received a backrub after pulling up his shirt, encouraged J to divorce her husband, and gave her a hug during which he pressed her breasts to his chest.

To find criminal intent on the part of Ohrtman, the court had to conclude that J's breasts were "intimate parts" as defined by statute and that his "touching" her was sexual contact. The court had no problem in finding that breasts are intimate parts. However, the court, after searching the dictionary and prior cases, ruled that hugging, absent other touching, does *not* constitute sexual contact within the meaning of the statute (*State v. Ohrtman* 1991).

This case raises three important points. First, clients are increas-ingly willing to sue counselors for contact of any kind. Although one could well wonder what kind of therapeutic milieu drinking beer and receiving a shirtless backrub might create, the *hug*, oddly, was the focus of the complaint. Second, social workers need to view hugs and other touching from the *client's* perspective, not their own. Ohrtman might have thought that J would immediately understand that his hug was meant in a totally nonerotic way. He assumed as much to his own detriment. Third, counselors need to assess closely the meaning attached to their touching *before* they proceed, even with what seems clearly to be nonerotic touching. One person's hug is another's sexual assault. Even if a client requests a nonerotic hug for assurance and comfort, the social worker needs to independently assess the likely emotional and psychodynamic consequences of any touching.

PRIVATE PRACTICE VERSUS PUBLIC SERVICE

This section places the conflict between government service and private licensing, as well as mediation, in an ethical perspective. These issues are related to dual relations because each issue, in its own way, involves a conflict of loyalties.

Professionals who work for the public must serve two masters. The first master is the ethics required by their respective professions. The second is the policies, procedures, and ethics of the agency or department. Sometimes these two masters can work in harmony; at other times they cannot.

In *Belmont v. California State Personnel Board* (1974), the California Court of Appeal upheld the suspension of two psychiatric social workers for willful disobedience of their employer. The two social workers refused to disclose information on individuals in their caseloads for inclusion in their department's computer systems, claiming that the information was privileged and confidential. The social workers cited the social worker code of ethics as evidence that they were acting within their professional capacities in protecting their clients' privacy.

The court did not agree. It held that the social workers were not entitled to invoke the statute of privileged communications and that they were required to obey a lawful departmental order. Thus, the court upheld their disciplinary actions.

The current NASW Code (IV, L) may obviate such conflicts in the future. It reads:

> Commitments to Employing Organization—The social worker should adhere to commitments made to the employing organization.

The provisions of the code (IV, L, 1, 3, and 4) continue to specify that social workers improve the efficiency of the agency, prevent agency discrimination, and use agency resources only for their intended purposes. Additionally, the NFSCSW Code (IV, c) reads: "Clinical social workers employed by an agency or clinic and also engaged in private practice conform to agency regulations regarding their dual roles."

These provisions seem to place the social worker's priorities in favor of the employing agency. This may not *necessarily* be so. These provisions must be read in light of other code provisions. For example, NASW Code (II, F) states that the "social worker's *primary* (author's emphasis) responsibility is to the client." When conflicts arise between the rules of agency or employer and those of the client, whose interest takes precedence? The answer is found in how statutes, or provisions in codes of ethics, are interpreted. Such interpretations are "statutory hermeneutics." Statutory hermeneutics is a highly important concept in interpreting one provision in light of other provisions, especially if they are, or appear to be, contradictory.

One statutory hermeneutic suggests that subsequent code provisions modify more primary provisions. In other words, the *primary* duty to clients is *modified* by the provisions to obey agency regulations. Significantly, the *Belmont* case reminds us that agency rules, while superseding the code provisions, must be lawful to be enforced. All codes of ethics must be read in light of *other* provisions as well as statutes and case law.

Mediation

At least since 1978, social workers have discussed using mediation to settle disputes among divorcing persons (Haynes 1978). Mediation is a form of alternative dispute resolution—"alternative" from the sometimes costly and contentious fora of law courts. Mediation is a service increasingly offered by social workers. Authors have discussed its practice implications for strategic planning in divorce (Weingarten 1986), family mediation for the elderly (Parsons and Cox 1989), and child protection cases (Palmer 1989).

There has been a lively but limited discussion of legal and ethical principles involved in the mediation process—particularly in the domain of dual relations. Authors have despaired over the "imprecise language" and absence of ethical theory (Gibson 1989) while maintaining the centrality of ethics in mediation practice (Grebe, Irvin, and Lang 1989). In 1991, NASW promulgated Standards of Practice for Social Work Mediators. How are these standards to be understood in light of the NASW Code of Ethics?

The only statutory hermeneutic the standards themselves offer is that the provision should be interpreted "within the ethical base and values explicated in the *NASW Code of Ethics*" (National Association of Social Workers 1991). It is unclear which ethical standard, if any, is to prevail. It can be argued that the statutory hermeneutic of specificity dictates that the specific standards for mediators take precedence over the general provisions of the NASW Code. NASW mediational standards present specific guidance and, because they are specifically promulgated to address mediation, stand above more general social and cultural norms in providing primary ethical norms. Each of the twelve standards promulgated is followed by interpretive paragraphs. Two standards apply most directly to dual relations issues.

Standard 2 (p. 3) reads, "Social work mediators should remain impartial and neutral toward all parties and issues in a dispute." This standard emphasizes the ethical principles of impartiality and neutrality. While these terms are not specifically defined, the interpretive statements distinguish between them. Impartiality means that the mediator acts without bias or favoritism. Neutrality requires that the social worker mediator "have no relationship with parties or vested interests in the substantive outcome that might interfere or appear to interfere with the ability to function in a fair, unbiased, and impartial manner" (p. 3). This needs an interpretation because of the significant points this single sentence makes.

First, both *relationships* and *vested interests* among parties and the outcome are prohibited. Relationships formed by the mediator with *one* of the parties in mediation pose clear threats to this standard. Vested interests could include financial and social interests. The mediator can attempt to sway the outcome of child custody or tangible assets disputes (real estate, pensions, degrees, insurance, etc.) if the mediator colludes with one of the mediated parties at any level. For example, where the mediator is also an instructor or trainer of one of the parties, an emotional and social and financial bias is present. Relationships can also include emotional obligations and social debts.

Second, both the *fact* and the *appearance* of impropriety are prohibited. Mediators need to be aware of how their practice appears and to be vigilant of behavior that may *look* like misconduct. For the purposes of protecting professional reputation, sometimes appearance *is* reality. For example, if it is disclosed (as in a lawsuit) that a party to mediation was also a student of the mediator, the appearance of impropriety exists. Even if the mediator acted in an impartial and neutral manner, both as a mediator and as an instructor, the claim could be made by the other mediated party that the potential misconduct worked to his or her detriment. Defending such claims is difficult, if not impossible. The *feeling* and *impression* of complete impartiality and neutrality is necessary for mediation to succeed.

Third, while Standard 2 does not state from whose perspective misconduct must be perceived, the perception must come from the mediated parties. If the decision comes from the mediator, his or her own judgment may have already been clouded by the emotional sway of a conflict of interest. Additionally, failure to disclose actual or potential conflict of loyalty or conflict of interest presents the *appearance* of impropriety. The standard should speak to this issue and should insist that *any* conflict of interest must be disclosed to all mediated parties, and that the mediation should proceed only after an informed consent to do so is documented.

If the mediator is involved in misconduct, at any level, with the mediation process, Standard 2 requires disclosure of the issue. Disclosures should be made in such a way as to ensure informed consent in order to continue the mediation process. Informed consent is a legal term that denotes specific characteristics. Consent is "informed" when the mediated parties know its exact nature and the likely consequences of the conflict of interest. The disclosure and the consent to continue mediation, if given, should both be fully documented. Documentation serves to provide a written record of the agreement and to clarify what is disclosed and what is agreed upon.

The second standard applicable to this discussion is Standard 11 (p. 7), which states:

> The mediator shall not use any information obtained during the mediation process for personal benefit or for the benefit of any group or organization with which the mediator is associated.

This standard is really a corollary of Standard 2. Standard 11 specifies that information gained in mediation cannot be used for the benefit of the mediator. This standard is the mediation equivalent of the prohibition against "insider trading." Insider trading laws prohibit those who, in the course of their jobs, gain access to information concerning future corporate takeovers, changes in personnel, or other stock market conditions that could give them an unfair advantage over other stock buyers. The 1980s proved to be a fertile field for both legitimate stock buyers and criminal indictments against insider traders who "earned" millions with inside information.

There are many examples of the information that mediators might gain. Divorce proceedings alone are rife with possibilities, including the price and conditions of sale of the couple's home, cars, or businesses—just a few of the financial assets that change hands in divorce proceedings. For tax purposes, the mediator may be tempted to suggest charitable causes with which he or she is familiar. Even with the most honorable intentions, such information is "mediational insider trading."

PROFESSIONAL NONJUDGMENTALISM
VERSUS SELF-EXAMINATION

This section addresses issues pertaining to the crucial distinction between professional nonjudgmentalism and self- examination. The NASW Code (II, G) states, "The social worker should make every effort to foster maximum self-determination on the part of clients." Certainly, the principle of self-determination is a cornerstone of social work practice. The social worker protects the client's right to decide for him or herself what is in his or her best interest. Another way of speaking about client self-determination is to speak about being nonjudgmental. Protecting client self-determination requires that social workers evaluate a client's decisions without considering their own wishes, needs, or ways of life, basing their evaluation upon the client's own best interests.

Being nonjudgmental does not mean that the social worker must be a potted plant, or an appendage to the client's decisions. Being non-judgmental is not the same as acquiescing to all the client's needs or demands. Self-determination does not mean blind acceptance of all the client's notions and needs. As already shown, some clients will try to seduce social workers. To allow the client to succeed in seduction is a warped version of client self-determination.

In fact, client self-determination is quickly being superseded by what might be called "statutory determination"—that is, clients and social workers have only those "rights" that are statutorily defined. For example, in chapter 3 the statutes specifically prohibiting the defense of client "consent" to sexual contact were discussed. These statutes effectively mean that clients do not have the legal power to consent to sexual activities with their psychotherapists. Additionally, the *Tarasoff* rulings, and related state statutes, "statutorily determine" what clients can and cannot legally do.

The following is a discussion of potential misconduct as it applies to the supervisor-supervisee relationship. This discussion is included here because this relationship is informed, to the extent that supervisors can separate being nonjudgmental from conducting the kind of self-criticizing analysis necessary to avoid supervisor-supervisee misconduct.

Educators, Trainers, and Supervisors

Writers are giving ethical conduct in supervision increasing scrutiny. Jacobs (1991) finds a similarity between two kinds of supervisor exploitation—incidents where the supervisor "counsels" the supervisee and incidents where there is sexual contact. Both kinds of exploitation involve suspect conduct relations because they divide the supervisory relationship. The supervisor sexually exploiting the supervisee wants a supervisee and a lover. In either case such a dual relationship conflicts the supervisory purpose with alternative purposes, creating conflict of interests and divided loyalties.

The incidence of supervisory dual relations may be considerable. In a study of female graduate students in psychology, researchers found that between 20 and 25 percent had sexual relations with their educators—most of whom had a working relationship with their students (Glaser and Thorpe 1986). Additionally, 31 percent of the respondents reported that they received sexual advances from their educators. Of these, 45 percent reported they received some form of punitive action when they declined advances. Such pressure for sexual relations is disturbing; even more disturbing is the frequency of retribution reported. Retribution for those students who refuse the sexual advances may indicate not only how entrenched such misconduct may be among professionals, but also how oblivious some educators are regarding their own culpability, as well as the legal consequences.

Misconduct among professional educators and supervisors is particularly harmful. Chapter 4 discussed the dynamics of misconduct in psychotherapy. The special harm in educator-supervisor dual relations can be to the *future* clients. If professional misconduct becomes acceptable, all future clients are at risk. The harm done in one generation is repeatable, like broken chromosomes, *ad infinitum.*

Training agreements and other legal and quasi-legal tools are being used to avoid legal liability (Gelman 1990). These agreements, and other supervisory "contracts," may be the single most effective tool in discouraging supervisory misconduct. A training agreement is a type of contract. The agreement is entered into by the field supervisor, field educator, or supervisor, and the student. Researchers have found that a high percent (86 percent) of field placements have such agreements, which include indemnification clauses and "hold harmless" clauses, and address liability of the placement employer (Gelman and Wardell 1988). Field placements are "real world" work opportunities for students in professional programs and "hold harmless" clauses purport to give up the right to sue someone.

While the legal effectiveness of "hold harmless" clauses is questionable, such clauses can include important agreements about the limits of the duties and responsibilities of all parties so as to avoid misconduct. Clauses could include the specific times, places, and manner of supervision. Such clauses should ensure that supervisory meetings do not result in appropriate social situations. Additionally, specification of topics to discuss and the limits to those topics could help prevent supervisory discussions from transforming themselves into personal counseling.

The preceding sections have addressed topics and issues relative to social work misconduct. Sometimes professional codes of ethics have been included to offer specific guidance. The following section offers four techniques or concepts, some considered previously, that can be used to avoid misconduct. They represent "defensive" social work. Defensive social work is both an attitude and an action designed to prevent ethical misconduct and legal liability.

DEFENSIVE SOCIAL WORK: FOUR ETHICAL RESPONSES

Four techniques and concepts discussed in this chapter bear repeating: disclosure, the demand for informed consent, divestiture, and documentation. These are the "4 Ds" of defensive social work with respect to ethics and law violations.

Disclosure

Disclosure has been discussed in a variety of situations. Disclosing the cost and the nature of gifts, the counseling of friends or relations, and potential conflicts of interest are appropriate uses of disclosure. Disclosure can be used in other settings as well, and is a useful tool to preempt potential misconduct across a broad spectrum of problems.

Disclosure includes informing, in writing, a supervisor or employer of gifts or other potential compromising relations. In potential conflicts of interest or conflicts of loyalty, the nature of the conflict should be cited as well as the parties involved and the points of conflict of interest or loyalty.

Demand for Informed Consent

Demand for Informed Consent is an often overlooked dimension of defensive social work practice. An informed consent should be standard practice for all facets of social work practice—from the initial contact through termination. An emphasis upon "demand" for informed consent is deliberately placed because of the essential nature of informed consent. Where clients cannot or do not give written, informed consent to treatment or for practice, and treatment or practice proceeds, the social worker is exposed to legal liability for services rendered.

In some states the elements of informed consent are statutorily set forth for certain services. Some states even *require* that clinicians offer informed consent information at the beginning of clinical work. The elements of informed consent relating to divulging client information, for example, are that the client understands exactly *what* information is divulged, *to whom* the information is divulged, *under what circumstances* the information is divulged, *when* the consent expires, and any *consequences* that divulging the information is likely to have upon the client. Informed consent is defined again in this book's glossary.

Divestiture

Divestiture means that all professional connections with the client must be severed. This theme is deliberately analogous to the "divestiture" of stocks, bonds, and other financial commitments to companies and countries for political or financial purposes. In the 1970s and 1980s some companies and universities "divested" stock and other ties with South Africa. Divestiture of a client is the professional equivalent for purposes of dual relations.

Divesting a client is more profound than merely terminating a client. Divesting a client means that the social worker will have no part in choosing a referral, no part in making any subsequent treatment decisions, and no further professional contact. Divesting a client, where potential misconduct arises, needs to be clear and unequivocal to protect the integrity of the social worker and the interests of the client.

While divestiture must be done expeditiously and unequivocally, it should not be done precipitously. Care should be taken to explain the ethical rationale for divestiture and to educate the client as to why such action is necessary. In fact, such education and explanation is part of an informed consent process.

Documentation

Documentation is the theme that ties all the above three themes together. It is now almost axiomatic that social workers need to document all phases of client contact—from beginning to end. Some supervisors and agencies are more scrupulous than others in demanding such documentation. Sometimes documentation is honored more in the breach than in the observance.

Ultimately, it is the social workers themselves who must persevere in documentation, because documentation is in their own best interest. Documenting protects the social worker because notes and process recordings can be used to verify the social worker's oral statements.

This chapter has described the ethical considerations of a number of issues currently affecting social workers. Procedures and methods of analysis have been suggested to clarify the issues involved. Additionally, the concept of a statutory hermeneutic has been introduced to help conceptualize how ethical code provisions can be synchronized or prioritized. The next chapter describes the law and social science surrounding prevention of misconduct. Several specific provisions, from both statutes and policies, are discussed.

REFERENCES

Belmont v. California State Personnel Board, 36 Cal. App. 3d 518, 111 Cal. Rptr. 607 (App. 1974).

Blum, J. (1993, July 3). 3 with HIV accused of attempted murder. *Washington Post,* B1 and B5.

Borys, D. (1988). Dual relationships between therapist and client: A national survey of clinicians' attitudes and practices. Unpublished doctoral dissertation. University of California, Los Angeles.

Cohen, E. (1990). Confidentiality, counseling, and clients who have AIDS: Ethical foundations of a model rule. *Journal of Counseling and Development,* 68, 282–86.

Fulero, S.M. (1988). *Tarasoff:* 10 years later. *Professional Psychology,* 19(2), 190.

Gelman, S.R. (1990). The crafting of fieldwork training agreements. *Journal of Social Work Education,* 26(1), 65–75.

Gelman, S.R., and Wardell, P.J. (1988). Who's responsible?: The field liability dilemma. *Journal of Social Work Education* 24 (1), 70–78.

Gibson, K. (1989). The ethical basis of mediation: why mediators need philosophers. *Mediation Quarterly,* 7(1), 41–50.

Glaser, R., and Thorpe, J. (1986). Unethical intimacy: A survey of sexual contact and advances between psychology educators and female graduate students. *American Psychologist,* 41(1), 43–51.

Grebe, S.C., Irvin, K., and Lange, M. (1989). A model for ethical decision making in mediation. *Mediation Quarterly,* 7(2), 133–48.

Haynes, J. (1978). Divorce mediator: A new role. *Social Work,* 23, 5–9.

Herlihy, B., and Corey, G. (1992). *Dual relations in counseling.* American Counseling Association: Alexandria, VA.

Holroyd, J., and Brodsky, A. (1977). Psychologists' attitudes and practices regarding erotic and nonerotic physical contact with patients. *American Psychologist, 32,* 843–49.

Holub, E.A., and Lee, S.S. (1990). Therapists' use of nonerotic physical contact: Ethical concerns. *Professional Psychology: Research and Practice,* 21(2), 115–17.

Jacobs, C. (1991). Violations of the supervisory relationship: An ethical and educational blind spot. *Social Work,* 36(2), 130–35.

National Association of Social Workers. (1991). *Standards of practice for social work mediators.* Silver Spring, MD: Author.

National Federation for Clinical Social Workers. (1985). *Code of ethics.* Author.

Palmer, S.E. (1989). Mediation in child protection cases: An alternative to the adversary system. *Child Welfare,* 68(1), 21–30.

Parsons, R.J., and Cox, E.O. (1989). Family mediation in elder caregiving decisions: An empowerment intervention. *Social Work,* 34(2), 122–26.

Pope, K., Tabachnick, B., and Keith-Spiegel, P. (1987). Ethics of practice: The beliefs and behaviors of psychologists as therapists. *American Psychologist, 42,* 993–1005.

Reamer, F.G. (1991). AIDS, social work, and the "duty to protect." *Social Work,* 36(1), 56–60.

Reidinger, P. (1987). Negligent sex. *ABA Journal, 73,* 75.

St. Germaine, J. (1993). Dual relationships: What's wrong with them? *American Counselor,* 2(3), 25–30.

State v. Ohrtman, 466 N.W. 2d 1 (Minn. App. 1991).

Tarasoff v. Regents of California, 17 Ca. App. 3d 741, 614 P.2d 728 (1976).

Weil, M., and Sanchez, E. (1983). The impact of the *Tarasoff* decision on clinical social work practice. *Social Service Review,* 57(1), 112–24.

Weingarten, H.R. (1986). Strategic planning for divorce mediation. *Social Work,* 31(3), 194–200.

Chapter 7

▶······················◀
Prevention and
Professional Responses
▶······················◀

INTRODUCTION

This chapter reviews suggestions for social worker professional organizations, agencies, and individual practitioners to prevent dual relations among their constituencies and clients. This chapter will discuss the role of ethical codes, education, and supervision in the professional control of dual relations.

THE SPIRITUAL-PSYCHOSOCIAL DYNAMICS OF PREVENTION

The dynamics of prevention correspond to the elements of responsibility for dual relations: personal, educational, organizational, and legal. These elements constitute an ecology of ethical resources, much like the ethical ecology of sexual misconduct discussed in chapter 5. This ecology of ethical resources is illustrated in figure 7.1. This chapter proceeds through the elements of this ecology one by one.

Personal Dynamics of Prevention

Clients see their individual social worker as the representative, even the embodiment, of the entire profession. In this way, the personal

Figure 7.1
Ecology of Ethical Resources

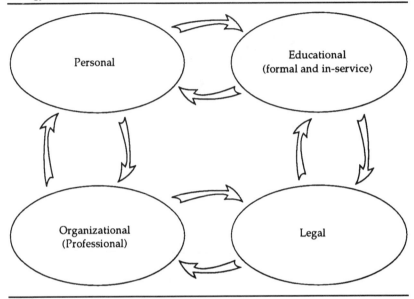

recapitulates the professional. The dynamics of the social worker begin with a professional and personal orientation and end with a relationship to larger and larger institutions and organizations. Personal dynamics proceed, in a reciprocal relationship, from the microcosm to the macrocosm.

  1. It is okay to be vulnerable, but not okay to violate. The social worker can recognize and acknowledge his or her vulnerability in two ways. First, the practice principles of empathy and unconditional acceptance currently predominate in the social work profession. These principles not only play an important therapeutic role for clients, but also help distinguish social workers from other helping professionals. The capacity for vulnerability is a double-edged sword. These practice principles render the social worker vulnerable to both the client's pain and to their manipulations—malicious and benign. Being empathetic and accepting does not mean that the social worker accepts the machinations of clients or colludes in their avoidance of therapeutic issues using deception and other means. Social workers need not feel guilty about placing appropriate limits on clients' behavior.

Social workers who recognize that they are vulnerable to sexual relations and other kinds of ethical misconduct are in the best position to guard against such conduct. Social workers who deceive themselves into thinking that they are immune from client sexual, financial, or social seduction fool only themselves. There is no professional substitute for raw self-examination. In some quarters this is called professional humility.

This is like asking someone to be his or her own therapist. The lawyer's adage "Those who represent themselves have fools for clients" can also apply to social workers. The loss of objectivity is at risk in either case. As a practical matter, however, too often professionals have no choice but to monitor themselves. Being a professional means having an enormous amount of professional discretion. Few people are looking over the social worker's shoulder. Thus, professionals must walk a tightrope between honoring the public concern for accountability and the necessity of making professional judgments with minimal outside interference. The "Potential Misconduct Window" provides a tool for ethical discretion. They provide a way for professionals to assess their behavior.

Another way social workers may exercise professional honesty is to submit to regular supervision with a trusted colleague. Supervision is not just a means to licensure, but an important *ongoing* part of social work practice. Social workers need "professional sanctuaries" where they can speak frankly of their frustrations with and attractions to clients.

Self-examination is neither fun nor easy. It costs time, effort, and pain. However, an additional way social workers may protect themselves and their clients is not to take professional roles so seriously as to be unable to laugh at themselves. This requires seeing the forest of the client's ultimate benefit rather than the trees of personal gain or professional control.

2. Name the dynamics. If a client suggests, or even intimates, some type of illicit misconduct, immediately tell the client what that means in professional terms. Saying aloud the professional term for illicit activities tends to lessen clients' attractions. Specifically naming misconduct and its therapeutic and ethical consequences tends to undermine its power and allure.

Naming the dynamics does not constitute accusations against the client. Saying aloud that misconduct proposed by the client constitutes illegal or unethical behavior and spelling such behavior out can be a profitable educative and therapeutic intervention. Such "naming" can and should be placed in the natural course of assessment and intervention strategies.

3. Keep current with law and ethical issues. Attending seminars and professional meetings, and reading articles on misconduct, law, and related issues further increases a professional sensitivity to ethical trends. Social workers should exercise discretion in the kind and content of seminars and classes advertising training and counsel on dual relations. Seminars and courses should be selected on the bases of well-understood criteria.

This criteria should include an examination of the legal, professional, ethical, and psychological dynamics involved in dual relations. Misconduct, by its very nature, requires interdisciplinary expertise. Expertise in the dynamics of misconduct is not the exclusive province of any one discipline. Choose seminars that cover the criminal and civil laws in the state where the social worker practices, that can interpret the causes of actions against social workers who engage in misconduct, and that can address legal trends. Choose training events that integrate spiritual psycho-social dynamics into the ecology of misconduct and that integrate the above two elements with state ethical provisions, ethical provisions from the NASW Code, or ethical codes of other professional societies.

Educational Dynamics of Prevention

The suggestions to prevention posited by Borys and Pope (1989) concentrate on dynamics properly in the province of educational institutions or other training opportunities. Some of these opportunities include programs exploring the nature, causes, and consequences of dual relations. While most authors have written on the negative aspects of sexualized dual relations, Borys and Pope cite others (Romeo 1978; Shephard 1971) that have posited a view that such relations may serve a therapeutically legitimate purpose. While legal and ethical codes must be affirmed, a full and frank professional discussion on the role and function of misconduct should be tolerated and encouraged by professional schools and organizations. The rule of law and ethical codes should not serve only as hammers against those who transgress. These sanctions should serve also as anvils to forge greater sensitivity among social workers toward ethical behaviors, to foster a fuller understanding of their roles as professionals and citizens, and to foment change in laws and statutes where needed.

Clinical coursework needs to integrate ethical and clinical implications of misconduct. Courses that address practice issues need to address the dynamics of misconduct as a consequence of clinical practice. Ethical determinations from social worker professional organizations need to be highlighted and discussed. Legal considerations are also part of this discussion.

Professional training institutions for social workers serve two additional purposes in this respect. First, educational institutions are in a unique position to initiate, support, and conduct research into the ethics of sexual and other misconduct. Second, professional training schools are in a unique position to interpret research results, communicate those results in a meaningful manner to students and others in the profession, and construct educational exercises to apply research to practice.

Institutions can issue clear standards as to what constitutes misconduct and the consequences for engaging in it. Such standards and procedures should include definitions of dual relations and conflicts of interest, the manner in which complaints will be investigated, agency or institutional responsibility toward the accused social worker during the investigative phase, the sanctions imposed if found guilty, and procedures to address the news media.

Administrators, clinical supervisors, and trainers can make explicit their adherence to ethical standards. They can accomplish this in two ways. They can administer their institutional standards conscientiously and consistently, and they can indicate, in both word and deed, that they take the standards seriously and expect employees to follow suit.

While dual relations and conflicts of interest are matters upon which reasonable people may disagree, procedures can be established that set guidelines for full disclosure of behavior that may constitute a conflict of interest or other misconduct. There are many "gray" areas of misconduct, but reporting gifts, outside meeting times (lunches, dinners, etc.), business and personal relations with clients outside the clinical setting, and other relations can be documented on disclosure forms.

Because social workers often serve clients outside normal office hours and enjoy considerable discretion with their time, official disclosure of times, places, dates and other information may seem restrictive on the part of the social worker and cumbersome on the part of administrators. However, such disclosure serves as both a system of accountability for the social worker and a supervisory tool for administrators. Given the propensity to sue both social workers and agencies and departments, such systems of accountability can provide defensive evidence if allegations of impropriety arise.

Organizational Dynamics of Prevention

This section addresses the opportunities available to professional organizations to prevent sexual and other misconduct. Borys and Pope (1989) offer suggestions that can be adapted by social work organizations, including explicit consequences for those found to have violated standards of practice.

Consequences for those who report possible misconduct should be explicit and standardized. These standards should protect the reporter from unfair consequences and at the same time establish clear responsibilities for reporting. Fairness and due process suggest that safeguards for reporters be established.

Such safeguards serve two purposes. They protect potential witnesses, and they protect the investigative and adjudicative process. Victims of misconduct are often witnesses to those allegations. Protections to victims who are witnesses can alleviate the fears of witness tampering, or the intimidation of testimony by those who have reason to alter testimony or to frighten witnesses from testifying.

Such protection also preserves the integrity of the investigative and adjudicative processes. Investigators need to know the formal processes for gathering facts, including the timing of gathering evidence, what facts need to be gathered, and how those facts need to be gathered and conveyed to the adjudicators. "Leading" witnesses has cost both informal and formal prosecutions their cases more than once. Leading a witness means that the prosecution asks questions in such a manner as to coerce a foregone conclusion or to steer the content or the style of the witness' response.

Another kind of protection valuable to witnesses is confidentiality. Providing confidentiality for victims protects them from possible intimidation or, perhaps more importantly, the *fear* of intimidation. California (Bus & Prof Code, Section 729(3)(d)) seeks to provide such protection. The statute reads:

> In the investigation and prosecution of a violation of this section, no person shall seek to obtain disclosure of any confidential files of other patients, clients, or former patients or clients of the psychotherapist.

Another illustration of administrative actions to prevent misconduct are employment policies and procedures. The appendix includes some examples of religious denominational policies designed to prevent and/or respond to clergy sexual misconduct. The policies are similar in some respects and dissimilar in others. For example, all the policies include systems for reporting, the taking of evidence, the prosecuting of alleged exploiters, and the sanctioning of those found guilty.

There is some variety, however, within these very broad parameters. First, all the policies require that the allegations be in writing to a committee or head of the ecclesiastical body. Written allegations are designed to protect both the accuser and the accused. The accused is protected because accusers are less likely to put a false or frivolous accusation in writing than in mere verbal accusations. Second, some policies contain statutes of limitations. These limitations require that the written accusations be filed within a certain period of time. Generally, once that statute of limitations expires, the claim is lost.

One provision dissimilar among the policies deals with how the accused is dealt with during the investigative stage. Some policies strike the balance of justice in favor of the accused's presumption of innocence by allowing the accused to remain in his or her professional position. Other policies strike the justice balance in favor of the accused (and other potential victims) by placing the accused on some kind of administrative leave or other sanction.

Code of Ethics Advisory Opinions

In the legal domain, the state attorney general will periodically issue "advisory opinions" for attorneys of that state specifying various issues arising from that state's legal code of ethics. These advisory opinions are designed to clarify specific issues that attorneys face in their practices. Advisory opinions are generally clear and to the point. While they do not have the force of law, they often provide more specific guidelines to practicing professionals than do provisions in the code of ethics.

State licensing boards and professional organizations can offer similar advisory opinions, specifically relating to social work standards of practice. The following is an example of an advisory opinion ("Tough decisions" 1992) issued by the Ethics Committee of the American Association of Counseling and Development (AACD), now the American Counseling Association (ACA):

> *Do the AACD Ethical Standards prohibit sexual relationships between members who are counseling professors and their students, and between supervisors and their supervisees?*
>
> Yes . . . The AACD Ethics Committee interprets "clients" broadly to include students, supervisees or any other individuals with whom a

member has a relationship that involves an inherent power differential. . . . The AACD Ethics Committee interprets this standard as prohibiting dual relations—with clients, students, or supervisees—that might impair the member's objectivity or professional judgment. Sexual intimacies constitute one type of dual relationship and, clearly a sexual relationship would likely cloud a professor's judgment in grading or otherwise evaluating a student.

This advisory opinion is helpful in that it answers the question simply and unequivocally in the affirmative; it directly connects the answer to relevant provisions in the code of ethics; and it provides a brief rationale to underscore the opinion. In this case the opinion states that such dual relations are likely to cloud the judgment and compromise objectivity.

LEGAL DYNAMICS OF PREVENTION

Chapters 2 and 3 of this book have described at length the civil and criminal law surrounding sexual misconduct. While these statutes certainly are designed to *deter* such behavior, they primarily *punish* behavior. Some states have designed laws specifically to prevent future sexual misconduct on the part of psychotherapists.

Legislative Interventions

At least one state has established a formula for the prevention of sexual exploitation by psychotherapists. Minnesota law (611A.24, 1985) directs the commissioner of corrections to establish an educational program, for both the public and professionals, concerning psychotherapist sexual exploitation. State governments, through their licensing boards, are in a good position to develop such models, procedures, and educational programs for three reasons. First, they have the expertise at their disposal. State agencies and departments bring an enormous, interdisciplinary array of expertise to bear on prevention research and response. Second, states have the coercive power of state government and licensure approval by which to apply these procedures. Third, state governments can influence, through education and the exercise of police powers, ethical behavior of all social workers practicing within the state's jurisdiction.

The Minnesota law offers several programs, below outlined, followed by the author's commentary.

1. Collect and distribute information on the problem of psychotherapist sexual exploitation. This law can establish systems for gathering the necessary data to reveal the scope of social

work sexual misconduct. The way in which the data is collected can influence how the data is interpreted and how useful the data can become. Simply collecting data on the frequency of complaints filed for sexual misconduct is insufficient to prepare "surgical strikes" against social worker sexual misconduct.

For clear, efficient, precise preventative measures, the data collected should specify the type of practice, the nature of the practice, and the client base where complaints of sexual misconduct occur. This information can provide clues to where state educational and enforcement efforts may be most usefully brought to bear. Additionally, the conceptual orientation of the social worker should be ascertained. This connection was discussed in chapter 4.

2. Educate the public and professionals about the administrative, civil, and criminal complaints and prosecution procedures. Professional education, addressing the right professional population, places the social workers "on notice" of the definitions of sexual misconduct and the sanctions imposed. While education alone probably is not enough to dissuade sexual misconduct arising out of personality disorders, sexual addiction, sexual narcissism, or untreated childhood sexual abuse, such education may sensitize social workers to sexual behaviors arising out of improper reactions to transference or out of ignorance of the impropriety of acting out sexually with clients.

To separate sexual misconduct from the more entrenched disorders and addictions mentioned above, a more stringent code is probably necessary. It is unreasonable, for example, to assume addictive or narcissistic behavior in the sexual realm would be easier to avert than addictions to alcohol or other drugs. The state's efforts should be geared to those social workers whose behavior is most likely to be amended.

3. Provide information and referral services, advocacy, crisis intervention, a statement of the rights of psychotherapy clients relating to sexual exploitation, and other assistance to victims of sexual exploitation. States have the systems and the personnel to effectively provide these services—systems to disseminate information and to train and equip personnel to respond to client complaints are already in place. Referral services can be a usual part of the complaint procedure.

State registration, certification, or licensing boards can provide statements as to the rights of sexually abused clients, and can require social workers to disseminate such statements. Many states currently require psychotherapists to disclose to clients their rights of privacy, confidentiality, and competency of the therapists. Social workers can similarly disclose the rights of abused clients.

4. Develop policy and procedure manuals and education and training programs for use by professionals, professional organizations, educational institutions, employers, and supervisors. This element of the Minnesota law has the benefit of drawing upon the expertise and resources of national and state organizations. Given the state of the art to date, sufficient educational materials are available to discuss the nature, the harm, and the legal consequences of social worker sexual and other misconduct. To this extent, state organizations and professional groups do not have to reinvent the sexual misconduct wheel in order to present factual, informative, and effective programming.

   As stated previously, any materials generated should be interdisciplinary in nature. The responsibility of sexual misconduct is not the province of any one profession and neither are the responses. Prosecutors, defense attorneys, survivors, social work practitioners from both the public and private sectors, social workers working with adults and children, as well as those practicing from a variety of theoretical orientations should be included.

5. Develop manuals, brochures, and other educational material for distribution to the public. Like the above point, developing effective brochures, videotapes, and single-page statements of client rights, and organizing seminars on social worker sexual misconduct, does not require starting from scratch. Developing such materials requires only the will to commit political and economic resources to do so.

   Distributing such materials can be handled in a variety of ways. Newly licensed, certified, or registered social workers can be given such materials as a matter of course. Continuing education courses can be required. Professional organizations can work with state agencies and educational institutions to provide guest lecturers on sexual and other misconduct. In-service training opportunities for agency workers are also useful tools.

6. Recommend the creation or modification of state laws or regulations on issues related to sexual exploitation. Perhaps the most fruitful area for interagency and interdisciplinary

teamwork is new legislation addressing psychotherapist misconduct. As seen previously, many states specifically address these issues in their state regulatory scheme of professions, their civil or criminal codes, or both.

These few states have cracked the window open, but much more work needs to be done. Other states can modify the civil and criminal exploitation laws to fit their own regulatory schemes. While most, if not all, states would attach civil liability for proven sexual misconduct, it is easier to address the substantive charge if procedural issues are clarified by statute. Questions as to the extent of employer liability, the statute of limitations, whether or not consent is a defense and the nature of "therapeutic deception" as an element of the liability are all issues that can be addressed in the statute. States can also establish schemes, like the Minnesota model, to prevent sexual and other misconduct in the first place.

The Duty to Report

Some states have enacted laws that require subsequent therapists to report the sexual misconduct of prior therapists when the subsequent therapist suspects the client has been abused. Such reporting laws are analogous to child abuse reporting laws. They are designed first to protect future victims of sexual exploitation by therapists and second to identify and punish perpetrators. Reporting laws can be criminal, civil, or administrative in nature. Wisconsin (940.22(3)) has enacted a criminal law, stating:

> If a therapist has reasonable cause to suspect that a patient or client he or she has seen in the course of professional duties is a victim of sexual contact by another therapist or a person who holds himself or herself out to be a therapist . . . as soon as practicable the therapist shall ask the patient or client if he or she wants the therapist to make a report under this subsection. The therapist shall explain that the report need not identify the patient or client as the victim. If the patient or client wants the therapist to make the report, the patient or client shall provide the therapist with a written consent to the report and shall specify whether the patient's or client's identity will be included in the report.

There are four elements of this law. First, social workers are specifically named "therapists" for the purposes of this statute (940.22(1)(i)). Second, the law is mandatory to the extent that it requires the therapist to ask the client if he or she wishes the therapist to make a report. Thus, the client controls whether or not the therapist makes a report. In this respect, this therapist exploitation

reporting law substantially differs from mandatory child abuse reporting laws. As in child abuse reporting laws, however, sanctions
are imposed for failure to report violations of the law. Wisconsin
provides that such violations constitute a misdemeanor (940.22(2)(d)).

Third, immunities are provided from civil or criminal liability for
making a report or record under this section. Immunities shield both
persons and institutions, and presume that all reports are made in
good faith. Such presumptions of good faith often can be challenged.
For example, a social worker who makes false reports to retaliate
against another therapist or out of other vindictiveness, or where the
social worker has reason to believe the report is false, rebuts the
"good faith" presumption.

Fourth, reports and records are kept confidential (940.22(4)).
Reports of sexual exploitation by the examining board, investigations,
and the district attorneys are not to be disclosed. Nor are the names
of the victims or alleged victims to be disclosed unless by written
consent of the victim. This law, with its emphasis upon consent of the
victim, protects the victim of sexual exploitation by psychotherapists
in several ways.

The law cannot, of course, abrogate the initial victimization, but
it can help to protect against "secondary victimizations." Secondary
victimizations are subsequent harms done to the victim by the
prosecutorial processes in which they are both a *victim* of a crime and
a government *witness* to that crime. As a witness to the alleged crime
against them, they must endure cross-examination and other rigors of
the prosecutorial process. The statutory requirement of written
consent by the victim to release his or her name protects the victim in
two ways. First, the victim may choose not to release his or her name
at all for purposes of prosecution. U.S. law provides that the state
may elect to bring criminal charges without the victim's consent or
cooperation, but this is not the norm. Second, the alleged perpetrator's choice can help persuade the alleged perpetrator to enter a guilty
plea. This avoids an expensive, public trial while also serving the
ends of justice.

PREVENTING SEXUAL HARASSMENT

Suggestions for preventing sexual harassment merit a separate section because of the distinct legal considerations. As discussed in
chapter 3, sexual harassment is dictated by statutory and case law.
While it is impossible to predict the future of harassment law, it can
be asserted with some certainty that such claims will intensify. It is

also possible to define probable areas where suits are likely to arise and to assert prevention techniques.

Administrative Policies and Procedures

Social work employers, both public and private, should promulgate and publicize policy and procedures addressing sexual harassment in their place of business (Howard 1991). The policies and procedures should clearly define unacceptable behaviors and processes for filing complaints, investigations, and defining sanctions. The procedures should seek to protect the due process rights of both the accused and the alleged victims. While this is not an easy balance to strike, many private companies and public institutions have established such procedures already and can be used as models.

Appendixes A, B, and C represent denominational and organizational policies and procedures designed to address sexual harassment in church and legal organizations. The policy posed by the State Bar of California is now passed and is part of California law. These policies are included to show the variety among them.

A section of such policies that should be expressly stated is the *rationale* for such a policy. This rationale can include principles of NASW Code that uphold the client's dignity and autonomy. Such a rationale can also incorporate new data on the legal and emotional consequences of sexual harassment. The rationale, as an educational statement, serves to reinforce the deliberate intentions of the overall policy.

Defining Unacceptable Sexual Behaviors

The primary reason for specifically defining prohibited sexual behaviors is to place workers on notice of proscribed behaviors. It can be noted that in appendix C the proposed California State Bar defines "sexual relations" as "sexual intercourse or the touching of an intimate part of another person for the purpose of sexual arousal, gratification, or abuse." In chapter 2 several criminal statutes were discussed that specifically defined the prohibited sexual activity.

It is unfair, and probably fruitless, to expect employees and supervisors to refrain from sexual harassment if they do not know from what behaviors to refrain. Chapter 3 included several examples of possible sexual harassment. Given the resistance of some individuals to curbing their own harassment, the persistence of harassing behaviors among some individuals, and the prevalence of sexual harassment charges, defining illegal or unacceptable sexual conduct is necessary to protect both employees and employers.

Management Education

The education of managers and supervisors is an essential component in the prevention of sexual harassment. Managers and supervisors control the livelihoods of their employees. Within that control over the livelihoods of others, managers and supervisors can hold money, careers, privilege, and futures for the furtherance of their legitimate business interests, or for selfish, personal gain. Given this power, managers and supervisors can exert considerable influence in significant ways.

Of all the positive efforts that managers and supervisors can exert, none is more important than setting personal examples. There is no substitute for employers who set personal examples of legal and ethical behavior regarding sexual misconduct. Employers who brook no behaviors close to sexual misconduct set the tone for others. This attitude places employees on notice that for those employees guilty of sexual misconduct, sanctions will be applied consistently and objectively. Putting the example more positively, employers who do not tolerate sexual misconduct make good role models for courteous, respectful employee relations.

Specific Policy Issues

After reading policies designed to prevent or to punish sexual misconduct, several issues arise. In striking the balance between protecting the rights of the accused and protecting real or potential victims, policies must address how to administratively treat the accused. Is administrative leave appropriate? With or without pay? Is this "preemptive sanction" already a suggestion of guilt without trial?

In addition, procedures for investigations and hearings should be established that safeguard both the "due process" rights of the accused and the freedom of the hearing officer to conduct a probing yet expeditious hearing. Such due process considerations might include whether accusations must be in writing, whether the accused can "cross-examine" his or her accuser, and whether a statute of limitations on accusations will be enforced.

Finally, any presumptions should be explicitly stated. For example, the State Bar of California's proposed policy *presumes* that sexual relations with a client violates the policy. This is an important presumption because there is no allowance for a defense once the sexual relations are proven. If any mitigating circumstances or defenses are administratively considered, they should be explicitly set forth.

The final section of this chapter describes specific practices for prevention. These practices are illustrative, not exhaustive or cumulative, and are offered as examples of how trainers, educators, and professional organizations may use interventions.

SPECIFIC PRACTICES AND ISSUES

The profession of social work has at its disposal several specific practice interventions and resources to address sexual misconduct. These interventions and resources have two features. First, they are already among the clinical intervention tools of many clinicians. They can be adapted to address specifically issues of sexual misconduct within a wide variety of clinical orientations. Second, they address issues raised about both the perpetrator and the survivors of sexual misconduct.

Law Cases and Case Studies

Case studies are employed by the social and behavioral sciences, as well as business schools and theological schools, to educate students in professional programs. Case studies offer the advantages of "real life" situations for students to synthesize data, organize relationships, analyze reactions, and formulate solutions. Of course, case studies can be used as material in studying ethical issues as well. Newspapers, magazine articles, and students' own personal experiences may be fruitful sources of case material.

A largely undiscovered source of case study material on misconduct are law cases. It is no coincidence that this book uses many law cases. The cases themselves determine the law, and the case facts present life situations that illustrate misconduct. There are several advantages in using law case material as the fact bases for case studies. First, as law cases are a matter of public record, there is no question of breaching confidentiality when using such material. Second, the cases are easily cited and documented. Third, the cases furnish legal resolutions. Fourth, as many of the law cases are reported in the popular and academic presses, additional background material is also available. How to locate and update legal materials is the basis of chapter 8.

Role Playing

Role playing can be an important tool for counselors-in-training to sensitize them to feelings and insights related to therapist seduction (Vasquez 1988). Creating and reinforcing empathy is a key factor in both intellectually and emotionally understanding the harm of sexual misconduct. This is an intervention tool useful in supervision, in-service training, and professional seminars as well.

Role playing has three components that make it an intervention of special importance in preventing sexual misconduct. First, as ·mentioned above, role playing is an experiential training and reaches the emotions as well as the intellect. Playing the roles of both the client and the social worker enables the social worker to experience what it might be like to be the object of seduction by a clinician, as well as to experience what it might be like to want to seduce a client. The second component, related to the first, is that role playing sensitizes the social worker to how clients can try to seduce them, and can sensitize social workers to how their own possibly seductive behavior can be experienced by clients. Third, participants can experience the impressions of others observing the role play. Observers can provide insights as to how the behavior looks from objective points of view.

Peer Assistance Programs

Peer assistance programs for impaired professionals, often designed to address drug and alcohol problems, may be adapted to address sexual misconduct. Essential treatment plans for professional rehabilitation have been identified (Schoener and Gonsiorek 1988). These plans include personal psychotherapy, practice limitations, and supervision. These avenues of address, specifically applied to social workers, are considered below. How the criminal justice systems, licensing or regulatory agencies, or professional organizations deal with social workers guilty of sexual exploitation is a matter of values.

While there is no small stigma attached to a criminal record, Americans value the ethic of rehabilitation after sentencing. To professionally dispose of social workers guilty of sexual exploitation without offering remediation and, ultimately, the chance to return to professional usefulness, is wasteful, inefficient, and contrary to the value, attached with all sanctions, that promotes resumption of these social workers' professional lives after they have "paid their debt to society." After an offender has been convicted and served a sentence, retribution must give way to rehabilitation. Such a possibility is attached to other criminal acts and should factor into social worker sexual misconduct as well.

Personal psychotherapy for perpetrators is no easy matter for the treating therapist. Treating a peer who is also a perpetrator introduces complicating factors into the counseling relationship. If the counseling is required or coerced by law or administrative sanctions, the inevitable resentments need to be confronted. The treating therapist will have to address the emotional fallout of treating a social worker ostracized from his or her own profession. The social worker may be unemployed, financially strained, shunned by former support groups, and avoided by family and friends.

There is also the issue of competence, both clinical and ethical. Who is competent to treat social workers who exploit their clients? This is not an area taught in most clinical practice programs. The baseline skills should include four constellations of competencies:

1. A thorough knowledge of the dynamics of social work exploitation, including both the clinical disorders and non-clinical descriptions of perpetrators. This knowledge should include the impacts on the survivors of such exploitation.
2. A thorough knowledge of the ethical and legal sanctions imposed by the social work professional organizations, by the state regulatory boards, and by state civil and criminal penalties. The treating clinician must understand the professional and personal impact on the perpetrator, and also the professional costs, liabilities, and values that sexual exploitation violates.
3. Clinical skills particularly adapted to perpetrators of sexual crimes. These skills may include, but not be limited to, self-esteem, behavioral modification, empathy, self-reflection, and confrontation.
4. Experience and supervision in counseling perpetrators of sexual offenses, particularly among the professions. As an example, there is the case of a woman sexually abused by her minister who later sought to report the abuse to the minister's immediate ecclesiastical supervisor. When she told her story to the supervisor, the supervisor himself had sexual relations with the woman, right in his office. Social workers must understand the tremendous power of sexuality.

The state of Texas illustrates a statutory approach to peer assistance programs (Health and Safety Code 467.001ff, 1991). The statute provides that a "professional association or licensing or disciplinary authority may establish a peer assistance program to identify and assist impaired professionals" with funding from a surcharge on professional licenses or license renewal fees. "Impaired professional" is a statutorily defined term that means an individual whose professional services are impaired by drugs or alcohol, or by reason of mental illness. Suspected "impaired professionals" may be reported by anyone suspecting impairment, and some individuals may be *required* to report. Those reporting are immunized from civil liability.

Once a licensing or disciplinary body receives an initial complaint, they have two choices. They may either *refer* the suspected professional to a peer assistance program or *require* the suspected professional to attend or complete a treatment course or rehabilitation program (467.006, 1991). The statute does not mention if or how the licensing board *verifies* that the suspected professional is, in fact, an "impaired" professional.

Such peer assistance programs can include, or become the basis for, declaring a professional impaired by reason of sexual misconduct. The sexual misconduct could be addressed in a peer assistance program, regardless of whether or not the misconduct arose from ignorance of the ethical standards, from addictive behaviors, or from personality disorders. Specially trained teams of peer counselors could address these issues as other peer counselors address drug abuse and mental illness.

Prior experience and supervision in counseling sexual perpetrators is designed to eliminate those counselors whose own sexual issues are not yet resolved. Sending a sexual perpetrator-therapist for psychotherapy to another sexually immature therapist is a dangerous proposition.

Practice limitations imposed upon the perpetrator create special problems for the social work profession. Given the variety of social work practices, from licensed clinicians to registered and certified professionals, perpetrators may be able to continue practicing by simply moving to another town or across state lines. Placing real practice limitations on social workers requires a system of monitoring professional activities and publicizing professional sanctions. Civil and criminal sanctions are already publicly noted in open court, in court decisions, and in newspapers.

The *NASW News* names those who have had sanctions imposed against them, the cause of the sanctions, the nature of the sanctions, and any changes in the sanctions. Such information could be officially passed to state NASW chapters for dissemination among its members. This may help with the "peer surveillance" of social workers who may be practicing contrary to imposed sanctions. The relationship between a supervisor and a social worker found guilty of sexual misconduct can be complex. First, the treating professional must have worked through his or her own issues of power, authority, anger, self-righteousness, and sexuality. Each of these issues can become emotional time bombs when counseling social workers guilty of sexual exploitation. Second, the treating therapist must address legal issues inherent in these cases. The offending client may be under court order to participate in individual or group counseling. Third, the client may have lost his or her job, family connections, and professional reputation. These factors make such rehabilitation and counseling materially different and require materially different preparation for the treating therapist.

Victim/Survivor Advocacy Groups

Victim/survivor advocacy and treatment for impaired professionals have been offered as resources for both survivors and perpetrators of therapist sexual exploitation (Hotelling 1988). In the past decade victims of crimes have played an increasingly important political role in advocating for victims' rights. Now several states have statutes specifically establishing victim input in sentencing decisions, parole hearings, and an array of financial and social services. Many states have also established "victim/witness" programs to prepare victims for court testimony, to coordinate the payment of food, lodging, and other travel expenses related to court, and to facilitate social services (including counseling) for victims.

Often, establishing and encouraging self-help survivor groups for victims is a part of victim/witness programs. Self-help groups, particularly for survivors of attempted homicide, play an important part in publicizing the role of victims in the judicial process, advocating for a voice for victims in the court of public opinion, and providing support. Survivor support groups, of course, can be formed for survivors of social worker sexual exploitation as well. Such groups can be instrumental in supporting their members during trials, through the ordeal of witnessing, and in seeking victims' compensation, as well as in advocating for judicial, criminal justice and statutory sensitivity to these crimes and the victims of these crimes.

Professional Liability Insurance

Liability insurance is different from other types of insurance in that it specifically ensures against malpractice liability and other professionally-related claims—as opposed to other business claims like "slip-and-fall" claims. Liability insurance is discussed here because many carriers of liability insurance also educate professionals about their exposure to professional liability, and because the insurance itself ensures against financial loss in defending against liability suits, and against the attendant financial judgments if the suits prove successful.

For the purposes of this discussion, two carriers of liability insurance will be addressed: the NASW Insurance Trust and the American Counseling Association (ACA) Insurance Trust. This discussion in no way intends to evaluate or promote the insurance policies illustrated. These policies are included only to discuss the coverage of alleged sexual involvement and misconduct.

A few preliminary remarks should be made about professional liability insurance. First, even if social workers are employed by an agency or department that has its own liability insurance that covers social worker employees, social workers should carry their own insurance, because the agency's insurance works for the *agency*, not the *individual* social worker. For example, if the insurance company decides to settle a suit against a social worker out of court, the agency may agree to do so, even if the social worker wants to prove his or her innocence in court. The social worker may be left with a tarnished reputation, without ever having the power to decide whether to take the claim to trial.

Additionally, social workers need their own insurance because they may be liable for agency fees or for damages against the agency if they do not have personal liability coverage (Contract clause 1991). This may happen when social workers sign "hold harmless" clauses as part of their employment agreements. Hold harmless clauses are contracts whereby the social worker agrees that the agency is not responsible for the negligent acts of the social worker. Thus, even if the agency's insurance company covers the social worker in the event of a successful lawsuit, the social worker may be responsible for money damages leveled against the agency. What protection agency liability gives on one hand may be taken away by "hold harmless" clauses on the other hand.

Second, social workers must be sure that their insurance carrier is safe. Three important questions should be satisfactorily addressed by the state insurance regulator or organizations like the A.M. Best Company before a social worker purchases from any carrier (Nelson 1991):

1. *Check the financial status of the company.* If the insurance carrier is experiencing financial troubles, they may be unable to pay off a claim promptly or at all.

2. *Check the company's record of claim payments.* This check should uncover whether the company makes payments promptly and fairly.

3. *Check the consistency of rates.* Fluctuations in rates may be a sign of problems with the company.

Both the NASW and the ACA Insurance Trusts can cover professional sexual involvement with clients. A portion of the text of each insurance brochure is repeated verbatim because of the language and policy pertaining to sexual involvement with clients. The NASW insurance brochure, "Every social worker needs malpractice insurance," states:

> Any claim where one of the allegations is sexual misconduct (including, but not limited to, an attempt or a proposed erotic physical contact with any patient or client or certain other persons) is subject to an aggregate sub-limit liability of $25,000. This is the most the insurance company will pay for damages for all claims of this type, no matter how many of them there are. This does not apply to defense costs.

The ACA insurance brochure "Do you really need professional liability insurance?" states:

> Among the most important exclusions are criminal acts, dishonesty, fraud, malicious acts of omission and discrimination. Causes which are covered by other types of insurance are also excluded. *Sexual misconduct is limited to an aggregate of $50,000* (emphasis in original).

Four issues raised by these brief statements should be addressed. First, any policy purchased should be carefully noted for its exclusions. Exclusions are acts or events that the insurance policy will not cover. Second, it should be noted that the policy limits ($25,000 and $50,000 respectively) are *aggregate* figures and may not cover the entire amount of damages assessed in a suit against the social worker. Many claims for sexual misconduct will ask for damages many times those figures. Third, these policy limits may not include the limits for *defending* against such claims. The NASW brochure states so explicitly. A social worker considering the ACA policy should examine the "defense" limits as well.

The fourth issue, whether insurance policies that "exclude" criminal acts or intentional torts mean to exclude sexual acts with clients, requires more discussion. In *Aetna Life and Casualty Company v. McCabe* (1983), a federal court ruled that even if the malpractice was intentional, the insurance company was obliged to cover the damages. The court also ruled that the policy had only one exclusion, not for intentional injury, and that the insured must be made aware of the exclusions in order for the exclusions to be enforced. In *L.L. v. Medical Protective Company* (1984), the appeals court ruled that the psychiatrist acted within the course of his professional services when engaging in client sexual relations. Thus, the insurance company had to cover the damages.

It is imperative that social workers examine the precise language of what actions the prospective policy covers and does not cover before buying. These cases illustrate the necessity of carefully considering the language of any insurance to be purchased as well as carefully considering how the insurance company may construe the coverage once a claim is filed. It is wise to speak directly to an insurance representative about coverage for sexual and other misconduct, even if the policy states coverage. The final note about insurance protection is that most professional insurance organizations conduct training programs about avoiding liability in the first place. For example, the ACA distributes a cassette tape titled "Liability Insurance Issues." It is available from ACA, 5999 Stevenson St., Alexandria, Virginia 22304 (703/823-8900).

This chapter has surveyed some important statutes in place to prevent sexual misconduct. It has also presented and discussed suggestions and policies related to misconduct. Chapter 8 explains how to access firsthand legal documents and legal materials. A specific example of locating legal materials is illustrated. Chapter 8 also suggests some legal texts useful for all social workers and concludes with a glossary of legal terms.

REFERENCES

Aetna Life and Casualty Company v. McCabe, 556 F.Supp.1342 (E.D. Pa. 1983).

Borys, D.S., and Pope, K.S. (1989). Dual relationships between therapist and client: A national study of psychologists, psychiatrists, and social workers. *Professional Psychology: Research and Practice,* 20(5), 283–93.

"Contract clause could boost liability limits." (1991). *NASW News,* 36(10), 154.

Hotelling, K. (1988). Ethical, legal, and administrative options to address sexual relations between counselors and clients. *Journal of Counseling and Development,* 67(4), 233–37.

Howard, S. (1991). Organizational resources for addressing sexual harassment. *Journal of Counseling and Development,* 69, 507–11.

L.L. v. Medical Protective Company, 362 N.W.2d 174 (1984).

Nelson, P.L. (1991). Is your insurance company safe? *Guideposts,* 34(5), 4 and 41.

Romeo, S. (1978, June) Dr. Martin Shephard answers his accusers. *Knave,* 19, 14–38.

Schoener, G.R., and Gonsiorek, J. (1988). Assessment and development of rehabilitation plans for counselors who have sexually exploited their clients. *Journal of Counseling and Development,* 67(4), 227–32.

Shephard, M. (1971). *The love treatment: Sexual intimacy between patients and psychotherapists.* New York: Wyden.

Torrey, S. (1989, October 4). Women lawyers in survey report bias, harassment. *The Washington Post,* D1 and D5.

"Tough Decisions." (1992). *Guideposts,* 34(11), 14.

Vasquez, M.J.T. (1988). Counselor-client sexual contact: Implications for ethics training. *Journal of Counseling and Development,* 67(4), 238–41.

Chapter 8

▶ ⋯⋯⋯⋯⋯⋯⋯⋯⋯ ◀

How to Find the Law Yourself

▶ ⋯⋯⋯⋯⋯⋯⋯⋯⋯ ◀

This chapter describes how social workers, with no legal background or legal training, can locate both statutes and case law. First, the advantages for social workers in finding the law themselves are described. The chapter then gives step-by-step instructions for locating law from several different starting points, including starting from statutes, cases, law reviews, and other legal references. An illustration of finding the law from a state (Minnesota) code index is described. The chapter concludes with a bibliography of illustrative samples of legal materials useful to social workers, and a glossary of terms.

WHY SHOULD YOU FIND THE LAW YOURSELF?

There are five reasons why a social worker needs to be able to find statutes and case law.

1. *Professional legal advice is expensive.* Some social workers have lawyers in their agencies or departments to whom they can turn for legal advice. Most social workers, however, do not enjoy this luxury. The ability to look up and examine statutes and cases does not and cannot replace legal counsel. Yet, social workers who can read statutes and cases can focus on

issues and formulate questions once legal counsel is sought. This can save time, when time is a valuable clinical and commercial commodity.

2. *Laws change.* Ten years ago there were no laws against psychotherapist sexual exploitation. In the next ten years, most states will probably enact them. Social workers who ignore changes in federal law and laws of the state in which they practice do so at their own risk.

3. *Law cases also change.* Different judges render different decisions for different states. Even social workers who keep abreast of general law through professional journals and seminars cannot be fully apprised of relevant law if they do not respond to the statutes and case law in their *particular* states.

4. *Social workers are, by ethical mandate and professional training, policymakers.* Public policy has its most profound and pervasive expression in public law. The form and content of statutes are important elements of public policy critique. Without understanding the language and text of laws, and how case law modifies or explains statutes, social workers cannot conduct a meaningful critique of public policy.

5. *As social science researchers, social workers must be able to interpret data firsthand.* Using secondhand sources too often results in second-rate research. To the extent that social workers can read statutes and case law firsthand, they can assess the results of others' research, analysis, and conclusions in their own terms and by their own standards, without reliance upon the opinions of others. This is true particularly because of the ubiquitous nature of law—a legal, economic, or political analysis of the law alone is adequate without a social analysis. This social analysis is a strength of the social work profession and should not be relinquished. Social workers have a professional interest, if not duty, to find and read the law firsthand.

FINDING A LAW LIBRARY

Finding a law library is easier than one might think. Libraries in law schools usually offer the widest array of services—at least the most *public* array of services. Most law school libraries welcome non-matriculated students to use their facilities and employ a staff which help the public use the facilities. It is helpful to establish a relationship with a law librarian before plunging into the stacks. The law librarians can offer specific instruction in both computerized and manual legal research. Computerized research is now possible through WestLaw and Lexis as well as other computerized systems for legislative and legal periodical searches. Law librarians also have at their disposal short books, published by legal publishers. Those social workers fortunate enough to have law schools nearby have more resources at their immediate disposal, but there are other avenues.

Other law libraries include those at larger colleges and universities, federal and state court libraries, and the libraries in law firms. Many colleges and universities have law periodicals, federal and state reporters of law cases, and state law codes. These resources are usually limited to the states in which the college or university resides or for which the university has a specialty, as periodicals are expensive to renew and the range of legal periodicals is enormous. Most likely they will have also U.S. Supreme Court reporters. As with law school libraries, university libraries with legal materials will have librarians to provide assistance.

Larger cities may host either a district or circuit federal court. Sometimes federal law libraries allow researchers to use their resources. These libraries typically will have the law codes for every state and an extensive collection of federal and state case reporters. Federal law libraries will also carry collections of legal periodicals. Other cities host state courts. State court libraries will have larger collections of that state's and county's materials. In fact, state courts probably hold the best collections of state and local materials.

The libraries in private law firms also have expensive and complete collections of legal materials. Obviously, law firms will gear their collections to the type of law the firm practices: criminal, tax, insurance, etc. Most law firms will also limit their collections to the state in which their attorneys practice. Social workers, through their own acquaintances or through other connections, probably can find a partner in a larger law firm with a library. Permission to use their library, as well as its librarian and duplicating machines, can often be secured.

With this array of resources available, few social workers are without some means to examine case law, statutes, and some legal periodicals. The next section describes ways of finding pertinent case law and statutes.

FEDERAL AND STATE LAW CODES

Federal and state law codes can be located through the indices of these codes. Federal laws and state laws are codified in volumes with indices. The specific statutes run serially through these volumes. Specific statutes can be located in two ways using the codes. First, if the social worker has a legal citation for a statute, the statute may be located directly. For example, if the citation is a New Jersey law cited at 9:6-8.8, find volume 9 in the code and proceed serially through the volume until you find the correct designation. The volume number and sometimes a topic of law will be located on the spine of each volume. This particular New Jersey citation is for that state's child abuse reporting statute. Most codes have titles for each statute and the social worker can read the heading to find the area of law he or she is seeking.

The second way of finding statutes from the codes themselves is by examining the index for either the name of the statute or act or the general kind of law (e.g., "child abuse" or "privileged communications"). The ease with which specific statutes can be discovered in the index is in direct proportion to the thoroughness of the index itself. In other words, some indices are more useful than others, and the social worker will have to be persistent and creative in seeking the terms for the statute in the index. For example, privileged communications for social workers may be found under "social workers," "privileged communications," or "confidential communications." Once the proper name for the statute has been found in the index, it will yield the code citation. Social workers should note all information given in the index—particularly *names* of volumes. States like California and New York have code volumes with names like "Bus & Prof" (Business and Professions) that indicate the type of law covered by that volume.

This same procedure will work for both federal and state law. The federal code has a daunting number of indices for its many volumes of laws. State codes have fewer volumes—even though states like New York and California have several volumes of codes and indices.

Social workers always need to check for updated statutes. Every year state and federal legislatures create, revise, or repeal statutes. It is imperative for legal researchers to know the current status of statutes in order to compile accurate, current legal research. Yearly supplements are provided for all statutes whether they be state or federal laws. These statutory supplements are also called "pocket parts" because many are located in the slotted back covers of hardbound volumes. It is less expensive to provide paperbound statutory updates than it is to replace hardbound volumes each year. Sometimes pocket parts are located in the shelves alongside the corresponding volumes.

The system of updating both statutes and cases, called *Shepard's Citations*, can also be used to track changes in state and federal case law. This manual system of updating laws is described more fully in the next section.

Legal codes are also an excellent way to discover case law related to those statutes. Many publishers of statutes *annotate* their codes with references to cases that interpret the relevant statutes. These annotations are a quick and efficient way of researching relevant cases on a given statute.

CASES

Locating cases and locating statutes from references within cases are important methods of finding law. Law cases are judicial decisions that interpret statutes within specific fact patterns. Judges must apply statutes and previous decisions (precedence) to the conduct of individuals.

Case law is an important clue, sometimes the determining factor, in interpreting statutes. It is worth noting that the U.S. Supreme Court has the right, even the duty, to overturn statutes and prior decisions deemed contrary to the U.S. Constitution. A casualty of constitutional scrutiny is the *Plessy v. Ferguson* decision (1896), which was overturned by *Brown v. Board of Education* (1954), striking down strictly segregated schools. It is worth noting too that the "privacy" right to abortion and the right to die are entirely judicial creations. No privacy right per se exists in the U.S. Constitution. In the *Cruzan* (1990) decision, which established the constitutional right for the family of a patient in a persistent vegetative state to refuse medical treatment, the U.S. Supreme Court reversed a Missouri Supreme Court decision reaching the opposite conclusion. Similarly, the twin cases of *Doe v. Bolton* (1973) and *Roe v. Wade* (1973) overturned statutes in Georgia and Texas respectively that criminalized abortion.

The authority of case law is in direct proportion to the jurisdiction of the court rendering the decision. The U.S. Supreme Court enjoys the broadest jurisdiction—ruling both federal and state courts. In the federal system the court below the Supreme Court is called the Circuit Court of Appeals, and the "lowest" (trial) federal courts are called district courts. Generally, cases begin at the district court levels and are appealed to the Circuit Courts. Proportionally speaking, the Supreme Court reconsiders very few of the thousands of cases requesting appeals—about two hundred of the five thousand that seek such review each year.

For the purposes of locating federal cases, each level of court has its own systems of case "reports," with its own designated system of citations. The citations reveal the court systems that they contain. The Supreme Court cases are contained in reporting systems designated as "U.S.," "S.Ct.," or "U.S.L.W." For example, a citation for the *Cruzan* decision is 110 S.Ct. 2841 (1990). The first number (110) is the volume number of the reporters series and the second number (2841) refers to the page number. The date refers to the year in which the decision was made. The Circuit Court reporter is either "F" (federal) or, in its current second edition, "F.2d." The District Court reporter is "F.Supp."

The levels of state courts are designated differently by different states. In Virginia, for example, the designations for the court jurisdictions follow the federal designations: the trial courts are "district courts" followed by the Circuit Court and the Virginia Supreme Court. However, New York State's trial court is called the Supreme Court, the appellate court is called the Supreme Court-Appellate Division, and the highest court is called the Court of Appeals.

Cases, like statutes, can be reversed, affirmed, or otherwise modified. A system of case updating has been established in both the computer databases mentioned below and in a manual system. This system, known as *Shepard's Citations,* shows when a case has been cited in a later case. For instance, *Shepard's* uses letters to indicate whether cases have been criticized ("c"), followed and cited as controlling ("f"), or affirmed ("a"). Other letters designate other modifications. *Shepard's Citations* is organized to coincide with both the regional and state law reports. *Shepard's* covers the federal reporting systems as well. Legal researchers always need to check for case changes—this updating is commonly known as "shepardizing."

Two different systems of reporting carry state court decisions. The first is the system that often has sets of volumes for the appellate courts of each state. For example, New York State has reporting systems that publish the major cases from the Appellate Division and the Court of Appeals.

The second system publishes the major cases from each state in "regional" reports. Each regional report includes several states. The reporter, the citation, and the states the regional reporter includes are listed below.

LAW REVIEWS

Another fertile source for firsthand legal documents are law reviews, the professional journals of the legal profession. Every law school in the United States publishes at least one law journal. Some schools publish two or more on selected kinds of law—environmental law,

Table 8.1
Regional Reports: Reporters, Citations, and States Included

Reporter	Citation	States Included
Atlantic	A. or A.2d	Connecticut, Delaware, District of Columbia, Maine, Maryland, New Hampshire, New Jersey, Pennsylvania, Rhode Island, Vermont
North Eastern	N.E., N.E.2d	Illinois, Indiana, Massachusetts, New York, Ohio
North Western	N.W., N.W.2d	Iowa, Michigan, Minnesota, Nebraska, North Dakota, South Dakota, Wisconsin
Pacific	P., P.2d	Alaska, Arizona, California, Colorado, Hawaii, Idaho, Kansas, Montana, Nevada, New Mexico, Oklahoma, Oregon, Utah, Washington, Wyoming
South Eastern	S.E., S.E.2d	Georgia, North Carolina, South Carolina, Virginia, West Virginia
South Western	S.W., S.W.2d	Arkansas, Kentucky, Missouri, Tennessee, Texas
Southern	So., So.2d	Alabama, Florida, Louisiana, Mississippi

international law, public policy, labor law, and the like. While a primary purpose for law reviews is to explicate trends and the history of legal developments for academicians and practicing attorneys, law reviews serve another extremely important function.

Law review articles typically have enormous amounts of footnotes per page of text—it is not uncommon for literally half of a page to be devoted to footnotes. These footnotes provide a wealth of cases and statutes yielding raw material for firsthand research. The footnotes will provide complete citations for both case names and statutes, as well as descriptions of the cases themselves. Finding an article addressing the social work research topic can yield a number of judicial decisions and statutes from several states.

Finding law reviews, and other legal journals, requires specialized research tools analogous to the *Guide to Social Work Literature*. There are two primary manual tools for locating law articles. The *Guide to Legal Periodicals* organizes citations by subject and author, by case, by statute, and by book review. The *Current Law Index* organizes its legal periodical citations by statute, by case, by subject, and by author. These volumes are consistently and periodically updated.

HORNBOOKS AND CASEBOOKS

Hornbooks are digests of various legal disciplines; casebooks contain the texts of major cases within an area of the law, along with questions and commentary. Hornbooks differ from casebooks in that hornbooks do not provide the text of cases, but rather place a multitude of cases into a coherent conceptual framework. Both hornbooks and casebooks are valuable sources of cases, and order cases by topic; most provide pocket parts for the newest cases publishable. A sample of hornbooks and casebooks especially relevant to social workers is provided below:

Clark, H.H. (1980). *Cases and problems on domestic relations.* St. Paul, MN: West Publishing.
    Includes 1,138 pages of casebook with commentary on the law of premarriage contracts, the marriage contract, abortion, divorce, and annulments.

Eisenberg, T. (1981). *Civil rights legislation.* Charlottesville, VA: Michie Company.
    Includes 960 pages of cases and commentary on legal remedies for civil rights violations, with an appendix including the U.S. Constitution, the Civil Rights Act of 1866, the Civil Rights Act of 1870, the Civil Rights Act of 1871, and the Civil Rights Act of 1875.

Keeton, W.P., Dobbs, D.B., Keeton, R.E., and Owen, D.G. (1984). *The law of torts.* St. Paul, MN: West Publishing.
    Includes 1,286 pages of hornbook including pocket parts covering such areas as negligence (including professional negligence), vicarious liability (the liability of employers), defamation, domestic relations, and immunities.

Lockhart, W., Kamisar, Y., Choper, J., and Shiffrin, S. (1986). *Constitutional law.* St. Paul, MN: West Publishing.
    Includes 1,601 pages of hornbook covering such areas as national legislative powers, separation of powers, protection of individual rights, freedom of expression and association, equal protection, and congressional enforcement of civil rights.

Weyrauch, W., and Katz, S. (1983). *American family law in transition.* Washington, DC: Bureau of National Affairs.
    Includes 629 pages of casebook covering such areas as marriage as a contract, common law marriage, privacy rights (including abortion) in marriage, state involvement in marriage (including Social Security benefits), and children in privity (including factors influencing custody decisions).

AMERICAN LAW REPORTS

There are several fine sets of volumes that summarize and explain current law. Among these are *Corpus Juris Secundum* and *American Jurisprudence*. Another extremely useful series of volumes for legal research is called the *American Law Reports*. The ALR is now in its fifth series—it has been updated five times in hardbound volumes, in addition to the pocket parts. It has separate volumes for state and federal law. The ALR categorizes legal topics into essays with case notes as citations. To look up a subject in the ALR, turn to volumes titled Index to Annotations.

For example, the topic of "social worker malpractice" is among the articles included in the fourth series of the ALR. The ALR citation for this section is 58 ALR4th 977. Consistent with case citations above noted, the "58" refers to the volume number and the "977" refers to the page number. This particular essay explains all the cases extant addressing social worker malpractice, including a discussion of the facts and the cases' relevance to this area of law. Additionally, the essay lists other ALR essays of related interest, including liability of hospitals or clinics for sexual relations with patients, liability of mental care facilities for patients committing suicide, and malpractice liability connected with diagnosis and treatment of mental disease. Consistent with volumes containing statutes, the ALR has pocket parts to keep the reader current.

FAMILY LAW REPORTER

Loose-leaf reporter systems are also available for specialized legal research. Loose-leaf binders (sometimes several volumes) are available in a number of different areas including Supreme Court decisions, tax law, and corporation law. These loose-leaf reporters allow for quick and regular printing of court decisions, administrative regulations, and statutory updates.

The Family Law Reporter is a loose-leaf reporter system published by the Bureau of National Affairs, Washington, D.C., which updates the law concerned with marriage, family, and related issues. Other topics covered include antenuptial agreements, divorce decrees and settlements, alimony, separation agreements, child custody, professional malpractice, and child abuse. Social worker malpractice is also covered as this liability relates to services rendered in the above professional contexts.

COMPUTERIZED LEGAL RESEARCH

Legal periodicals, cases, and statutes are also accessible by computerized search—the system called *InfoTrak* is such a database. By entering the research topic, case name, or name of statute, a list of both American and foreign law articles is disclosed.

For example, when the heading "Custody of Children" is entered, several subheadings appear, including "moral and religious aspects." Under this subheading a number of journal and law newspaper articles are cited. A sample is included below.

> What rights do parents have over kids' religious training? by Albert Momjian 42 col in. v11 Pennsylvania Law Journal-Reporter Nov 21 '88 p3 col 1

> Religion vs. custody? Parents' faith increasingly an issue in cases. by Deborah Cassens Moss i1 v74 ABA Journal Nov1 '88 p32(2)

> Religious considerations in custody disputes. (Great Britain) by Bernadette A. Walsh v18 Family Law June '88 p198-200

Thus, *InfoTrak* has accessed state, national, and international law material related to the requested subject through one of many subheadings.

Two major databases for legal research are *Lexis* and *WestLaw*. These large computer systems access a wide array of legal materials. They can access cases, statutes, and legal periodicals. They can quickly show case updates and are now commonly used among legal professionals.

The following section illustrates how a typical legal search might proceed. While other searches may proceed from different points, this illustrative search begins with finding a statute from the index of a state code.

AN EXAMPLE OF LOCATING THE LAW FROM STATE CODE INDICES

The following exercise illustrates how to locate and update state statutes, cases, and other legal materials starting from state indices. The state of Minnesota was chosen because it has provided both case and statutory law for this book. Figure 8.1 is a page from the index for the Minnesota state code. The upper left and right columns show the subject titles "Crimes and Offenses" and "Criminal Sexual Conduct." Under "criminal sexual conduct" is the subtitle "psychotherapists," with its reference number 609.344. It should be noted that not all state

Figure 8.1
Minnesota State Code Index

CRIMES

CRIMES AND OFFENSES—Cont'd
Wiretapping,
  Access to store communications, **626A.26**
  Devices, **626A.03**
  Injunctions, **626A.25**
X-ray equipment, **144.1211**
Zebra mussels, **18.317**

CRIMINAL ACT
Defined,
  Concealing evidence, **609.495**
  Racketeering, **609.902**

**CRIMINAL AND JUVENILE JUSTICE INFORMA-
TION POLICY GROUP**
Generally, **299C.65**

CRIMINAL APPREHENSION BUREAU
Accounts and accounting, drivers licenses revocation reex-
  aminations, fees, **171.29**
Child protection background checks, **299C.60 et seq.**
Pardons and reprieves, copies, **638.02**
Privileges and immunities, children protection background
  checks, **299C.64**

CRIMINAL CODE
Numbering scheme, **299C.65**

CRIMINAL GANGS
Defined, crime committed for benefit of, **609.229**
Gangs, generally, this index

CRIMINAL HISTORY DATA
Adult day care, disqualification, reconsideration, **245A.04**
Child protection background checks, **299C.60 et seq.**
Criminal history score, computation, **244.10**
Currency exchanges, license applicants, **53A.03**
Defined,
  Fire department access, **299F.035**
Fire department access, **299F.035**
Gambling,
  Managers, **349.167**
Harassment offenders, mental health assessments, **13.99**
Hazardous substances and waste, transportation, licenses,
  221.035
Inspection, public, **13.87**
International student exchange visitor placement organi-
  zations, **5A.04**
Public data, **13.87**
  Inspection, **13.87**
School bus drivers, **171.321**
  Crimes against minors, license cancellations, **171.3215**

CRIMINAL JUSTICE AGENCIES
Defined,
  Fire department access to criminal history data,
  299F.035

**CRIMINAL JUSTICE DATA COMMUNICATIONS
NETWORK**
Revenue, department of, access, **270.062**
Security clearance, federal security clearances, access,
  299C.46
State agencies,
  Access, **299C.46**
  Connections, authorization, **299C.48**

CRIMINAL NEGLIGENCE
Pregnant women, death or injuries to unborn children,
  609.21

CRIMINAL SEXUAL CONDUCT
See, also, Sexual Offenses, generally, this index
Abuse of Children, this index
Age, mistake, defenses,
  Fourth degree, **609.345**
  Third degree, **609.344**

CRIMINAL SEXUAL CONDUCT—Cont'd
Assessments, **609.3452**
Clergy, **609.344 et seq.**
Community-based sex offender program evaluation, **241.67**
Conditional release, sex offenders, **609.346**
Confidential or privileged information, offender assess-
  ments, **609.3452**
Consent, defenses, **609.341 et seq.**
Evidence,
  Psychotherapists, patients personal or medical history,
    609.347
Fabricated allegations of sexual assault, evidence showing
  tendency, **609.347**
Feticide, felony-murder, **609.2661**
Fifth degree, **609.3451**
  County attorneys, prosecution, **388.051**
Fines and penalties,
  Fifth degree, **609.3451**
Fourth degree,
  Fifth degree, **609.3451**
  Psychotherapists, **609.345**
Health care professional, false representation, **609.344,
  609.345**
Life sentence, **609.346**
Mistake,
  Defense of, **609.344**
Orders of court, treatment, offenders, **609.3452**
Pregnant women, unborn children, felony-murder,
  609.2661
Previous conduct of victim, evidence, **609.347**
Psychopathic personality commitments, statewide judicial
  panel, **526.115**
Psychotherapists, **609.344 et seq.**
Registration, sex offenders, **243.166**
Second and subsequent offenses, **609.346**
Sexual penetration,
  Fourth degree criminal sexual conduct, psychothera-
    pists, **609.345**
Stay, imposition or execution of sentence, **609.342 et seq.**
Thirty-year sentence, **609.346**
Treatment programs, stay of sentence, **609.346**
Unborn children, felony-murder, **609.2661**
Victims,
  Previous sexual conduct, evidence, **609.347**

CRIMINAL VEHICULAR HOMICIDE AND INJURY
Generally, **609.21**
Drivers licenses, revocation, **171.17**

CRISIS ASSISTANCE
Defined, childrens mental health, **245.4871**

CRISIS SERVICES
Defined, family preservation grants, **256F.03**

CRITERIA
Defined, health care cost containment, antitrust exceptions, **62J.2912**

CROP HAIL ADJUSTER
Defined, insurance, **72B.02**

CROP OWNER'S LIENS
Liens and incumbrances, generally. Agricultural Prod-
  ucts, this index

CROP PRODUCTION INPUT
Defined,
  Agricultural production inputs sales, discounts, **325E.35**

CROP VALUE
Defined, agricultural crops, liens, **557.11**

CROSS COUNTRY SKIING
Passes, sales and use tax, exemption, **297A.25**
Sales and use tax, electricity used to make snow, **297A.25**

*Reprinted with permission from Minnesota Statutes Annotated, Copyright © by West Publish-
ing Company.*

168

indices have their sexual exploitation statutes listed under psycho-therapist. Often it is necessary to explore other headings such as "sexual crimes" or "exploitation."

Once the code reference number is obtained, in this case "609.344," the researcher can go directly to that state statute. In Minnesota the psychotherapist exploitation statutes run from sections 609.341 to 609.346. These sections include a definition section and four separate degrees of criminal sexual misconduct. Section 609.345, illustrated in figure 8.2, denotes criminal sexual conduct in the fourth degree. As can be seen, this statute explicitly names psychotherapists in this criminal activity under subsections "h," "i," and "j." Each of these subsections defines ways in which social workers can be charged with this crime. Social workers are defined as psychothera-pists for the purposes of this statute in section 609.341. Penalties are also defined for each degree of the offense. For example, in the criminal conduct in the fourth degree, the penalty can be imprison-ment for not more than five years, a fine of not more than $10,000, or both.

An extremely important part of the statute are the annotations published at the end. These annotations include the history of the statute, law review commentaries, and notes of decisions. Each of these annotations can yield important legal data. The notes of decisions indicate that several cases have been tried under this statute (see figure 8.3, notes 1/2 and 6). Especially important for this book is the *State v. Ohrtman* (1991) case, because it involves a psychotherapist. Notes on this case and the case citation are included in this annota-tion. With the case citation, the social worker can examine the case itself firsthand.

The front page of the *Ohrtman* case (figure 8.4) is reproduced to show what a law case looks like from the regional report. (Regional reports were discussed previously in this chapter.) This first page of a law case reveals the parties to the case, the court that decided the case, the date the case was decided, a synopsis of the case, the holding (decision) of the case, a series of numbers and legal areas, and the beginning of the case facts. The arrangement of the case in this fashion is done by West Publishing—not by the court.

Each element noted on the first page tells a great deal about the case. The court deciding this case was the Minnesota Court of Appeals; this means that the case was appealed. The "Syllabus of the Court" indicates that the state appealed the "lower," trial court's decision to dismiss the complaint against Ohrtman. The paragraph under the case name indicates that the state lost its appeal of the earlier decision to dismiss the charge. Finally,

Figure 8.2
Minnesota State Code

CRIMINAL CODE

§ 609.345

age of his multiple victims, his abuse of a position of trust, and psychological harm he caused his victims; sentence was substantially greater than presumptive sentence for felony-murder. State v. Poole, App.1992, 489 N.W.2d 537, affirmed 499 N.W.2d 31.

15. Child support

Father, who had been below age of consent for sexual intercourse under criminal sexual conduct statutes at time of conception, was civilly responsible for supporting child resulting from that union. Jevning v. Cichos, App.1993, 499 N.W.2d 515.

609.345. Criminal sexual conduct in the fourth degree

Subdivision 1. Crime defined. A person who engages in sexual contact with another person is guilty of criminal sexual conduct in the fourth degree if any of the following circumstances exists:

(a) the complainant is under 13 years of age and the actor is no more than 36 months older than the complainant. Neither mistake as to the complainant's age or consent to the act by the complainant is a defense. In a prosecution under this clause, the state is not required to prove that the sexual contact was coerced;

(b) the complainant is at least 13 but less than 16 years of age and the actor is more than 48 months older than the complainant or in a position of authority over the complainant and uses this authority to cause the complainant to submit. In any such case, it shall be an affirmative defense which must be proved by a preponderance of the evidence that the actor believes the complainant to be 16 years of age or older;

(c) the actor uses force or coercion to accomplish the sexual contact;

(d) the actor knows or has reason to know that the complainant is mentally impaired, mentally incapacitated, or physically helpless;

(e) the complainant is at least 16 but less than 18 years of age and the actor is more than 48 months older than the complainant and in a position of authority over the complainant, and uses this authority to cause the complainant to submit. Neither mistake as to the complainant's age nor consent to the act by the complainant is a defense;

(f) the actor has a significant relationship to the complainant and the complainant was at least 16 but under 18 years of age at the time of the sexual contact. Neither mistake as to the complainant's age nor consent to the act by the complainant is a defense;

(g) the actor has a significant relationship to the complainant, the complainant was at least 16 but under 18 years of age at the time of the sexual contact, and:

(i) the actor or an accomplice used force or coercion to accomplish the contact;

(ii) the complainant suffered personal injury; or

(iii) the sexual abuse involved multiple acts committed over an extended period of time.

Neither mistake as to the complainant's age nor consent to the act by the complainant is a defense;

(h) the actor is a psychotherapist and the complainant is a patient of the psychotherapist and the sexual contact occurred:

(i) during the psychotherapy session; or

(ii) outside the psychotherapy session if an ongoing psychotherapist-patient relationship exists.

Consent by the complainant is not a defense;

(i) the actor is a psychotherapist and the complainant is a former patient of the psychotherapist and the former patient is emotionally dependent upon the psychotherapist;

(j) the actor is a psychotherapist and the complainant is a patient or former patient and the sexual contact occurred by means of therapeutic deception. Consent by the complainant is not a defense;

(k) the actor accomplishes the sexual contact by means of deception or false representation that the contact is for a bona fide medical purpose. Consent by the complainant is not a defense; or

Reprinted with permission from Minnesota Statutes Annotated, Copyright © by West Publishing Company.

Figure 8.3
Minnesota State Code Annotations

Law Review Commentaries

Guilty of the crime of trust: Nonstranger rape. Beverly Balos & Mary Louise Fellows, 75 Minn. L.Rev. 599 (1991).

Notes of Decisions

Instructions 11
Medical purpose 9
Sentence and punishment 10
Sexual contact 7
Sufficiency of evidence 8
Validity ½

½. Validity

Statute making it criminal sexual conduct to accomplish sexual penetration or sexual contact by means of false representation that [penetration or contact] is for bona fide medical purpose by health care professional was not unconstitutionally vague either on its face or as applied to conduct of defendant, a licensed doctor who practiced in areas including obstetrical and gynecological care, but allegedly made sexual contact and sexual penetration with patients for nonmedical reasons. State v. Poole, 1993, 499 N.W.2d 31.

Statutes, criminalizing sexual contact accomplished by false representation that contact is for bona fide medical purpose by health care professional, were not ambiguous, as to whether false representation could be implied, as applied to doctor who saw patients for medical reasons, in an examining room at his clinic, where entire examination was implicitly for medical purposes. State v. Poole, App.1992, 489 N.W.2d 537, affirmed 499 N.W.2d 31.

Statutes criminalizing sexual contact accomplished by false representation that contact was for bona fide medical purpose by health care professional were subject to reasonable construction and established adequate guidelines to govern law enforcement. State v. Poole, App.1992, 489 N.W.2d 537, affirmed 499 N.W.2d 31.

Medical doctor convicted of criminal sexual conduct for acts committed against female patients could not bring facial challenge to statutes criminalizing sexual contact accomplished by means of false representation of bona fide medical purpose; statutes did not reach constitutionally protected conduct. State v. Poole, App.1992, 489 N.W.2d 537, affirmed 499 N.W.2d 31.

Defining "touching" within meaning of fourth-degree criminal sexual conduct to include nonsexual hugs would render statute excessively vague. State v. Ohrtman, App.1991, 466 N.W.2d 1.

Right to privacy did not protect counselor who engaged in sexual activity, although private and "consensual," arising directly out of religious counseling relationship, so as to render invalid this section proscribing as criminal sexual conduct psychotherapist-patient sexual penetration; sexual activity arising out of such a relationship violated counselor's duty to patient and might properly be regulated by police power of state. State v. Dutton, App.1990, 450 N.W.2d 189.

2. Lesser offenses

It was proper to submit lesser-included offenses of second and fourth-degree criminal sexual conduct in prosecution for first-degree criminal sexual conduct, even though the issue of penetration, as opposed to contact, which is the difference in the offenses, was not specifically distinguished in victim's testimony. State v. Kobow, App.1991, 466 N.W.2d 747, review denied.

Second and fourth-degree criminal sexual conduct are lesser-included offenses of first-degree criminal sexual conduct. State v. Kobow, App. 1991, 466 N.W.2d 747, review denied.

4. Force or coercion

"Coercion" required for conviction of fourth-degree criminal sexual conduct does not require force or actual threat. State v. Day, App.1993, 501 N.W.2d 649.

Conviction of therapist for fourth-degree criminal sexual conduct was supported by evidence that he took complete control of counseling session, grasped patient's hands, and virtually compelled her, despite her protests, to engage in sexual touching. State v. Day, App.1993, 501 N.W.2d 649.

In prosecution for fourth-degree criminal sexual conduct, there was no error in instructing that "coercion" means words or circumstances that forced complainant to submit to sexual contact, while omitting statutory reference to fear of bodily harm or confinement. State v. Day, App.1993, 501 N.W.2d 649.

5. Victim's testimony or statements

Conviction of criminal sexual conduct in fourth degree was supported by sufficient evidence, despite alleged inconsistency between victim's testimony and her statements to police. State v. Totimeh, App.1988, 433 N.W.2d 921, review denied.

Sufficient evidence supported defendant's conviction for criminal sexual conduct; victim's testimony was positive and largely unimpeached, and State produced other corroborating evidence including her prompt complaint, her emotional state, and physical and medical evidence as testified to by neutral witnesses. State v. Stafford, App.1987, 404 N.W.2d 918.

6. Consent

Actual consent to sexual touching of patient by psychotherapist during counseling session is irrelevant to charge of fourth-degree criminal conduct; equivalent of coercion is assumed by counselor/counselee relationship. State v. Ohrtman, App. 1991, 466 N.W.2d 1.

Reprinted with permission from Minnesota Statutes Annotated, Copyright © by West Publishing Company.

Figure 8.4
Ohrtman Case—Page 1

STATE v. OHRTMAN　　　Minn. **1**
Cite as 466 N.W.2d 1 (Minn.App. 1991)

STATE of Minnesota, Appellant,

v.

Steven Ray OHRTMAN, Respondent.

No. C3–90–1872.

Court of Appeals of Minnesota.

Feb. 12, 1991.

Defendant was charged with fourth-degree criminal sexual conduct for sexual contact during counseling. The District Court, Blue Earth County, James C. Harten, J., granted motion to dismiss, and State appealed. The Court of Appeals, Davies, J., held that the hug given by the defendant who was a pastor during a counseling session with a female parishioner was not a sexual "touching" within meaning of criminal sexual conduct statute.

Affirmed.

Randall, J., concurred in result.

1. Criminal Law ☞13.1(1)

Criminal statute is unconstitutional if it does not give fair warning to defendant of proscribed conduct. U.S.C.A. Const. Amends. 5, 14.

2. Criminal Law ☞13.1(1)

Statute is unconstitutionally vague if legislature fails to draw bright line to determine where criminality begins.

3. Assault and Battery ☞65

Actual consent to sexual touching of patient by psychotherapist during counseling session is irrelevant to charge of fourth-degree criminal conduct; equivalent of coercion is assumed by counselor/counselee relationship. M.S.A. § 609.345, subd. 1(h).

4. Assault and Battery ☞59

"Touching" within meaning of criminal sexual conduct statute means contacts designed primarily to create sensory feel of touch primarily by hand, fingers, or other organ used for feeling, including mouth or penis and excludes nonsexual hug in which

chest touches breasts. M.S.A. § 609.345, subd. 1(h).

See publication Words and Phrases for other judicial constructions and definitions.

5. Assault and Battery ☞59

Defining "touching" within meaning of fourth-degree criminal conduct statute to include nonsexual hugs would render statute excessively vague. M.S.A. § 609.345, subd. 1(h); U.S.C.A. Const.Amends. 5, 14.

6. Assault and Battery ☞59

Pastor's hug of female parishioner during counseling session which compressed parishioner's breasts against his chest was not "touching" within meaning of fourth-degree criminal conduct statute. M.S.A. § 609.345, subd. 1(h).

Syllabus by the Court

The conduct alleged in this case is not a "touching" of the intimate parts within the definition of the offense of fourth degree criminal sexual conduct.

Hubert H. Humphrey, III, Atty. Gen., St. Paul, Ross E. Arneson, Blue Earth County Atty., Mankato, for appellant.

Peter Thompson, Thompson & Lundquist, Ltd., Minneapolis, Charles A. Adamson, Mankato, for respondent.

Considered and decided by RANDALL, P.J., and FORSBERG and DAVIES, JJ.

OPINION

DAVIES, Judge.

This is an appeal by the state from an order dismissing a complaint charging fourth degree criminal sexual conduct (sexual contact by a psychotherapist) under Minn.Stat. § 609.345, subd. 1(h) (1990). We affirm.

FACTS

Respondent Steven Ohrtman, the pastor of a Mankato church, was charged with fourth degree criminal sexual conduct allegedly committed against J., a parishioner, during a counseling session.

Reprinted with permission from North Western Reporter, Second Series, Copyright © by West Publishing Company.

numbers and legal areas, such as "criminal law" and "assault and battery" denote decisions of the court, which are explained at length later in the case.

The final figure (figure 8.5) shows *Shepard's Citations*, the volumes that update cases and statutes. To locate any updates ("shepardize") in the *Ohrtman* case, first locate the volume number of the regional reporter (466) and find the corresponding number in the *Shepard's* volume (middle right). Second, find the page number of the case (1) and locate the corresponding number in *Shepard's*. One case citation is located. As the *Ohrtman* case is relatively recent, few citations are expected. This citation (501 N.W. 2d 653) is without a preceding letter; thus, this case does not affirm, reverse, overturn, or modify the decision. Upon examination, this case refers only to the *Ohrtman* case. "Shepardizing" statutes works the same way.

ANNOTATED BIBLIOGRAPHY

The following books are useful research and practice tools for social workers and other professionals. While some are designed specifically for lawyers, they are handy reference material for professionals whose work is influenced by law.

Books

Black, H.C. (1979). *Black's law dictionary*. St. Paul, Minn.: West.

This is perhaps the premier law dictionary and an indispensable tool for lay legal research. This volume has almost 1,500 pages of terms, defined in both theory and practice, with some case citations.

Burton, S.J. (1985). *An introduction to law and legal reasoning*. Boston: Little, Brown & Co.

This work explains the process of legal reasoning and how "families of cases" contribute to legal precedent. Especially helpful are sections on the judicial process and the roles of legal theory and the legal community.

Federal Judicial Center. (1980). *Federal courts and what they do*. Washington, D.C.: Author.

This pamphlet is a little gem. It offers concise discussions of the process of the federal judiciary, how cases move up and down the appellate ladder, some important legal principles, and a brief glossary of legal terminology. The pamphlets are available from the Federal

Figure 8.5
Shepard's Report

Vol. 465	NORTHWESTERN REPORTER, 2d SERIES				
—172—	**—380—**	**—531—**	**—731—**	**—852—**	**—155—**
504NW305	lv app den	506NW437	SPB	Md	499NW³128
	in 439Mch938		1NEAdv¹1596	623A2d190	
—183—	in 439Mch944	**—537—**			**—158—**
		Tex	**—732—**	**—857—**	
Cir. 8	**—394—**	859SW16	505NW⁸714	507NW⁵412	505NW²124
994F2d³492					
	j 501NW593	**—551—**	**—737—**	**—865—**	**—211—**
—238—					
	—395—	j 500NW462	499NW75	504NW151	US cert den
499NW⁷721		505NW817	j 504NW835		in 116LE169
f 499NW722	503NW¹²915			**—887—**	in 112SC210
502NW896	e 506NW⁷607	**—561—**	**—743—**		
f 502NW⁵897				N M	**—215—**
506NW⁸754	**—404—**	j 499NW346	SPB	853P2d731	
Mass		j 501NW155	1NEAdv³79		499NW283
617NE996	507NW²892	j 506NW866		**—898—**	502NW869
	Cir. 8		**—752—**		
—242—	819FS¹853	**—568—**		499NW315	**—221—**
			503NW²172		
S D	**—412—**	Case 2	507NW²676	**—906—**	502NW¹137
f 501NW369					
	507NW¹884	lv app den	**—756—**	499NW321	**—239—**
—252—		in 505NW583		504NW151	
	—419—		507NW⁶659		501NW²868
504NW¹420		**—569—**	SPB		
504NW²421	Cir. 8		1NEAdv⁶1581	**Vol. 466**	**—281—**
D C	816FS⁵1362	Case 2	2NEAdv²236		
626A2d32		506NW³911	2NEAdv¹240	**—1—**	Case 1
	—424—		2NEAdv²589		
—266—		**—573—**	502NW²497	501NW653	s 114LE97
	499NW⁵47				s 115LE1108
501NW⁷892	499NW⁶47	s 496US933	**—773—**	**—49—**	s 116LE22
501NW⁹892	503NW¹808	s 110SC3208			s 111SC2008
j 501NW894	504NW¹243		506NW¹48	Cir. 8	s 112SC26
	504NW¹274	**—625—**		815FS⁶1280	s 112SC44
—272—	Cir. 5		**—777—**		
	813FS⁵486	499NW28		**—56—**	**—287—**
501NW¹541			(5A³1078)		
	—453—	**—633—**		502NW¹427	f 502NW344
—285—			**—787—**		508NW191
	499NW72	j 507NW¹ 7		**—71—**	
507NW410	502NW¹¹475		Md		**—302—**
		—66:—	624A2d496	500NW²190	
—317—	**—472—**				lv app den
		j 501NW5 2	**—800—**	**—73—**	in 439Mch862
505NW14	504NW¹⁰296				in 439Mch866
		—664—	r 120LE174	f 507NW¹⁴477	
—342—	**—483—**		r 112SC2447		**—305—**
		r 120LE59	s 500NW667	**—101—**	
502NW¹709	505NW¹⁰756	r 112SC2365	s 116LE27		501NW185
502NW²709	f 505NW¹758	s 116LE23	s 112SC49	Case 2	
502NW³709		s 117LE103			**—309—**
502NW⁶710	**—490—**	s 117LE405	**—812—**	504NW²556	
502NW⁵711		s 117LE613		506NW⁵726	Iowa
503NW⁶913	f 507NW¹349	s 112SC45	j 501NW410		501NW²521
505NW9		s 112SC931	j 501NW411	**—111—**	
	—520—	s 112SC1156	502NW²136		**—311—**
—365—		s 112SC1467	507NW⁶124	US cert den	
	503NW⁴279			in 111SC2239	506NW558
lv app den	503NW⁵279	**—696—**	**—829—**		
in 439Mch852				**—120—**	**—315—**
504NW714	**—525—**	503NW⁵518	503NW⁴365		
506NW¹599				cc 501NW756	499NW¹445
	507NW¹111	**—721—**	**—833—**	500NW205	500NW¹482
—376—	508NW⁹22				504NW190
	Cir. 7	f 499NW⁵508	504NW427	**—148—**	506NW¹552
507NW²218	809FS⁹699				506NW¹911
				f 502NW¹532	508NW¹163

Judicial Center, the Dooley Madison House, 1520 H. Street, N.W. Washington, D.C. 20005, 202-633-6011.

Garner, B.A. (1987). *A dictionary of modern legal usage*. New York: Oxford University Press.
     This 587 page volume offers definitions of most commonly-used legal terms. It also has a brief, but useful, bibliography.

Periodicals

Law schools and law organizations publish useful periodicals for social work practitioners and researchers. While some of these periodicals are distributed to members of Sections of the American Bar Association, they are available at most law school libraries, court libraries, and law firm libraries.

Family Advocate, published by the American Bar Association's Family Law Section. Concise articles for the practicing lawyer on a broad range of topics including divorce, child custody, professional privileges, court testimony, marriage contracts, and privacy issues.

Family Law Quarterly, another periodical published by the Family Law Section of the American Bar Association. This periodical publishes lengthy, scholarly articles with numerous charts and footnotes. The topics, again, are broad, including divorce and custody determinations, the law for marriages and single parents, domestic violence, the court testimony of professionals, and mediation. Particularly helpful dimensions of this periodical are periodic compendiums of "family law in the fifty states" and an annual survey of periodical literature on family law.

Human Rights, published by the Section of Individual Rights and Responsibilities of the American Bar Association. This journal examines current issues in civil liberties and civil rights. It is very readable and full of useful resources for training and educational use.

Pamphlets

Legal research is often aided by pamphlets prepared by state and county agencies and departments. These legal resources are particularly helpful in describing and explaining specific areas of law from specific jurisdictions.

Crime Victims in Virginia, by the Department of Criminal Justice Services. In a dozen pages this pamphlet briefly covers how to report crimes to law enforcement officials, the criminal justice system after arrest, pretrial hearings, bail, protective orders, when to appear in court, sentencing, and appeals.

Help for Crime Victims, by the Virginia Division of Crime Victim's Compensation. This pamphlet describes the process of filing a claim for a crime victim's compensation, including how and when a claim must be filed, the qualifications a victim must meet, what benefits are available, and how to file an appeal.

Understanding Your Domestic Relations Rights in Virginia, by the Metropolitan Richmond Women's Bar Association. This pamphlet describes general legal principles including court procedures, divorce, spousal support, child support, custody and visitation, property settlement, and protective orders and injunctions. Other states may have similar pamphlets.

Videos

Videotapes increasingly play important roles in education and training. Below is an example of a general video that explains the processes of both civil and criminal litigation.

Understanding the Courts: Anatomy of a Criminal Case and Anatomy of a Civil Case, with instructor's guide and viewer's guide. $25 for package from the American Bar Association, Order fulfillment, 750 North Lake Shore Drive, Chicago, Ill. 60611.

GLOSSARY OF LEGAL TERMS AND CONCEPTS

The following are definitions of legal terms used in this book. Each definition is adapted for social workers.

Appeal. A party who loses a lower court decision asks a higher court to review the case—hoping for a decision in his or her favor. Criminal cases, custody cases, and even social security decisions have appeal processes. It is important to note that the appeal process of each court or administrative court decision is governed by rules—and in most cases such rules are strictly enforced.

Cause of Action. The legal terminology for the specific wrong alleged in a civil suit. In some states "social worker malpractice" is a *cause of action.* Other states do not legally recognize such a cause of action. In those states the *causes of action* against social workers may be "intentional infliction of emotional distress" or "breach of fiduciary duty." This book has also discussed the *cause of action* against social workers for "psychotherapist sexual exploitation."

Civil law. Essentially, this is private law, advocated by private attorneys. For example, social worker malpractice law is civil law. Conversely, criminal law is public law, specifically derived from the criminal code. See *criminal law.*

Criminal law. The public law, investigated by public officials (investigators, police), prosecuted by public officials (district attorneys, etc.), and penalized by public officials (sheriff's office, prison officials).

Dicta. Non-binding comments of judges in a law case. *Dicta* must be distinguished from the holding of the case. See *holding.*

Holding. The judicial ruling of the case. This holding is a specific application of the law to the facts involved. See *dicta.*

Immunity. A legal excuse for liability for an otherwise wrongful act. Some social workers may have been immunized under the doctrines of the "charitable" or "sovereign" immunities. The "charitable" immunities, severely curtailed now in most jurisdictions, have been used by religious or non-for-profit organizations. The "sovereign" immunity, used by governments at all levels, has much more legal vitality.

Informed Consent. This "consent" requires that the person giving consent must *know* and *understand* the implications of that consent as well as the consequences of such consent. For example, a client's *informed consent* to have the social worker discuss his or her case with others would have to specify *who* will discuss the information, *what* information will be discussed, *what limits,* if any, will be placed upon what information is divulged, and *when* the sharing will stop.

Jurisdiction. Each court has its own power and authority. The court with the greatest jurisdiction in the United States is the Supreme Court, because it can overturn *any* law—either federal or state. The highest state courts have jurisdiction over their states. In the federal system of courts, the lowest courts are the district courts. The district courts have jurisdiction over federal cases within a geographic parameter. The federal appellate courts are called circuit courts.

Legal counsel. A licensed lawyer. Lawyers need to be licensed in each state where they practice law.

Liability. A legal determination deciding legal culpability or responsibility.

Malpractice. A legal term meaning "professional negligence." *Malpractice* against social workers is a cause of action recognized by some courts and ignored by others. See *negligence.*

Negligence. The basis for liability. A legal determination of *negligence* must be found prior to liability. The four traditional elements of *negligence* are: duty, breach of duty, damages, and proximate cause. See *malpractice.*

Precedence. Cases are decided upon consistent legal principles. Judges will cite earlier cases to show they are relying upon the precedence previously established. Precedence gives continuity to court decisions. A severe departure from this line of precedence is unusual, but it does occur.

Torts. A sub-type of the civil law dealing with harm to others. Social worker malpractice is a type of torts. Other types of torts include personal injury or "slip and fall" cases.

Vicarious Liability. Liability that is attached to the actions of others. Employer liability is a type of vicarious liability. In employer liability the employer is held responsible for the *tort* (wrongful) actions of employees. Thus, the supervisors and employers of social workers may be liable for the negligent or wrongful acts of social workers.

REFERENCES

Brown v. Board of Education, 347 U.S. 483 (1954).
Cruzan v. Director, Missouri Department of Health, 110 S. Ct. 2841 (1990).
Doe v. Bolton, 410 U.S. 179 (1973).
Plessy v. Ferguson, 163 U.S. 537 (1896).
Roe v. Wade, 410 U.S. 113 (1973).
Shepard's Northwestern Reporter. *Shepard's Citations, 90*(7), 141
State v. Ohrtman, 466 N.W. 2d 1 (Minn. App. 1991).

Appendix A

▶ ⋯⋯⋯⋯⋯⋯⋯⋯⋯ ◀
The Sexual Misconduct Policy of the Presbyterian Church (USA)
▶ ⋯⋯⋯⋯⋯⋯⋯⋯⋯ ◀

A. Principles of Conduct

The basic principles guiding this policy are as follows:

1. Sexual misconduct is a violation of the role of pastors, employees, volunteers, counselors, supervisors, teachers, and advisers of any kind who are called upon to exercise integrity, sensitivity, and caring in a trust relationship. It breaks the covenant to act in the best interests of parishioners, clients, co-workers, and students.

2. Sexual misconduct is a misuse of authority and power which breaches Christian ethical principles by misusing a trust relation to gain advantage over another for personal pleasure in an abusive, exploitive, and unjust manner. If the parishioner, student, client, or employee initiates or invites sexual content in the relationship, it is the pastor's, counselor's, officer's or supervisor's responsibility to maintain the appropriate role and prohibit a sexual relationship.

3. Sexual misconduct takes advantage of the vulnerability of children and persons who are less powerful to act for their own welfare. It is antithetical to the gospel call to work as God's servant in the struggle to bring wholeness to a broken world. It violates the mandate to protect the vulnerable from harm.

B. Victims and Families

The governing body, entity, and response team will offer treatment and care to the alleged victims of sexual misconduct and their families. It has sometimes been the case that the victim or family is so angry and alienated from the church that offers of help have been perceived as insincere or attempts at a cover-up. If the victim or family at first refuses, the church should continue to offer help. Above all the church should not act in a self-protective manner by ignoring the victims and their families.

Although the extent of the damage to the victims of sexual misconduct will vary from person to person, being influenced by such factors as the degree or severity of abuse, the age and emotional condition of the victim, personality dynamics, and the importance of the religious faith, the governing body, entity, and response team is to assume in all cases that the victim has been wounded by the experience.

Feelings of guilt, shame, anger, mistrust, lowered self-esteem, unworthiness, and feelings of alienation from God, self, the religious community, and family are frequent injuries suffered by victims. It is important for the response team to be sensitive to the victim's pain and need for healing, and to act by making appropriate pastoral care available.

C. Congregations or Employing Entity

The governing body, employing entity, and response team should be aware of the problems a congregation or employing entity may experience resulting from allegations of sexual misconduct by a minister, employee, or volunteer. The allegations may polarize the congregation or organization, damage morale, and create serious internal problems. Efforts should be taken to recognize and identify the problems and heal the damage done to the congregation or organization.

D. The Accused

The governing body or entity shall offer treatment and care for the accused as well as alleged victims and families. If the accused is a minister, this is the responsibility of the Committee on Ministry G-11.0501. Persons accused of rape or other sexual offenses do not inspire sympathy. When criminal charges are filed some accused cannot get bail and are sometimes forced to spend extended periods of time in prison while awaiting trial. While there, they have been known to have been abused by guards or other prisoners. There is evidence that men accused of rape find it more difficult to obtain a lawyer than people accused of other crimes. News media often give much attention to the arrest and opening of the trial, while little or nothing is said when the accused is acquitted. Many false accusations are filed in cases of sexual harassment, child molestation, and sexual misconduct. For these and other reasons it is important that representatives of the governing body or other entities do not make a presumption of guilt or over-react to lurid charges.

When a person is acquitted of charges, it is important for the governing body or entity to see that the acquittal is publicized as widely as possible within their power to do it when requested to do so by the accused.

E. The Non-Victim Accuser

In many cases the non-victim accuser is the parent, guardian or other advocate for a child who has been the victim of sexual misconduct. Because of the child's minority status an adult is requested to file the action on behalf of the child.

In cases where the victim is an adult, the non-victim accuser shall observe the following guidelines:

1. For their own protection the non-victim accuser should have something in writing from the victim detailing the charges.

2. The non-victim accuser should be certain the victim is willing to come forward to testify if an action is filed.

3. Some objective evidence of the sexual misconduct should be available to substantiate the charges (e.g., medical test results, motel receipts, proof of repeated telephone calls, etc.) otherwise the victim and/or the non-victim accuser could be subject to a suit for filing a false charge which may damage a person's reputation and diminish his/her ability to obtain future employment. For this reason it is not wise for staff of any governing body or entity to be the accuser unless that person is also the victim.

Risk Management

A. Implementation

The General Assembly urges all governing bodies and related entities including colleges, universities, and theological institutions to establish policies, procedures, and practices related to sexual misconduct. Governing bodies and entities are to take appropriate steps to inform members, employees, volunteers, and students of the standards of conduct and the procedures for effective response when receiving a report of sexual misconduct. Governing bodies are reminded of their duty to cooperate with secular authorities in the investigation and prosecution of violations of law.

In part the structures and procedures for responding to allegations of sexual misconduct are mandated by the Book of Order, such as the roles of the committee on ministry and the special disciplinary committee (see G-11.0502 and D-7.0800). When child sexual abuse or other misconduct that violates criminal laws is alleged, the secular authorities will immediately take control of the investigation and disposition of charges against the accused. Governing bodies and entities must cooperate with secular authorities in any secular investigation of sexual misconduct. The governing body or entity has a duty to make its inquiry and enforce disciplinary procedures if warranted when it can be done without interfering with the secular authority or in cases when civil authorities have dropped action in the case.

Response to complaints of sexual misconduct in the course of employment will be governed by the governing body's or entity's existing personnel policy. The same allegations may also result in charges filed against a church member or minister under the Rules of Discipline, and may lead to temporary or permanent removal from membership or office.

Implementation of this *churchwide* policy will require governing bodies and their entities to adopt educational programs to prevent sexual misconduct, and to provide training in pastoral and disciplinary procedures.

B. Liability and Insurance

A governing body or entity can be held liable for harm caused by sexual misconduct of a minister or employee based on a number of legal theories *such as* negligent hiring and supervision. Governing bodies and entities must take such potential liability into consideration when establishing hiring and supervisory practices.

Governing bodies and entities should regularly inform their liability insurance carriers of the activities and programs they operate or sponsor and of the duties and responsibilities of officers, employees, and volunteers. The standard insurance policy must be enhanced by endorsements to cover specific exposures such as camps, day-care operations, shelters, or other outreach programs.

It is also recommended that governing bodies and entities obtain an endorsement to their general liability insurance policy specifically covering sexual abuse and molestation. Such coverage may provide for legal defense expenses and judgments in civil suits brought against the organization, its officers, directors, or employees.

C. Employment Practices

1. Record Keeping

Accurate record keeping is an essential part of hiring and supervision practices. Every governing body and entity should maintain a personnel file on every employee including ministers. The file should contain the application for employment, any employment questionnaires, reference responses and other documents related to this policy.

2. Prescreening Applicants

Governing bodies and entities are urged to establish stringent hiring practices. If an applicant is unknown to the employer, the employer should confirm the applicant's identity by requiring photographic identification such as a driver's license.

Part of pre-employment screening should include specific questions related to discovering previous complaints of sexual misconduct. Governing bodies and entities should ask persons seeking ministerial calls or employment in non-ordained positions questions such as:

a. Has a civil or criminal or ecclesiastical complaint ever been filed against you alleging sexual misconduct by you?
b. Have you ever resigned or been terminated from a position for reasons relating to allegations of sexual misconduct by you?
c. If so, indicate the date, nature and place of these allegations, and the name, address, and phone number of your employer at the time.
d. Have you been required to receive professional treatment, physical or psychological, for reasons related to sexual misconduct by you?
e. If so, please give a short description of the treatment including the date, nature of treatment, place and name, address and phone number of the treating physician or other professional.

A sample employment questionnaire is attached as Exhibit A for adaptation by governing bodies and entities. The questions included in this sample may be integrated into a standard employment questionnaire along with other necessary questions.

3. References

The employing governing body or entity is responsible for contacting references for prospective ministers, employees, or volunteers. A written record of conversations or correspondence with references should be kept in the minister's/employee's personnel file. (See Exhibit B for a sample reference form).

In dealing with ministers when transferring from one position to another in the matter of sexual misconduct clearance, the governing body could assume responsibility for previous employer reference checks through the synod executive, executive presbyter, or other authorized persons who would report to the committee on ministry either that there had been no reported sexual misconduct, or that the committee should inquire into reported sexual misconduct.

The person within the governing body or entity authorized to give a reference is obligated to give truthful information regarding allegations, inquiries, and administrative or disciplinary action related to sexual misconduct of the applicant. The response, however, must be limited to information contained within the written summary prepared as part of the response team or governing body report. The response, however, must be limited to information that is a matter of public record (e.g., presbytery minutes) or in the applicant's own personnel file which is maintained by the governing body or other entity.

If false or misleading information is given or relevant information is withheld, the applicant will be eliminated from consideration.

Applicants should be informed of negative comments regarding sexual misconduct and shall be given an opportunity to submit additional references or to give other evidence to correct or respond to harmful information obtained from a reference.

D. Distribution

Copies of this policy shall be distributed to all governing body and entity offices and shall be distributed to all employees and volunteers, and be available to all church members. It is intended for use by church members, church officers, employees, and volunteers. The policy shall be made available to persons who *accuse others of misconduct, including those who are* or claim to be victims of sexual misconduct and their families. The policy will be available to those serving on special disciplinary committees, committees on ministry, and response teams.

Upon receipt of this policy, personnel in high-risk occupations must sign a written acknowledgment of receipt (Exhibit C). This acknowledgment shall be kept in the person's personnel file.

E. Volunteers

While these guidelines are intended for volunteers, no requirement for screening and application is usually applied. The increase of litigation requires that local churches do a better job of screening and supervising unpaid volunteers. If the volunteer is new or unknown to your church, some informal checking may be wise before allowing him/her to work in high-risk positions such as youth advisor, children's worker, lay counselor, boy or girl scout leader, or camp counselor.

Appendix B

▶ ⋯⋯⋯⋯⋯⋯⋯⋯⋯⋯ ◀

The Sexual Misconduct Policy of the N.W. District of the American Lutheran Church (1987)

▶ ⋯⋯⋯⋯⋯⋯⋯⋯⋯⋯ ◀

POLICY FOR DEALING WITH AN ALLEGED OCCURRENCE OF SEXUAL MISCONDUCT

Any complaint or allegation of sexual misconduct (as defined in this policy) shall be brought to the immediate attention of the Bishop (or his/her representative). If circumstances warrant, the Bishop may immediately suspend the accused pastor temporarily from his/her pastoral duties with the congregation or agency he/she serves (with pay and without prejudice); in this event, the Bishop shall notify the congregation or agency of the investigation and insure that the congregation has adequate pastoral services during this period.

In carrying out his/her responsibility to "seek to remove any cause from complaint," the Bishop shall call upon the Special Committee on Pastoral Ethics (a subcommittee of the District Executive Board) to meet with person(s) bringing the complaint forthwith in order to:

A1. hear her/his allegations directly

A2. request that complainant(s) prepare a written complaint

A3. request permission from complainant(s) to use the written complaint and her/his name in discussion with the accused pastor

A4. attempt to secure the complainant(s)' willingness, if requested, to appear before the District Executive Board in a formal hearing

A5. outline the process which will be followed in response to the complaint

Once the written complaint is received and if the Special Committee believes that there is sufficient cause for concern that there may have been some violation of professional ethics, the Special Committee shall meet with the accused pastor in order to:

B1. present him/her with the formal, written complaint

B2. hear his/her response to complaint directly (may be verbal and/or written)

B3. outline the process which will be followed in response to the complaint; emphasizing the presumption of innocence and the right to due process

B4. make available a summary of the pastor's response to the complainant for comment

If there is sufficient cause for concern that there may have been some violation of professional ethics, the Special Committee shall proceed.

The Special Committee shall presume the innocence of the accused pastor until unethical conduct is proven.

The Special Committee shall not ask the complainant and the accused pastor to meet together during this phase of the process.

If not already accomplished, in order to protect the rights of the accused pastor and to protect the complainant(s) and congregation from possible harm during the investigation:

C1. the Special Committee shall recommend to the Bishop a temporary suspension of the pastor from pastoral duties, with pay and without prejudice.

C2. the Bishop shall notify the congregation or agency of the investigation, temporarily suspend the accused pastor, and appoint another to serve temporarily. The temporary pastor shall be fully informed of the circumstances of the temporary suspension in order to minister effectively with the congregation.

The Special Committee shall fully investigate the accusation through information and documentation from the complainant, the accused pastor, and other credible sources as appear appropriate.

Based on the investigation carried out by the Special Committee, it shall, using its best judgment, determine the veracity of the complaint and recommend action to the Bishop as follows:

D1. IF THE ALLEGATIONS ARE NOT SUBSTANTIATED by the Special Committee, the investigation will cease and every effort will be made to exonerate the pastor. A record of the process and its conclusion will be provided for the pastor and may be included in his/her personnel file. A public statement of exoneration by the Bishop may be made if the pastor so chooses. The Bishop and Special Committee shall respond with care and concern to the complainant(s) and to the congregation or agency as appropriate.

D2. IF THE ALLEGATIONS ARE SUBSTANTIATED by the Special Committee and the offense and consequences of the misconduct are determined to be relatively MINOR, the Special Committee will recommend that the Bishop shall take the following steps:

a. issue an *educative advisory* in response to a situation which is not necessarily unethical but shows poor professional judgment. He/she should provide clear guidance in order to accomplish the necessary corrective.

b. issue an *educative warning* in response to a situation of unquestionably inappropriate and unwise behavior but which is not clearly unethical. It is expected that this clear warning will bring a cessation of the behavior.

c. issue a *reprimand* in response to a situation which involves unethical behavior but which resulted in relatively minor consequences. This action will be recorded and placed in the pastor's file.

The Bishop, using his/her best judgment and in light of the recommendation of the Special Committee, will determine what action to take and will meet with the complainant, the accused pastor, and representatives of the congregation or agency (separately) to communicate and explain the action taken. This action will be communicated in writing to all parties as well.

D3. IF THE ALLEGATIONS ARE SUBSTANTIATED by the Special Committee and the consequences of the misconduct are determined to be relatively Major, the Bishop shall recommend that the District Executive Board hear the case. The District Executive Board shall proceed with a hearing to determine its action in this matter utilizing the section on Disciplinary Action, ALC Constitution and Bylaws, (Section 7.24.20–28.)

If the District Executive Board finds the accused engaged in unethical behavior, they shall take one of the following steps:

d. *Censure* the pastor is response to clearly unethical behavior which was persistent and resulted in (or could have resulted in) serious harm to others. This action shall be recorded and placed in the pastor's personnel file but not result in suspension. Restitution and rehabilitation may be recommended.

e. *Suspend the pastor temporarily* from the clergy roster in response to unethical conduct which resulted in harm to others and to the ministry. Protection of others from further harm is paramount. The suspension shall continue until there is clear evidence of rehabilitation and restoration of the pastor. (See below "Response to Offending Pastor.") At that time, the pastor may petition the District Executive Board for cessation of the suspension.

f. *Suspend the pastor permanently* from the clergy roster in response to unethical conduct which resulted in substantial harm to others, the church, and the ministry and, in the face of which, there is little possibility of rehabilitation and restoration to ministry. Protection of others from harm and protection of the integrity of the ministry are paramount.

Any of these actions shall be recorded and placed in the pastor's permanent file.

D4. APPEAL PROCESS: The appeal process shall be followed as outlined in the ALC Constitution and Bylaws.

Once the Executive Board has made its determination and taken a disciplinary position, the following steps should be utilized.

Responses to the Offending Pastor:

Confrontation of the offending pastor with the disciplinary action taken by the Bishop and/or Executive Board should be understood to be a pastoral and caring act of the church. It provides the greatest potential for both vocational and personal redemption and healing. Confession and/or acknowledgment of responsibility for the alleged misconduct shall be regarded as an important first step in the possible restoration of the offending pastor to effective ministry. The expression of remorse by the offending pastor, while genuine, shall not be deemed as adequate assurance that the misconduct will not be repeated. Repentance, that is, fundamental change of heart and practice, shall be regarded as the basic measure of possible restoration to ministry. While forgiveness may be forthcoming, formal absolution should be withheld until there is therapeutic intervention and subsequent evidence of change.

A requirement of therapeutic evaluation and/or treatment may be utilized in combination with any of the six levels of response as listed above. This requirement should be clearly communicated and monitored as appropriate over time.

A requirement of payment for restitution of the victim(s) by the offending pastor may be made as a condition of the rehabilitation process and possible return to the clergy roster.

The Bishop may limit the ministry of the offending pastor during the rehabilitation process and may appoint a trained supervisor to monitor the limited ministerial functions.

Evaluation and/or treatment should be carried out by therapists specially qualified to deal with sexual offenses and sensitive to issues of professional ethics. A qualified therapist should be selected by the offending pastor from a list provided by the Bishop. Assistance will be made available for the spouse and the family. Possible reinstatement of the pastor on the clergy roster shall be dependent upon the therapist, supervisor, Bishop and members of the Special Committee concluding that the pastor is sufficiently capable of effective ministry again.

The office of Support to Ministries shall be notified of the disciplinary actions of the Executive Board so that no offending pastor may move to another District without notice to that District and his/her potential employers.

Responses to the victim(s):

The Bishop and Executive Board shall respond to the victim(s) of the misconduct by the offending pastor with sensitivity and care. An appropriate pastor or lay leader shall be named and offered to the victim(s) early in the process to serve as advocate and support, interpreter of the process, and pastoral presence.

A list of qualified therapists shall be provided to the victim(s) to be utilized at their choice. While this does not imply financial responsibility on the part of the District, the District Executive Board may offer financial support for this purpose. The District Executive Board may direct the offending pastor to make restitution to cover these expenses as a condition of restoration to office.

Where there are multiple victims identified, an opportunity should be made for these persons to meet together throughout the process.

Response to the congregation or agency:

The Bishop and a representative of the District Executive Board shall meet with the local church or agency board and communicate the results of the hearing process with special attention to the disciplinary action taken and its implications.

The Bishop shall, in conjunction with the local church or agency board, notify each member of the church or agency in writing of the particulars of the charges, their resolution and action taken by the District Executive Committee.

The Bishop or Synod Council shall make available a trained resource person who can assist the local church or agency in whatever ways necessary to address their concerns so as to bring healing to their brokenness.

Appendix C

The California State Bar Rule

Rule 3-120. Sexual Relations With Client

(A) For purposes of this rule, "sexual relations" means sexual intercourse or the touching of an intimate part of another person for the purpose of sexual arousal, gratification, or abuse.

(B) A member shall not:
  (1) Require or demand sexual relations with a client incident to or as a condition of any professional representation; or
  (2) Employ coercion, intimidation, or undue influence in entering into sexual relations with a client; or
  (3) Continue representation of a client with whom the member has sexual relations if such sexual relations cause the member to perform legal services incompetently . . .

(C) Paragraph (B) shall not apply to sexual relations between members and their spouses or to ongoing consensual sexual relations which predate the initiations of the lawyer-client relationship.

(D) Where a lawyer in a firm has sexual relations with a client but does not participate in the representation of that client, the lawyers in the firm shall not be subject to discipline under this rule solely because of the occurrence of such sexual relations.

(E) A member who engages in sexual relations with his or her client will be presumed to violate rule 3-120, paragraph (B)(3). This presumption shall only be used as a presumption affecting the burden of proof in disciplinary proceedings involving alleged violations of these rules. "Presumption affecting the burden of proof" means that presumption defined in Evidence Code sections 605 and 606.

Discussion

Rule 3-120 is intended to prohibit sexual exploitation by a lawyer in the course of a professional representation. Often, based upon the nature of the underlying representation, a client exhibits great emotional vulnerability and dependence upon the advice and guidance of counsel. Attorneys owe the utmost duty of good faith and loyalty to clients. (See, e.g. *Greenbaum v. State Bar* (1976) 15 Cal.3d 893, 903 [126 Cal. Rptr. 785]; *Alkow v. State Bar* (1971) 3 Cal. 3d 924, 935 [92 Cal. Rptr. 278]; *Cutler v. State Bar* (1969) 71 Cal. 2d 241, 251 [78 Cal. Rptr. 172]; *Clancy v. State Bar* (1969) 71 Cal. 2d 140, 146 [77 Cal. Rptr. 657].) The relationship between an attorney and client is a fiduciary relationship of the very highest character and all dealings between an attorney and client that are beneficial to the attorney will be closely scrutinized with the utmost strictness for unfairness. (See, e.g., *Giovanazzi v. State Bar* (1980) 28 Cal. 3d 465, 472 [169 Cal. Rptr. 581]; *Benson v. State Bar* (1975) 13 Cal. 3d 581, 586 [119 Cal. Rptr. 297]; *Lee v. State Bar* (1970) 2 Cal. 3d 927, 939 [88 Cal.Rptr. 361]; *Clancy v. State Bar* (1969) 71 Cal. 2d 140, 146 [77 Cal. Rptr. 657]). Where attorneys exercise undue influence over clients or take advantage of clients, discipline is appropriate. (See, e.g. *Magee v. State Bar* (1962) 58 Cal. 2d 423 [24 Cal. Rptr. 839]; *Lantz v. State Bar* (1931) 212 Cal. 213 [298 P. 497]). In all client matters, a member is advised to keep client's interests paramount in the course of the member's representation.

For purposes of this rule, if the client is an organization, any individual overseeing the representation shall be deemed to be the client. (See rule 3-600.)

Although paragraph (C) excludes representation of certain clients from the scope of rule 3-120, such exclusion is not intended to preclude the applicability of other Rules of Professional Conduct . . .

Index